796

my **revisi⊙n** notes

AQA A-level

PE

Sue Young,
Symond Burrows and
Michaela Byrne

HODDER
EDUCATION
AN HACHETTE UK COMPANY

Acknowledgements

The Publishers would like to thank the following for permission to reproduce copyright material.

p.32 © Shutterstock/Maxisport; **p.33** © Shutterstock/Pal2iyawit; **p.42** © ALLSTAR PICTURE LIBRARY/Alamy Stock Photo; **p.118** © Andres Rodriguez – Fotolia; **p.126** © Undrey/Shutterstock; **p.144** *l* © Steve Russell/Toronto Star via Getty Images, *r* © Adam Pretty/Getty Images; **p.149** © Popperfoto/Getty Images; **p.151** © Jaroslav Uher/ Fotolia.

Every effort has been made to trace all copyright holders, but if any have been inadvertently overlooked, the Publishers will be pleased to make the necessary arrangements at the first opportunity.

Although every effort has been made to ensure that website addresses are correct at time of going to press, Hodder Education cannot be held responsible for the content of any website mentioned in this book. It is sometimes possible to find a relocated web page by typing in the address of the home page for a website in the URL window of your browser.

Hachette UK's policy is to use papers that are natural, renewable and recyclable products and made from wood grown in sustainable forests. The logging and manufacturing processes are expected to conform to the environmental regulations of the country of origin.

Orders: please contact Bookpoint Ltd, 130 Milton Park, Abingdon, Oxon OX14 4SE. Telephone: +44 (0)1235 827720. Fax: +44 (0)1235 400401. Email education@ bookpoint.co.uk. Lines are open from 9 a.m. to 5 p.m., Monday to Saturday, with a 24-hour message answering service. You can also order through our website: www.hoddereducation.co.uk

ISBN: 978 1 5104 0522 6

© Sue Young, Symond Burrows and Michaela Byrne 2017

First published in 2017 by
Hodder Education,
An Hachette UK Company
Carmelite House
50 Victoria Embankment
London EC4Y 0DZ

www.hoddereducation.co.uk

Impression number   10 9 8 7 6 5 4 3 2

Year   2022   2021   2020   2019   2018

Cover photo © bizoon/123RF

Illustrations by Integra

Typeset by Integra Software Services Pvt. Ltd., Pondicherry, India
Printed in Spain

A catalogue record for this title is available from the British Library.

Get the most from this book

Everyone has to decide his or her own revision strategy, but it is essential to review your work, learn it and test your understanding. These Revision Notes will help you to do that in a planned way, topic by topic. Use this book as the cornerstone of your revision and don't hesitate to write in it – personalise your notes and check your progress by ticking off each section as you revise.

Tick to track your progress

Use the revision planner on pages 4 and 5 to plan your revision, topic by topic. Tick each box when you have:

- revised and understood a topic
- tested yourself
- practised the exam questions and gone online to check your answers and complete the quick quizzes.

You can also keep track of your revision by ticking off each topic heading in the book. You may find it helpful to add your own notes as you work through each topic.

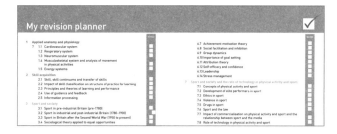

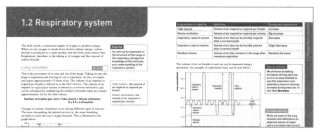

Features to help you succeed

Exam tips

Expert tips are given throughout the book to help you polish your exam technique and maximise your chances in the exam.

Typical mistakes

The author identifies the typical mistakes candidates make and explains how you can avoid them.

Now test yourself

These short, knowledge-based questions provide the first step in testing your learning. Answers are online.

Definitions and key words

Clear, concise definitions of essential key terms are provided where they first appear.

Key words from the specification are highlighted in bold throughout the book.

Revision activities

These activities will help you to understand each topic in an interactive way.

Exam practice

Practice exam questions are provided for each topic. Use them to consolidate your revision and practise your exam skills.

Summaries

The summaries provide a quick-check bullet list for each topic.

Online

Go online to check your answers to the exam questions and try out the extra quick quizzes at **www.hoddereducation.co.uk/myrevisionnotes**

My revision planner

REVISED

Answers and quick quizzes at **www.hoddereducation.co.uk/myrevisionnotes**

Now test yourself answers and exam practice answers online

Countdown to my exams

6–8 weeks to go

- Start by looking at the specification — make sure you know exactly what material you need to revise and the style of the exam. Use the revision planner on pages 4 and 5 to familiarise yourself with the topics.
- Organise your notes, making sure you have covered everything on the specification. The revision planner will help you to group your notes into topics.
- Work out a realistic revision plan that will allow you time for relaxation. Set aside days and times for all the subjects that you need to study, and stick to your timetable.
- Set yourself sensible targets. Break your revision down into focused sessions of around 40 minutes, divided by breaks. These Revision Notes organise the basic facts into short, memorable sections to make revising easier.

REVISED ☐

2–6 weeks to go

- Read through the relevant sections of this book and refer to the exam tips, exam summaries, typical mistakes and key terms. Tick off the topics as you feel confident about them. Highlight those topics you find difficult and look at them again in detail.
- Test your understanding of each topic by working through the 'Now test yourself' questions in the book. Check your answers online.
- Make a note of any problem areas as you revise, and ask your teacher to go over these in class.
- Look at exemplar papers. They are one of the best ways to revise and practise your exam skills. Write or prepare planned answers to the exam practice questions provided in this book. Check your answers online and try out the extra quick quizzes at **www.hoddereducation. co.uk/myrevisionnotes**
- Use the revision activities provided in the book to try out different revision methods. For example, you can make notes using mind maps, spider diagrams or flash cards.
- Track your progress using the revision planner and give yourself a reward when you have achieved your target.

REVISED ☐

One week to go

- Try to fit in at least one more timed practice of an entire past paper and seek feedback from your teacher, comparing your work closely with the mark scheme.
- Check the revision planner to make sure you haven't missed out any topics. Brush up on any areas of difficulty by talking them over with a friend or getting help from your teacher.
- Attend any revision classes put on by your teacher. Remember, he or she is an expert at preparing people for exams.

REVISED ☐

The day before the exam

- Flick through these Revision Notes for useful reminders, for example the exam tips, exam summaries, typical mistakes and key terms.
- Check the time and place of your examination.
- Make sure you have everything you need — extra pens and pencils, tissues, a watch, bottled water, sweets.
- Allow some time to relax and have an early night to ensure you are fresh and alert for the exam.

REVISED ☐

My exams

AS PE Paper 1 (7581)

Date:..

Time:..

Location:..

A-Level PE Paper 1 (7582/1)

Date:..

Time:..

Location:..

A-Level PE Paper 2 (7582/2)

Date:..

Time:..

Location:..

Answers and quick quizzes at **www.hoddereducation.co.uk/myrevisionnotes**

1.1 Cardiovascular system

The cardiovascular system is the body's transport system. It includes the heart and the blood vessels. During exercise, an efficient cardiovascular system is extremely important, as the heart works to pump blood through the various blood vessels to deliver oxygen and nutrients to the working muscles and gather waste products such as carbon dioxide.

Cardiac conduction system

REVISED

When the heart beats, the blood needs to flow through it in a controlled manner – in through the atria and out through the ventricles. Heart muscle is described as being **myogenic** as the beat starts in the heart muscle itself with an electrical signal in the **sinoatrial node (SAN)**. This electrical signal then spreads through the heart in what is often described as a wave of excitation (similar to a Mexican wave) in the following order:

- From the SAN, the electrical impulse spreads through the walls of the atria, causing them to contract (atrial systole).
- The impulse then passes through the **atrioventricular node (AVN)**, where it is delayed for approximately 0.1 seconds to enable the atria to contract fully before ventricular systole begins.
- The impulse then travels through the bundle of His, which branches into two bundle branches, and into the Purkinje fibres, which spread throughout the ventricles, causing them to contract (ventricular systole).

> **Exam tip**
>
> While structure is not tested in the exam, a good grasp of how the components of the cardiovascular system are arranged and organised will enable you to better understand how the system functions.

> **Myogenic:** originating in muscle tissue.
>
> **Sinoatrial node (SAN):** a small mass of cardiac muscle found in the wall of the right atrium that generates the heartbeat. It is more commonly called the pacemaker.
>
> **Atrioventricular node (AVN):** relays the impulse between the upper and lower sections of the heart.

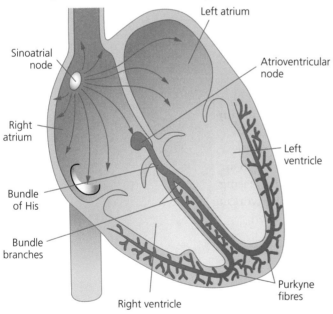

Figure 1.1a **The cardiac conduction system**

Now test yourself

TESTED

1 Identify the order in which a cardiac impulse travels.

Answer online

Factors affecting the change in rate of the conduction system

The conduction system ensures that heart rate increases during exercise to allow the working muscles to receive more oxygen. As discussed on the previous page, the heart generates its own impulses from the SAN, but the rate at which these cardiac impulses are fired can be controlled by the mechanisms outlined below.

Neural control mechanism

This involves the sympathetic nervous system, which stimulates the heart to beat faster, and the parasympathetic nervous system, which returns the heart to its resting level. These two systems are co-ordinated by the cardiac control centre located in the **medulla oblongata** of the brain.

The cardiac control centre is stimulated by chemoreceptors, baroreceptors and proprioceptors and will then send an impulse through either the sympathetic system to the SAN to increase heart rate or the parasympathetic system to the SAN to decrease heart rate:

Chemoreceptors → detect increase in blood carbon dioxide → cardiac control centre → sympathetic system → SAN increases heart rate

Baroreceptors → detect increase in blood pressure → cardiac control centre → parasympathetic system → SAN decreases heart rate

Proprioceptors → detect increase in muscle movement → cardiac control centre → sympathetic system → SAN increases heart rate

> **Medulla oblongata:** the most important part of the brain as it regulates processes that keep us alive.

> **Typical mistake**
>
> Don't be vague, tell the examiner what the receptors detect. For example, chemoreceptors detect an increase in carbon dioxide during exercise – don't just say chemical changes!

Now test yourself

TESTED

2 Identify and explain the role of chemoreceptors and proprioceptors in increasing heart rate.

Answer online

Hormonal control mechanism

Hormones can also have an effect on heart rate. The release of adrenaline during exercise is known as hormonal control. Adrenaline is a stress hormone that is released by the sympathetic nerves and cardiac nerve during exercise. It stimulates the SAN (pacemaker), which results in an increase in both the speed and force of contraction, therefore increasing cardiac output. This results in more blood being pumped to the working muscles so they can receive more oxygen for the energy they need.

Impact of physical activity and sport on stroke volume, heart rate and cardiac output

Stroke volume

This is the volume of blood pumped out by the heart ventricles in each contraction. On average, the resting stroke volume is approximately 70 ml.

Stroke volume depends upon the following:
- **Venous return** – when this increases, stroke volume will also increase.
- The elasticity of cardiac fibres – this is concerned with the degree of stretch of cardiac tissue during the diastole phase (when the heart is relaxed) of the cardiac cycle. The more the cardiac fibres can stretch, the greater the force of contraction. A greater force of contraction can increase the **ejection fraction**. This is called Starling's law.

> **Ejection fraction:** the percentage of blood pumped out by the left ventricle per beat.
>
> **Venous return:** the return of blood to the right side of the heart via the vena cava.

Answers and quick quizzes at **www.hoddereducation.co.uk/myrevisionnotes**

- The contractility of cardiac tissue (myocardium) – the greater the contractility of cardiac tissue, the greater the force of contraction. This results in an increase in stroke volume as well as the ejection fraction.

Stroke volume in response to exercise

Stroke volume increases as exercise intensity increases. However, this is only the case for up to 40–60 per cent of maximum effort. Once a performer reaches this point, stroke volume plateaus as the ventricles simply do not have as much time to fill up with blood and so cannot pump as much out.

Heart rate

This is the number of times the heart beats per minute. On average, the resting heart rate is approximately 72 beats per minute.

Heart rate range in response to exercise

Heart rate increases with exercise, but how much it increases is dependent on the intensity of the exercise. Heart rate will increase in direct proportion to exercise intensity: the higher the intensity, the higher the heart rate. Heart rate does eventually reach a maximum. Maximum heart rate can be calculated by subtracting your age from 220. An 18-year-old will have a maximum heart rate of 202 beats per minute:

220 – 18 = 202

A trained performer has a greater heart rate range because their resting heart rate is lower and their maximum heart rate increases.

The following graphs illustrate what happens to heart rate during maximal exercise such as sprinting and submaximal exercise such as jogging.

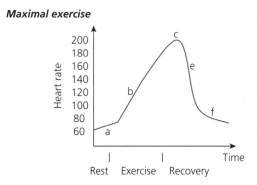

Maximal exercise

Submaximal exercise

a = *Anticipatory rise* due to hormonal action of adrenaline which causes the SAN to increase heart rate

b = *Sharp rise in* heart rate due mainly to anaerobic work

c = Heart rate continues to rise due to maximal workloads stressing the anaerobic systems

d = *Steady state* as the athlete is able to meet the oxygen demand with the oxygen supply

e = *Rapid decline* in heart rate as soon as the exercise stops

f = *Slower recovery* as body systems return to resting levels; heart rate needs to remain elevated to rid the body of waste products, for example lactic acid

Figure 1.1b Heart rate responses to maximal and submaximal exercise

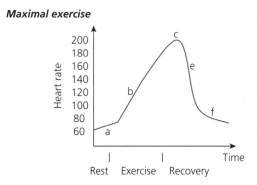

Regular aerobic training will result in more cardiac muscle. When the cardiac muscle becomes bigger and stronger, this is known as **cardiac hypertrophy**. Consequently, a bigger, stronger heart will enable more blood to be pumped out per beat (i.e. stroke volume), which means the heart does not have to pump as often. This is known as **bradycardia** and when this occurs, oxygen delivery to the muscles improves as there is less oxygen needed for contractions of the heart.

Cardiac output

This is the volume of blood pumped out by the heart ventricles per minute. It can be calculated using the following equation:

Cardiac output (Q) = Stroke volume (SV) x Heart rate (HR)

$$Q = 70 \times 72$$

$$Q = 5040 \text{ ml } (5.04 \text{ l})$$

It can be seen from this calculation that if heart rate or stroke volume increases, then cardiac output will also increase.

Cardiac output in response to exercise

During exercise, there is a large increase in cardiac output due to an increase in heart rate and an increase in stroke volume. Cardiac output will increase as the intensity of exercise increases until maximum intensity is reached. Then it plateaus (evens out).

The following table shows the differences in cardiac output in a trained and an untrained individual, both at rest and during exercise. The individuals in this example are both aged 18, so their maximum heart rate will be 202 beats per minute.

	Stroke volume x Heart rate = Cardiac output (SV x HR = Q)
Exercise untrained	120 ml x 202 = 24.24 litres
Exercise trained	170 ml x 202 = 34.34 litres

	Stroke volume x Heart rate = Cardiac output (SV x HR = Q)
Rest untrained	70 ml x 72 = 5.04 litres
Rest trained	84 ml x 60 = 5.04 litres

During exercise, the increase in maximum cardiac output will have huge benefits for the trained performer as they will be able to transport more blood to the working muscles and therefore more oxygen.

Now test yourself

TESTED ☐

3 (a) Define the terms 'cardiac output' and 'stroke volume' and explain the relationship between them.
  (b) Explain how training affects cardiac output and its components.

Answers online

Cardiac hypertrophy: when the heart becomes bigger and stronger due to a thickening of the muscular wall.

Bradycardia: when there is a decrease in resting heart rate to below 60 beats per minute.

Exam tip

Maximum heart rate is calculated as 220 minus your age.

Typical mistake

At rest, cardiac output for both the trained and untrained performer stays the same. It is *maximum* cardiac output that changes.

Impact of physical activity and sport on the health of the individual

Heart disease

Coronary heart disease (CHD) is the leading cause of death both in the UK and around the world. It occurs when your coronary arteries, which supply the heart muscle with oxygenated blood, become blocked or start to narrow by a gradual build-up of fatty deposits. This process is called **atherosclerosis** and the fatty deposits are called atheroma. High blood pressure, high levels of cholesterol, lack of exercise and smoking can all cause atherosclerosis.

> **Atherosclerosis:** when arteries harden and narrow and become clogged up by fatty deposits.

High blood pressure

Blood pressure is the force exerted by the blood against the blood vessel wall. This pressure comes from the heart as it pumps the blood around the body. High blood pressure puts extra strain on the arteries and heart and if left untreated increases the risk of heart attack, heart failure, kidney disease, stroke or dementia. Regular aerobic exercise can reduce blood pressure. It lowers both systolic and diastolic pressure by up to 5–10 mmHg, which reduces the risk of a heart attack by up to 20 per cent.

Cholesterol levels

There are two types of cholesterol:
- LDL (low-density lipoproteins) transport cholesterol in the blood to the tissues and are classed as 'bad' cholesterol since they are linked to an increased risk of heart disease.
- HDL (high-density lipoproteins) transport excess cholesterol in the blood back to the liver where it is broken down. These are classed as 'good' cholesterol since they lower the risk of developing heart disease.

Regular physical activity lowers bad LDL cholesterol levels. At the same time, it significantly increases good HDL cholesterol levels.

Stroke

The brain needs a constant supply of oxygenated blood and nutrients to maintain its function. The energy to work all the time is provided by oxygen delivered to the brain in the blood. A stroke occurs when the blood supply to part of the brain is cut off, causing damage to brain cells so they start to die. This can lead to brain injury, disability and sometimes death. There are two main types of stroke:
- Ischaemic strokes are the most common form and occur when a blood clot stops the blood supply.
- Haemorrhagic strokes occur when a weakened blood vessel supplying the brain bursts.

Research has shown that regular exercise can help to lower your blood pressure and help you maintain a healthy weight, which can reduce your risk of stroke by 27 per cent.

Now test yourself

TESTED

4 What effect does regular physical activity have on blood pressure and cholesterol levels?

Answer online

> **Revision activity**
>
> Create a table to summarise how physical activity can have an effect on heart disease, high blood pressure, cholesterol levels and strokes.

Cardiovascular drift

Cardiovascular drift is characterised by a progressive decrease in stroke volume and arterial blood pressure, together with a progressive rise in heart rate. It occurs during prolonged exercise in a warm environment, despite the intensity of the exercise remaining the same. A reduction in plasma volume occurs from the increased sweating response of the body and this reduces venous return and stroke volume. Heart rate then increases to compensate and maintain cardiac output.

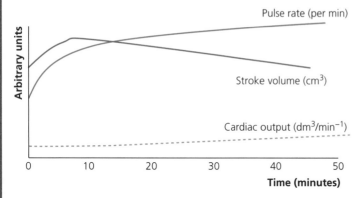

Figure 1.1c Graph to show cardiovascular drift

Exam tip

Cardiovascular drift → HR increases and stroke volume decreases → occurs after 10 minutes in warm conditions → caused by reduced plasma volume → reduced venous return → cardiac output increases due to more energy needed to cool the body/sweat

Blood vessels

Several different blood vessels carry blood from the heart, distribute it round the body, then return it back to the heart (systemic circulation) and transport deoxygenated blood from the heart to the lungs and oxygenated blood back to the heart (pulmonary circulation).

Each blood vessel is slightly different in structure:
- Veins transport deoxygenated blood back to the heart (with the exception of the pulmonary vein), have thinner muscle/elastic tissue layers, blood is at low pressure and they have valves and a wider lumen.
- Arteries transport oxygenated blood around the body (with the exception of the pulmonary artery), and have the highest pressure, thick and elastic outer walls and thick layers of muscle, a smaller lumen and a smooth inner layer.
- Capillaries are only wide enough to allow one red blood cell to pass through at a given time. This slows down blood flow and allows the exchange of nutrients with the tissues to take place by diffusion.

Revision activity

Create a spider diagram to highlight the key structures of arteries, veins and capillaries.

Now test yourself
TESTED

5 Explain why arteries have the highest pressure.

Answer online

Blood pressure

REVISED

Blood pressure is the force exerted by the blood against the blood vessel wall and is often referred to as:

Blood flow x Resistance

During exercise, the heart contracts with more force so that blood leaves the heart under high pressure in order for the muscles to receive the extra oxygen they require. This is the **systolic** pressure or pressure of contraction. The lower pressure as the ventricles relax is the **diastolic** pressure.

Blood pressure is measured at the brachial artery in the upper arm. A typical reading at rest is:

$$\frac{120}{80} \text{ mmHg (millimetres of mercury)}$$

Blood pressure is different in the various blood vessels and is largely dependent on the distance of the blood vessel from the heart.

> **Systolic:** when the ventricles are contracting.
>
> **Diastolic:** when the ventricles are relaxing.

> **Exam tip**
>
> It is easy to remember that blood pressure increases during exercise but make sure you can explain why.

Now test yourself

TESTED

6 Give an average blood pressure reading and identify what happens to blood pressure during exercise.

Answer online

Venous return mechanisms

REVISED

Venous return is the return of blood to the right side of the heart via the vena cava. Up to 70 per cent of the total volume of blood is contained in the veins at rest. This means that a large amount of blood can be returned to the heart when needed. During exercise, the amount of blood returning to the heart (venous return) increases.

Active mechanisms are needed to help venous return:
- The skeletal muscle pump – when muscles contract and relax, they change shape. This change in shape means that the muscles press on the nearby veins and cause a pumping effect and squeeze the blood towards the heart.
- The respiratory pump – when muscles contract and relax during breathing in and breathing out, pressure changes occur in the thoracic (chest) and abdominal (stomach) cavities. These pressure changes compress the nearby veins and assist blood to return to the heart.
- Pocket valves – it is important that blood in the veins only flows in one direction. The presence of valves ensures that this happens. This is because once the blood has passed through the valves, they close to prevent the blood flowing back.
- There is a very thin layer of smooth muscle in the walls of the veins. This helps squeeze blood back towards the heart.
- Gravity helps the blood return to the heart from the upper body.

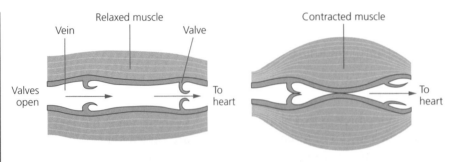

Figure 1.1d **The skeletal muscle pump**

Impact of blood pressure on venous return

When systolic blood pressure increases, there is also an increase in venous return as the pressure in the blood vessels is higher so the blood travels quicker. When systolic blood pressure decreases, there is a decrease in venous return as the pressure in the various blood vessels has dropped so blood flow slows down.

Venous return is also determined by a pressure gradient:

$$\frac{\text{Venous pressure (P}_\text{V}) - \text{Right atrial pressure (P}_\text{RA})}{\text{Venous vascular resistance R}_\text{V}}$$

To simplify this, increasing right atrial pressure decreases venous return and decreasing right atrial pressure increases venous return.

Transportation of oxygen

REVISED

Oxygen can be transported as follows:
- 3 per cent dissolves into plasma
- 97 per cent combines with haemoglobin to form oxyhaemoglobin.

At the tissues, oxygen is released from oxyhaemoglobin due to the lower pressure of oxygen that exists there. The release of oxygen from oxyhaemoglobin to the tissues is referred to as oxyhaemoglobin dissociation. In the muscle, oxygen is stored by **myoglobin**. This has a higher affinity for oxygen and will store the oxygen for the **mitochondria** until it is used by the muscles.

Oxyhaemoglobin dissociation curve

The oxyhaemoglobin dissociation curve helps us to understand how haemoglobin in our blood carries and releases oxygen. The curve represents the relationship between oxygen and haemoglobin.

Myoglobin: often called 'muscle haemoglobin'. It is an iron-containing muscle pigment in slow twitch muscle fibres which has a higher affinity for oxygen than haemoglobin. It stores the oxygen in the muscle fibres which can be used quickly when exercise begins.

Mitochondria: often referred to as the 'powerhouse' of the cell, as respiration and energy production occur there.

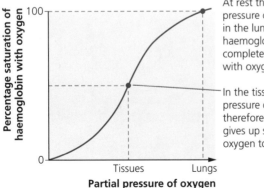

At rest the high partial pressure of oxygen in the lungs means haemoglobin is almost completely saturated with oxygen

In the tissues, the partial pressure of oxygen is lower, therefore the haemoglobin gives up some of its oxygen to the tissues

Figure 1.1e **The oxyhaemoglobin dissociation curve**

From this curve you can see that in the lungs there is almost full saturation (concentration) of haemoglobin but at the tissues the partial pressure of oxygen is lower.

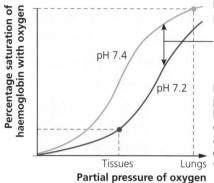

Figure 1.1f The effect of changing acidity on the oxyhaemoglobin dissociation curve

During exercise, this S-shaped curve shifts to the right. This is because when muscles require more oxygen, the dissociation of oxygen from haemoglobin in the blood capillaries to the muscle tissue occurs more readily. This shift is known as the **Bohr shift**.

Three factors are responsible for this increase in the dissociation of oxygen from haemoglobin, which results in more oxygen being available for use by the working muscles:

● Increase in blood temperature – when blood and muscle temperature increases during exercise, oxygen will dissociate from haemoglobin more readily.

● Partial pressure of blood carbon dioxide increases – as the level of blood carbon dioxide rises during exercise, oxygen will dissociate quicker from haemoglobin.

● Blood pH – more carbon dioxide will lower the pH in the body. A drop in pH will cause oxygen to dissociate from haemoglobin more quickly (Bohr shift).

Now test yourself   TESTED ☐

7 During exercise, the oxyhaemoglobin curve shifts to the right. Explain why this happens and the effect that this change has on oxygen delivery to the muscles.

Answer online

> **Bohr shift:** when an increase in blood carbon dioxide and a decrease in blood pH results in a reduction of the affinity of haemoglobin for oxygen.

> **Typical mistake**
>
> When giving the causes of the Bohr shift, don't forget the word 'blood'. (*Blood* pH, *blood* carbon dioxide levels, *blood* temperature).

Redistribution of blood   REVISED ☐

The distribution of blood flow is different at rest compared to during exercise. During exercise, the skeletal muscles require more oxygen, so more blood needs to be redirected to them in order to meet this increase in oxygen demand. The redirecting of blood flow to the areas where it is most needed is known as shunting or the **vascular shunt mechanism** and is important to ensure:

● More blood goes to the heart, because the heart muscle needs oxygen to beat faster and with more force.

● More blood goes to the muscles, as they need more oxygen for energy and more blood is needed to remove waste products such as carbon dioxide and lactic acid.

> **Vascular shunt mechanism:** the redistribution of cardiac output.

- More blood goes to the skin, because energy is needed to cool the body down.
- Blood flow to the brain remains constant, as it needs oxygen for energy to maintain function.

It is also important to ensure the gut is empty, as a full gut would result in more blood being directed to the stomach instead of the working muscles. This would have a detrimental effect on performance, as less oxygen is being made available.

Control of blood flow

Both blood pressure and blood flow are controlled by the vasomotor centre, located in the medulla oblongata of the brain. During exercise, chemical changes – such as increases in carbon dioxide and lactic acid – are detected by chemoreceptors. These receptors stimulate the vasomotor centre which then redistributes blood flow through **vasodilation** and **vasoconstriction**. Vasodilation is when the blood vessel widens to increase blood flow into the capillaries, and vasoconstriction is when the blood vessel narrows to decrease blood flow. In exercise, more oxygen is needed at the working muscles, so vasodilation will occur in the arterioles supplying these muscles, increasing blood flow and bringing in the much-needed oxygen, whereas vasoconstriction will occur in the arterioles supplying non-essential organs such as the intestines and liver.

Pre-capillary sphincters also aid blood redistribution. They are tiny rings of muscle located at the opening of capillaries. When they contract, blood flow is restricted through the capillary and when they relax blood flow is increased.

Vasodilation: the widening of the blood vessels to increase blood flow into the capillaries.

Vasoconstriction: the narrowing of the blood vessels to reduce blood flow into the capillaries.

Exam tip

During exercise, the muscles require more oxygen so we have to direct more blood to them.

Now test yourself

TESTED

8 (a) Why does blood flow to the skin and heart increase during exercise?
  (b) Explain why there is a need for an increase in blood flow to the skeletal muscles during exercise and how this is achieved.

Answers online

Arterio-venous difference (A-VO$_2$ diff)

REVISED

This is the difference between the oxygen content of the arterial blood arriving at the muscles and the venous blood leaving the muscles. At rest, the **arterio-venous difference** is low, as not much oxygen is required by the muscles. But during exercise much more oxygen is needed from the blood for the muscles, so the arterio-venous difference is high. This increase will affect gaseous exchange at the alveoli, so more oxygen is taken in and more carbon dioxide is removed. Training also increases the arterio-venous difference, as trained performers can extract a greater amount of oxygen from the blood.

Arterio-venous difference (A-VO$_2$ diff): the difference between the oxygen content of the arterial blood arriving at the muscles and the venous blood leaving the muscles.

Now test yourself

TESTED

9 What do you understand by the term 'arterio-venous difference' and what happens to this during exercise?

Answer online

Exam practice

1 During a game, a defender will work at various intensities. Describe how cardiac output increases when a defender is working at a higher intensity. [3]
2 Heart rate can be controlled by the heart itself. Explain how this occurs. [3]
3 What are the effects of cardiac hypertrophy and bradycardia on the heart during exercise? [3]
4 What factors determine blood pressure in blood vessels? [3]
5 Where is myoglobin found in the body and what is its role during exercise? [2]
6 How would performing a cool-down help venous return? [2]

Answers and quick quizzes online

ONLINE

Summary

You should now be able to:
- describe the cardiac conduction system
- explain the hormonal, neural and chemical regulation of responses during physical activity and sport
- describe the role of chemoreceptors, baroreceptors and proprioceptors in regulation of responses during physical activity
- understand the impact of physical activity and sport on cardiac output, stroke volume and heart rate, and explain the relationship between them in trained/untrained individuals and maximal/submaximal exercise
- understand Starling's law
- identify how physical activity can affect heart disease, high blood pressure, cholesterol levels and strokes

- explain cardiovascular drift
- understand the venous return mechanisms
- explain blood pressure using the terms 'systolic' and 'diastolic' and identify the relationship venous return has with blood pressure
- describe the transportation of oxygen and be able to explain the roles of haemoglobin and myoglobin
- understand the oxyhaemoglobin dissociation curve
- explain the Bohr shift
- explain how blood is redistributed during exercise through vasoconstriction and vasodilation
- explain arterio-venous oxygen difference (A-VO$_2$ diff).

1.2 Respiratory system

The body needs a continuous supply of oxygen to produce energy. When we use oxygen to break down food to release energy, carbon dioxide is produced as a waste product and the body must remove this. Respiration, therefore, is the taking in of oxygen and the removal of carbon dioxide.

Lung volumes

REVISED

This is the movement of air into and out of the lungs. Taking air into the lungs is inspiration and moving air out is expiration. At rest, we inspire and expire approximately 0.5 litres of air. The volume of air inspired or expired per breath is referred to as the **tidal volume**. The volume of air inspired or expired per minute is referred to as **minute ventilation** and can be calculated by multiplying the number of breaths taken per minute (approximately 12) by the tidal volume:

Number of breaths (per min) x Tidal volume = Minute ventilation
12 x 0.5 = 6 litres/min

Changes in minute ventilation occur during different types of exercise. The more demanding the physical activity is, the more breathing increases to meet the extra oxygen demand. This is illustrated in the graph below:

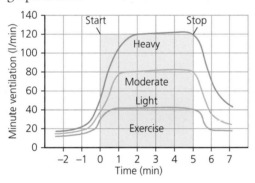

Figure 1.2a The respiratory response to various intensities of exercise

At rest, we still have the ability to breathe in and breathe out more air than just the tidal volume. This extra amount of air inspired is the **inspiratory reserve volume (IRV)** and the extra amount expired is the **expiratory reserve volume (ERV)**. Exercise will have an effect on these lung volumes.

Residual volume is the amount of air that remains in the lungs after maximal expiration, because we can never totally empty our lungs, even when we have exhaled as much as possible.

The following table defines the five lung volumes you need for your exam and identifies the changes that take place in these volumes during exercise:

> **Exam tip**
>
> You will not be examined on the structure of the lungs or the respiratory airways but knowledge of this will help your understanding of the respiratory system.

> **Tidal volume:** the volume of air inspired or expired per breath.
>
> **Minute ventilation:** the volume of air inspired or expired per minute.

> **Inspiratory reserve volume (IRV):** the volume of air that can be forcibly inspired after a normal breath.
>
> **Expiratory reserve volume (ERV):** the volume of air that can be forcibly expired after a normal breath.
>
> **Residual volume:** the amount of air that remains in the lungs after maximal expiration.

Lung volume or capacity	Definition	Change during exercise
Tidal volume	Volume of air inspired or expired per breath	Increase
Minute ventilation	Volume of air inspired or expired per minute	Big increase
Inspiratory reserve volume	Volume of air that can be forcibly inspired after a normal breath	Decrease
Expiratory reserve volume	Volume of air that can be forcibly expired after a normal breath	Slight decrease
Residual volume	Volume of air that remains in the lungs after maximum expiration	Remains the same

The volume of air we breathe in and out can be measured using a spirometer. An example of a spirometer trace can be seen below:

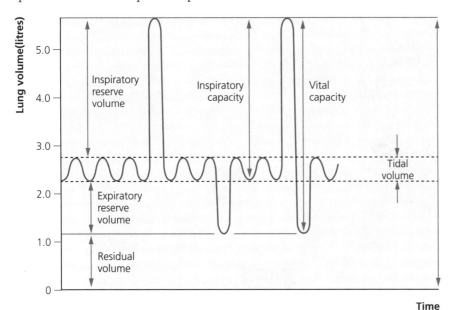

Figure 1.2b Spirometer trace of respiratory air

Now test yourself

TESTED ☐

1 What do you think will happen to the graphical representation of residual volume during exercise?

Answer online

Gaseous exchange

REVISED ☐

Gaseous exchange is concerned with:

● getting oxygen in the air into the lungs so that it can diffuse into the blood and be transported to the cells of the body
● the removal of carbon dioxide from the blood so it can diffuse into the lungs and into the air.

The terms **partial pressure** and **diffusion** are used when describing the gaseous exchange process. Quite simply, all gases exert a pressure. Oxygen makes up only a small part of air (approximately 21 per cent) so it therefore exerts a partial pressure. Diffusion is the movement of gas molecules from an area of high concentration or partial pressure to an area of low concentration or partial pressure. Since gases flow from an area of high pressure to an area of low pressure, it is important that as air

Gaseous exchange: the movement of oxygen from the air into the blood, and carbon dioxide from the blood into the air.

Typical mistake

Exam questions mentioning gas exchange want an explanation of the movement of both oxygen and carbon dioxide. Too often answers only mention one of these.

moves from the alveoli to the blood and then to the muscle, the partial pressure of oxygen of each is successively lower.

Gaseous exchange at the alveoli

The alveoli are responsible for the exchange of gases between the lungs and the blood, and their structure is designed to help gaseous exchange. Their walls are very thin (only one cell thick), which means there is a short diffusion pathway. This is because there are only two layers of cells from the air in the alveoli to the blood. An extensive capillary network surrounds the alveoli, so they have an excellent blood supply. They have a huge surface area because there are millions of alveoli in each lung, which allows for a greater uptake of oxygen.

> **Partial pressure:** the pressure exerted by an individual gas when it exists within a mixture of gases.
>
> **Diffusion:** the movement of gas molecules from an area of high concentration or partial pressure to an area of low concentration or partial pressure.

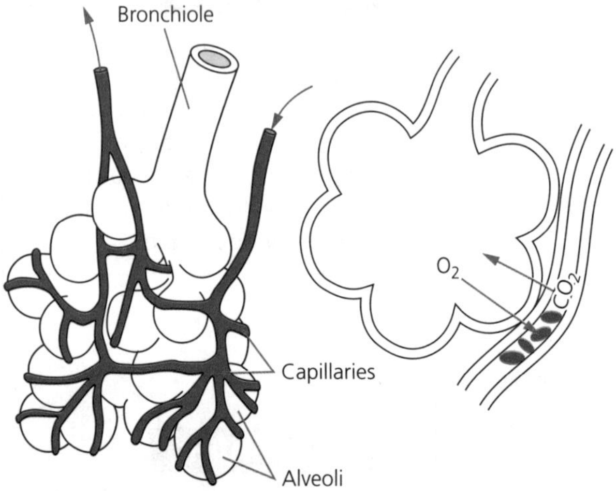

Figure 1.2c **The alveoli**

Now test yourself

TESTED ☐

2 Identify two structural features of the alveoli and explain how they assist in the diffusion of respiratory gases.

Answer online

The partial pressure of oxygen (pO_2) in the alveoli (100 mmHg) is higher than the partial pressure of oxygen in the capillary blood vessels (40 mmHg). This is because oxygen has been removed by the working muscles, so its concentration in the blood is lower and therefore so is its partial pressure. The difference in partial pressure is referred to as the **concentration/diffusion gradient**. The bigger this gradient, the faster diffusion will be. Oxygen will diffuse from the alveoli into the blood until the pressure is equal in both.

> **Exam tip**
>
> The diffusion pathway of oxygen is: alveoli → blood → muscles

The movement of carbon dioxide occurs in the same way but in the reverse order. This time, the partial pressure of carbon dioxide in the blood entering the alveolar capillaries is higher (46 mmHg) than in the alveoli (40 mmHg), so carbon dioxide diffuses into the alveoli from the blood until the pressure is equal in both.

> **Concentration/diffusion gradient:** this explains how gases flow from an area of high concentration to an area of low concentration. The steeper this gradient, the faster diffusion occurs.

Gaseous exchange at the muscles

The partial pressure of oxygen has to be lower at the tissues than in the blood for diffusion to occur. As such, in the capillary membranes surrounding the muscle the partial pressure of oxygen is 5 mmHg and

> **Exam tip**
>
> The diffusion pathway of carbon dioxide is: muscles → blood → alveoli

it is 100 mmHg in the blood. This lower partial pressure allows oxygen to diffuse from the blood into the muscle until equilibrium is reached. Conversely, the partial pressure of carbon dioxide in the blood (40 mmHg) is lower than in the tissues (46 mmHg), so again diffusion occurs and carbon dioxide moves into the blood to be transported to the lungs.

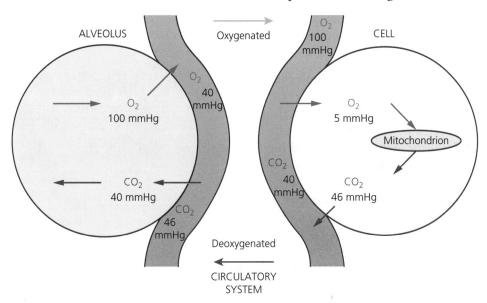

Figure 1.2d Movement of O_2 and CO_2 in the body due to partial pressures

Now test yourself

TESTED

3 Explain how the gas exchange system operates at the muscles.

Answer online

Regulation of pulmonary ventilation during exercise

REVISED

There are three factors involved in the regulation of **pulmonary ventilation** during exercise:

- neural control
- chemical control
- hormonal control.

Neural and chemical regulation of pulmonary ventilation

The nervous system controls pulmonary ventilation automatically through two systems: sympathetic and parasympathetic. Both of these cause opposite effects because their activating chemicals are different. The sympathetic nervous system prepares your body for exercise so it will increase how fast you breathe, whereas the parasympathetic nervous system will do the opposite and lower your breathing rate. The respiratory centre located in the medulla oblongata of the brain controls the rate and depth of breathing and uses both neural and chemical control.

An increased concentration of carbon dioxide in the blood stimulates the respiratory centre to increase respiratory rate. The respiratory centre has two main areas:

> **Pulmonary ventilation:** simply means breathing!

> **Exam tip**
>
> Neural control involves the brain and the nervous system, and chemical control is concerned with blood acidity.

- The inspiratory centre is responsible for inspiration and expiration.
- The expiratory centre stimulates the expiratory muscles during exercise.

The inspiratory centre sends out nerve impulses via the phrenic nerve to the inspiratory muscles (diaphragm and external intercostals) to cause them to contract. This stimulation acts for approximately 2 seconds and then the impulses stop and passive expiration occurs due to the elastic recoil of the lungs.

The respiratory centre responds mainly to changes in blood chemistry. During exercise, blood acidity increases as a result of an increase in the plasma concentration of carbon dioxide and an increase in lactic acid production. These changes are detected by chemoreceptors, which are found in the carotid artery and the aortic arch, and they send impulses to the inspiratory centre to increase ventilation until the blood acidity has returned to normal. To achieve this, the respiratory centre sends impulses down the phrenic nerve to stimulate more inspiratory muscles: namely the sternocleidomastoid, scalenes and pectoralis minor. As a result the rate, depth and rhythm of breathing increase.

Role of proprioceptors and baroreceptors in the regulation of pulmonary ventilation

- Proprioceptors: these detect an increase in muscle movement and provide feedback to the respiratory centre to increase breathing during exercise.
- Baroreceptors: a decrease in blood pressure detected by baroreceptors in the aorta and carotid arteries results in an increase in breathing rate.

Exam tip

The order of neural/chemical control for increased inspiration during exercise is:

Receptors → medulla oblongata → phrenic nerve → inspiratory muscles (diaphragm, external intercostals, sternocleidomastoid, scalenes and pectoralis minor)

The order of neural/chemical control for expiration during exercise is:

Receptors → medulla oblongata → intercostal nerve – abdominals and internal intercostals

---

Now test yourself

TESTED ☐

4 Explain the role of proprioceptors and baroreceptors in the regulation of pulmonary ventilation.

Answer online

Hormonal regulation of pulmonary ventilation during exercise

Adrenaline is often referred to as the body's activator and is released in response to exercise. As a result, breathing rate increases in preparation for exercise and the demand to take in more oxygen and remove more carbon dioxide.

> **Adrenaline:** the hormone that increases breathing rate in preparation for exercise.

Impact of poor lifestyle choices on the respiratory system

REVISED

Smoking affects oxygen transport because the carbon monoxide from cigarettes combines with haemoglobin in red blood cells much more readily than oxygen. This reduces the oxygen-carrying capacity of the blood, which increases breathlessness during exercise. Smoking can also cause the following:

- irritation of the trachea and bronchi
- reduced lung function and increased breathlessness caused by swelling and narrowing of the lungs' airways
- damage to the cells lining the airways from cigarette smoke, leading to a build-up of excess mucus in the lungs; this results in a smoker's cough in an attempt to get rid of the mucus
- reduction in the efficiency of gaseous exchange, which can increase the risk of COPD (chronic obstructive pulmonary disease).

Exam practice

1 Explain how the gas exchange system operates at the lungs. [4]
2 Explain the role of chemoreceptors in changing breathing rate during exercise. [4]
3 How does smoking affect oxygen transport? [2]
4 Identify what happens to the following lung volumes during exercise: tidal volume, inspiratory reserve volume and residual volume. [3]

Answers and quick quizzes online

ONLINE

Summary

You should now be able to:
- understand the following lung volumes: residual volume, expiratory reserve volume, inspiratory reserve volume, tidal volume and minute ventilation
- understand the impact of physical activity and sport on these lung volumes
- explain gaseous exchange of oxygen and carbon dioxide at the alveoli and muscles, through the principles of diffusion and partial pressures

- understand the hormonal, chemical and neural regulation of pulmonary ventilation during physical activity
- explain the role of chemoreceptors, proprioceptors and baroreceptors in the regulation of pulmonary ventilation during exercise
- understand the effect of poor lifestyle choices such as smoking on the respiratory system.

1.3 Neuromuscular system

When we exercise, the nervous system plays a crucial role recruiting different muscle fibre types, depending on the demands of the activity. It adjusts the strength of contraction and, with the use of sensory organs, can allow a muscle to stretch further in proprioceptive neuromuscular facilitation (PNF).

Nervous system

The sympathetic and parasympathetic nervous systems are part of the peripheral nervous system. Their role is to transmit information from the brain to the parts of the body that need to adjust what they are doing to prepare for exercise:
- The sympathetic nervous system prepares the body for exercise and is often referred to as the 'fight or flight response'.
- The parasympathetic nervous system has the opposite effect of the sympathetic system, relaxing the body and slowing down many high-energy functions. It is often explained by the phrase 'rest and relax'.

> **Exam tip**
>
> The sympathetic system is 'fight or flight' – it fires up the body for exercise. The parasympathetic system is 'rest and relax' – it slows everything down.

Types of muscle fibre

There are three main types of muscle fibre.
- slow oxidative (type I)
- fast oxidative glycolytic (type IIa)
- fast glycolytic (type IIx).

Type I fibres are known as 'slow twitch' and type II fibres are known as 'fast twitch'. Our skeletal muscles contain a mixture of all three types of fibre but not in equal proportions. This mix is mainly genetically determined.

Slow twitch fibres (type I)

These fibres have a slower contraction speed than fast twitch fibres and are better adapted to lower intensity exercise such as long-distance running. They produce most of their energy (ATP) aerobically (using oxygen) and therefore have specific characteristics that allow them to use oxygen more effectively

> **Exam tip**
>
> Slow twitch fibres contract slower and do not fatigue quickly, so they tend to be used by endurance runners who use the aerobic system to supply the majority of their energy.

Fast twitch fibres (type II)

These fibres have a much faster contraction speed and can generate a greater force of contraction. However, they also fatigue very quickly and are used for short, intense bursts of effort. They produce most of their energy anaerobically (without oxygen). As mentioned above, there are two types of fast twitch fibre:
- Type IIa fast oxidative glycolytic fibres are more resistant to fatigue and are used for events such as the 1500 m in athletics where a longer burst of energy is needed.
- Type IIx fast glycolytic fibres these fatigue much quicker than type IIa and are used for highly explosive events such as the 100 m in athletics where a quick, short burst of energy is needed.

Now test yourself

TESTED

1 Identify two sporting activities where slow twitch fibres are important.

Answer online

Characteristics of slow and fast twitch muscle fibres

All three fibre types have specific characteristics that allow them to perform their role successfully. These can be found in the table below.

Characteristic	Type I	Type IIa	Type IIx
Contraction speed (m/sec)	Slow (110)	Fast (50)	Fast (50)
Motor neurone size	Small	Large	Large
Motor neurone conduction capacity	Slow	Fast	Fast
Force produced	Low	High	High
Fatigability	Low	Medium	High
Mitochondrial density	High	Medium	Low
Myoglobin content	High	Medium	Low
Capillary density	High	Medium	Low
Aerobic capacity	Very high	Medium	Low
Anaerobic capacity	Low	High	Very high
Myosin ATPase/glycolytic enzyme activity	Low	High	Very high

These characteristics can be divided into two groups: functional or structural. A functional characteristic is what the fibre does and a structural characteristic concerns the make-up of the fibre.

Functional characteristics	Structural characteristics
● Contraction speed (m/sec) ● Motor neurone conduction capacity ● Force produced ● Fatigability ● Aerobic capacity ● Anaerobic capacity ● Myosin ATPase/glycolytic enzyme activity	● Motor neurone size ● Mitochondrial density ● Myoglobin content ● Capillary density

Typical mistake

Read the exam question carefully. If the question is not specific and just asks for characteristics, you can answer with both structural and functional characteristics. However, mistakes occur when a question specifies either structural or functional characteristics.

Revision activity

Make a list of all the characteristics of each fibre type and then explain how they are suited to producing ATP aerobically and anaerobically.

Now test yourself

TESTED

2 A football goalkeeper will use type IIx fibres when he jumps explosively to make a save. Can you give two functional characteristics of this fibre type?

Answer online

Motor unit

A **motor unit** consists of a motor neurone and a group of muscle fibres. Only one type of muscle fibre can be found in one particular motor unit. Muscle fibres work with the nervous system so that a contraction can occur. The motor neurone transmits the nerve impulse to the muscle fibre. Each motor neurone has branches which end in the neuromuscular junction on the muscle fibre.

> **Motor unit:** a motor neurone and its muscle fibres.

All or none law

Once the motor neurone stimulates the muscle fibres, either all of them contract or none of them contract. It is not possible for a motor unit to partially contract. This is called the **all or none law**. Here, a minimum amount of stimulation, called the threshold, is required to start a contraction. If the sequence of impulses is equal to or more than the threshold, all the muscle fibres in a motor unit will contract. However, if the sequence of impulses is less than the threshold, no muscle action will occur.

How to increase the strength of contraction

A basketball player jumping up for a rebound needs to exert as much force as possible to gain enough height to win the rebound. In order to increase the strength or force exerted by her quadriceps muscle to extend her knee as she jumps, the following need to take place:

- **Wave summation.** The greater the frequency of stimuli, the greater the tension developed by the muscle. This is referred to as **wave summation**, where repeated activation of a motor neurone stimulating a given muscle fibre results in a greater force of contraction. Each time the nerve impulse reaches the muscle cell, calcium is released. In simple terms, calcium needs to be present for a muscle to contract. If there are repeated nerve impulses with no time to relax, calcium will build up in the muscle cell. This produces a forceful, sustained, smooth contraction which is referred to as a **tetanic contraction**.

> **All or none law:** where a sequence of impulses has to be of sufficient intensity to stimulate *all* of the muscle fibres in a motor unit in order for them to contract. If not, *none* of them contract.
>
> **Wave summation:** where there is a repeated nerve impulse with no time to relax, so a smooth, sustained contraction occurs rather than twitches.
>
> **Tetanic contraction:** a sustained powerful muscle contraction caused by a series of fast repeating stimuli.

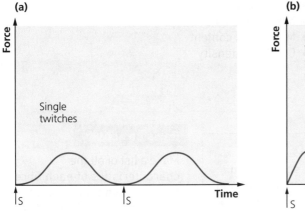

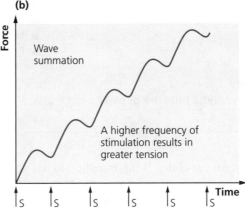

Figure 1.3a a) Low-frequency stimuli; **b)** high-frequency stimuli leading to increased tension

- **Spatial summation.** This occurs when impulses are received at the same time at different places on the neurone which add up to fire the neurone. It involves the recruitment of additional, bigger motor units and fast twitch fibres within a muscle to develop more force. Activation of these motor units is staggered, which enables a sustained muscle contraction to be maintained as some motor units are contracting while others are relaxing, delaying fatigue.

> **Spatial summation:** when the strength of a contraction changes by altering the number and size of the muscle's motor units.

Now test yourself

TESTED ☐

3 Contraction of different types of muscle fibre involves the use of motor units. What do you understand by the term 'motor unit' and how are motor units involved in the process of spatial summation?

Answer online

Proprioceptive neuromuscular facilitation (PNF)

REVISED ☐

Proprioceptive neuromuscular facilitation (PNF) is an advanced stretching technique. It is also considered to be one of the most effective forms of flexibility training for increasing range of motion. There are a few different PNF techniques, but the most practical is the **CRAC** technique.

CRAC: stands for contract–relax–antagonist–contract.

Role of muscle spindles and golgi tendon organs in PNF

In PNF, muscle action has to be controlled in order for movement to be effective. There are several internal regulatory mechanisms that make this possible. Proprioceptors are sensory organs in the muscles, tendons and joints that inform the body of the extent of movement that has taken place. Muscle spindles and golgi tendon organs are types of proprioceptors.

Muscle spindles

Muscle spindles are very sensitive proprioceptors that lie between skeletal muscle fibres. They are often called stretch receptors as they provide information (excitory signals) to the central nervous system about how fast and how far a muscle is being stretched. The central nervous system then sends an impulse back to the muscle telling it to contract, which triggers the stretch reflex. This reflex action causes the muscle to contract to prevent overstretching, reducing the risk of injury.

Muscle spindles: proprioceptors that detect how far and how fast a muscle is being stretched and produce the stretch reflex.

Golgi tendon organs

These are found between the muscle fibre and tendon. They detect levels of tension in a muscle. When the muscle is contracted isometrically in PNF, they sense the increase in muscle tension and send inhibitory signals to the brain, which allows the antagonist muscle to relax and lengthen. This is known as **autogenic inhibition**.

Autogenic inhibition: where there is a sudden relaxation of the muscle in response to high tension. The receptors involved in this process are golgi tendon organs.

a)  b)  c)

Figure 1.3b PNF in practice

a) Here, the individual performs a passive stretch with the help of a partner and extends the leg until tension is felt. This stretch is detected by the muscle spindles. If the muscle is being stretched too far, then a stretch reflex should occur.

b) The individual then isometrically contracts the muscle for at least ten seconds by pushing their leg against their partner who supplies just enough resistance to hold the leg in a stationary position. Remember, golgi tendon organs are sensitive to tension developed in a muscle, and during an isometric contraction they are activated and the inhibitory signals they send override the excitory signals from the muscle spindles, therefore delaying the stretch reflex.

c) As the leg is passively stretched again, the golgi tendon organs are responsible for the antagonist muscle relaxing, which means the leg stretches further. This process can be repeated until no more gains are possible.

Exam practice

1 The training that elite performers undertake may include proprioceptive neuromuscular facilitation (PNF) stretching. Explain the role of the muscle spindle apparatus and golgi tendon organs during PNF stretching. [5]
2 Describe the structural characteristics of the main muscle fibre type used by a triathlete. [4]
3 Explain how the force of muscle contraction can be varied to ensure that skills are executed correctly. [8]

Answers and quick quizzes online

ONLINE

Summary

You should now be able to:
- identify the characteristics and functions of the three muscle fibre types: slow twitch (type I), fast oxidative glycolytic (type IIa) and fast glycolytic (type IIx) for a variety of sporting activities
- understand the role of the sympathetic and parasympathetic nervous systems
- explain the recruitment of muscle fibres through motor units
- understand the terms 'spatial summation', 'wave summation', 'all or none law' and 'tetanic contraction'
- explain the role of the two proprioceptors, muscle spindles and golgi tendon organs, in PNF.

1.4 Musculoskeletal system and analysis of movement in physical activities

Joint types and articulating bones

REVISED

The following table summarises joint type and **articulating bones**:

Joint	Joint type	Articulating bones
Ankle	Hinge	Talus, tibia, fibula
Knee	Hinge	Femur, tibia
Hip	Ball and socket	Pelvis, femur
Shoulder	Ball and socket	Scapula, humerus
Elbow	Hinge	Radius, ulna, humerus

Articulating bones: bones that meet and move at the joint.

Exam tip

While you do not need to be able to label a skeleton, you do need to know the names of the bones that articulate at the ankle, knee, hip, shoulder and elbow.

Planes and axes

REVISED

Joint actions

Joint actions in the sagittal plane about a transverse axis

Flexion, extension/hyper-extension, plantar-flexion and dorsi-flexion occur in a sagittal plane about a transverse axis:

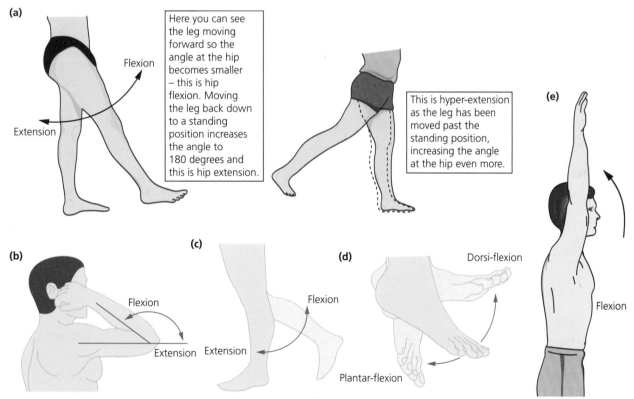

(a)

Flexion

Extension

Here you can see the leg moving forward so the angle at the hip becomes smaller – this is hip flexion. Moving the leg back down to a standing position increases the angle to 180 degrees and this is hip extension.

This is hyper-extension as the leg has been moved past the standing position, increasing the angle at the hip even more.

(e)

(b)

Flexion

Extension

(c)

Flexion

Extension

(d)

Dorsi-flexion

Plantar-flexion

Flexion

Figure 1.4a Joint actions on a sagittal plane about a transverse axis at the a) hip, b) elbow, c) knee, d) ankle and e) shoulder

Joint actions in the frontal plane about a sagittal axis

Abduction and **adduction** occur in a frontal plane about a sagittal axis:

> **Abduction:** movement away form the midline of the body.
>
> **Adduction:** movement towards the midline of the body.

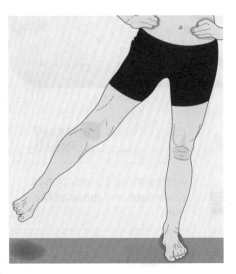

Figure 1.4b Hip abduction

Joint actions in the transverse plane about a longitudinal axis

Horizontal adduction and horizontal abduction occur in the transverse plane about a longitudinal axis. This joint action occurs in the shoulder when the arm is held straight out in front at a 90-degree angle to the body and parallel to the ground and is either moved across the body (horizontal adduction) and or away from the body (horizontal abduction).

Now test yourself

TESTED

1 Can you identify the joint actions occurring in the shoulder, hip and ankle as the performer moves from A to B in the following picture?

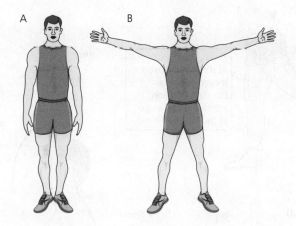

Answers online

Agonists and antagonists

REVISED

● Agonist is the muscle responsible for the movement that is occurring.
● Antagonist is the muscle that works in opposition to the agonist (to help produce a co-ordinated movement).

You need to learn the main agonists and antagonists for each of the joint actions:

Joint action	Agonist	Antagonist
Elbow flexion	Biceps	Triceps
Elbow extension	Triceps	Biceps
Ankle plantar-flexion	Gastrocnemius	Tibialis anterior
Ankle dorsi-flexion	Tibialis anterior	Gastrocnemius
Knee flexion	Hamstrings	Quadriceps
Knee extension	Quadriceps	Hamstrings
Hip flexion	Iliopsoas or hip flexors	Gluteals
Hip extension/hyper-extension	Gluteals	Hip flexors
Hip adduction	Adductors (adductor brevis/longus/magnus)	Tensor fascia latae and gluteus medius/minimus
Hip abduction	Tensor fascia latae and gluteus medius/minimus	Adductors (adductor brevis/longus/magnus)
Hip horizontal adduction	Adductors	Tensor fascia latae and gluteus medius/minimus
Hip horizontal abduction	Tensor fascia latae and gluteus medius/minimus	Adductors
Shoulder flexion	Anterior deltoid	Latissimus dorsi
Shoulder extension/hyper-extension	Latissimus dorsi	Anterior deltoid
Shoulder horizontal abduction	Latissimus dorsi	Pectorals
Shoulder horizontal adduction	Pectorals	Latissimus dorsi
Shoulder adduction	Posterior deltoid/latissimus dorsi	Middle deltoid/supraspinatus
Shoulder abduction	Middle deltoid/supraspinatus	Posterior deltoid/latissimus dorsi

Revision activity

Write the names of all the agonists and antagonists on sticky notes and stick them on your body at the correct location.

Types of muscular contraction

REVISED

Isotonic contraction

Isotonic contraction is when a muscle contracts to create movement:
- Concentric contraction is when a muscle shortens under tension.
- Eccentric contraction is when a muscle lengthens under tension.

Typical mistake

Eccentric is the type of contraction most misunderstood. Remember it is a contraction so the muscle cannot be relaxing, it is lengthening under tension.

Exam tip

An eccentric contraction usually occurs in the downward phase of most movements when the muscle is acting as a brake, for example the triceps in the downward phase of a press-up.

Isometric contraction

This is when a muscle can contract without actually lengthening or shortening, and the result is that no movement occurs, e.g. the crucifix position in gymnastics.

Now test yourself

2 Complete the movement analysis table of the hip, knee and ankle action in the drive phase of running.

Joint	Joint action	Plane and axis	Agonist	Type of contraction
Hip				
Knee				
Ankle				

Answers online

Exam practice

1 The figure below shows an overarm throw.

Complete the table below to identify the joint actions, names of the main agonists and type of contraction taking place at the elbow and shoulder as the performer passes the ball. [6]

Joint	Joint action	Main agonist	Type of contraction
Elbow			
Shoulder			

→

2 Weightlifters need to ensure that they prepare physically and psychologically in order to perform in a competitive situation. The photo shows a weightlifter who has moved into the squat position prior to attempting her lift.

Complete the table to identify the joint action, main agonist and type of muscle contraction taking place at the knee and ankle joints as the weightlifter moves downwards from a standing position into the squat position. [6]

Joint	Joint action	Agonist	Type of contraction
Knee			
Ankle			

Answers and quick quizzes online

ONLINE

Summary

You should now be able to:
- identify the type of joint and articulating bones for the ankle, knee, hip, shoulder and elbow
- recognise the actions in these joints that occur in the sagittal plane/transverse axis as flexion, extension, hyper-extension, plantar-flexion and dorsi-flexion
- recognise and identify that abduction and adduction occur in the frontal plane about a sagittal axis
- recognise and identify that horizontal adduction and horizontal abduction occur in the transverse plane about a longitudinal axis
- state the main agonists and antagonists for the actions occurring at the joints
- explain the types of muscle contraction: isotonic (concentric, eccentric) and isometric.

1.5 Energy systems

Energy transfer in the body

In the body, the energy we use for muscle contractions comes from **adenosine triphosphate (ATP)**, which is the only usable form of chemical energy in the body. The energy we derive from the foods we eat, such as carbohydrates, is broken down to release energy that is used to form ATP (which consists of one molecule of adenosine and three (tri) phosphates).

The energy that is stored in ATP is released by breaking down the bonds that hold this compound together. Enzymes are used to break down compounds, and in this instance ATP–ase is the enzyme used to break down ATP, leaving adenosine di-phosphate (ADP) and an inorganic phosphate (Pi).

> **Adenosine tri-phosphate (ATP):** the only usable form of energy in the body.

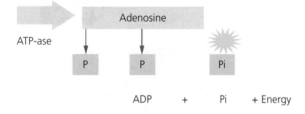

Figure 1.5a ATP–ase breaks down ATP to produce ADP + Pi + energy

The body has to constantly rebuild ATP by converting the ADP and Pi back into ATP. We can re-synthesise ATP from three different types of chemical reaction in the muscle cells; these reactions are fuelled by either food (carbohydrates, fats and protein) or a chemical called phosphocreatine, which is found in the muscles. The conversion of these fuels into energy takes place through one of three energy systems:
- aerobic
- ATP–PC
- anaerobic glycolytic.

Aerobic system

When exercise intensity is low and oxygen supply is high, e.g. jogging, the aerobic system is the preferred energy pathway.

The aerobic system has three stages as it works to provide energy: **glycolysis**, **Krebs cycle** and **electron transport chain**.

Stage 1: glycolysis

This first stage is anaerobic, so it takes place in the **sarcoplasm** of the muscle cell. Glycolysis is the breakdown of glucose into pyruvic acid (discussed in more detail under the anaerobic glycolytic system later). For every molecule of glucose undergoing glycolysis, a net of two molecules of ATP is formed.

Before the pyruvic acid produced in glycolysis can enter the next stage (Krebs cycle), it splits into two acetyl groups and is then carried into the Krebs cycle by coenzyme A.

> **Glycolysis:** the breakdown of glucose into pyruvic acid.
>
> **Krebs cycle:** a series of cyclical chemical reactions that take place using oxygen in the matrix of the mitochondria.
>
> **Electron transport chain:** this involves a series of chemical reactions in the cristae of the mitochondria where hydrogen is oxidised to water and 34 molecules of ATP are produced.
>
> **Sarcoplasm:** the fluid that surrounds the nucleus of a muscle fibre; the site where anaerobic respiration takes place.

Stage 2: Krebs cycle

Acetyl coenzyme A diffuses into the matrix of the mitochondria and a complex cycle of reactions occurs in a process known as the Krebs cycle. Here, acetyl coenzyme A combines with oxaloacetic acid, forming citric acid. Hydrogen is removed from the citric acid and the rearranged form of citric acid undergoes 'oxidative carboxylation', which simply means that carbon and hydrogen are given off. The carbon forms carbon dioxide, which is transported to the lungs and breathed out, and the hydrogen is taken to the electron transport chain. The reactions that occur result in the production of two molecules of ATP.

Fats can also enter the Krebs cycle. Stored fat is broken down into glycerol and free fatty acids for transportation by the blood. These fatty acids then undergo a process called **beta oxidation**, whereby they are converted into acetyl coenzyme A, which is the entry molecule for the Krebs cycle. From this point on, fat metabolism follows the same path as glycogen metabolism. More ATP can be made from one molecule of fatty acids than one molecule of glucose, which is why in long-duration, low-intensity exercise, fatty acids will be the predominant energy source – but this does depend on the fitness of the performer.

> **Beta oxidation:** a process where fatty acids are broken down to generate acetyl-CoA, which enters the Krebs cycle.

Stage 3: electron transport chain

Hydrogen is carried to the electron transport chain by hydrogen carriers. This occurs in the cristae of the mitochondria. The hydrogen splits into hydrogen ions and electrons and they are charged with potential energy. The hydrogen ions are oxidised to form water, while the hydrogen electrons provide the energy to re-synthesise ATP. Throughout this process 34 molecules of ATP are formed.

Now test yourself
TESTED ☐

1 Summarise the stages of the Krebs cycle.

Answer online

> **Exam tip**
>
> As well as learning the key points of each energy system, make sure you can identify when the aerobic system is the predominant method of producing energy.

ATP–PC system

This is an energy system using **phosphocreatine (PC)** as its fuel. PC is an energy-rich phosphate compound found in the sarcoplasm of the muscles. It can be broken down quickly and easily to release energy to re-synthesise ATP. Its rapid availability is important for a single maximal movement, such as the long jump take-off or shot put.

> **Revision activity**
>
> Draw a diagram starting with glucose at the top and try to summarise all three stages of the aerobic system.

How it works to provide energy

The ATP–PC system is an **anaerobic** process and re-synthesises ATP when the enzyme creatine kinase detects high levels of ADP. It breaks down the phosphocreatine in the muscles to phosphate and creatine, releasing energy:

> Phosphocreatine (PC) → Phosphate (Pi) + Creatine (C) + Energy

This energy is then used to convert ADP to ATP in a coupled reaction:

> Energy → Pi + ADP → ATP

> **Phosphocreatine (PC):** an energy-rich phosphate compound found in the sarcoplasm of the muscles.
>
> **Anaerobic:** a reaction that can occur without the presence of oxygen.

> **Exam tip**
>
> The ATP–PC system is the predominant energy system for high-intensity, short-duration activity lasting between 5 and 8 seconds. For high-intensity activity lasting less than 3 seconds, energy will be provided from just the breakdown of ATP.

Now test yourself

TESTED

2 What are the key points you need to remember for the ATP/PC energy system?

Answer online

Short-term lactate anaerobic system/ anaerobic glycolytic system

The short-term lactate anaerobic system, also called the anaerobic glycolytic system, provides energy for high-intensity activity for longer than the ATP–PC system. However, how long this system lasts depends on the fitness of the individual and how high the intensity of the exercise is. Working flat out to exhaustion will mean the system will last a much shorter time (hence 'short-term'). This is because the demand for energy is extremely high. An elite athlete who has just run the 400 m in under 45 seconds will not be able to run it again immediately at the same pace. However, reduce the intensity a little and the system can last longer, up to 2–3 minutes, because the demand for energy is slightly lower.

How it works to provide energy

When the PC stores are low, the enzyme glycogen phosphorylase is activated to break down the glycogen into glucose, which is then further broken down to pyruvic acid by the enzyme phosphofructokinase. This process is called anaerobic glycolysis and takes place in the sarcoplasm of the muscle cell where oxygen is not available. Since this is an anaerobic process, the pyruvic acid is then further broken down into lactic acid by the enzyme lactate dehydrogenase (LDH).

During anaerobic glycolysis, energy is released to allow ATP re-synthesis. The net result is two molecules of ATP are produced for one molecule of glucose broken down. (There are actually four moles of ATP produced but two are used to provide energy for glycolysis itself).

> **Exam tip**
>
> The key points about glycolysis are:
> - breakdown of glucose to pyruvic acid
> - produces two molecules of ATP
> - during intense exercise, pyruvic acid converted into lactic acid.

Energy continuum of physical activity

REVISED

The '**energy continuum**' is a term used to describe which energy system is used for different types of physical activity and sport. It refers to the contribution that the different energy systems make to the production of energy, depending on the intensity and duration of exercise. The three energy systems do not work independently of one another. They all contribute during all types of activity, but one of them will be the predominant energy provider. The *intensity* and *duration* of the activity are the factors that decide which will be the main energy system in use.

> **Energy continuum:** a term which describes which type of energy system is used for different types of physical activity and sport. The contribution of each system depends on the intensity and duration of exercise.

Answers and quick quizzes at **www.hoddereducation.co.uk/myrevisionnotes**

Intensity	Duration of performance	Energy supplied by
Very high	Less than 10 seconds	ATP–PC
High to very high	8–90 seconds	ATP–PC and anaerobic glycolytic
High	90 seconds to 3 minutes	Anaerobic glycolytic and aerobic
Low to medium	3+ minutes	Aerobic

Now test yourself

3 Decide on the intensity and duration of the following examples in a game of football and then decide which energy system would be the predominant energy provider:
- short 10m sprint into space to receive the ball
- making a quick break on attack over the length of the pitch
- jogging to keep in position.

Answers online

The energy continuum is often explained in terms of thresholds. The ATP–PC/anaerobic glycolytic threshold is the point at which the ATP–PC energy system is exhausted and the lactic acid system takes over. This is shown in Figure 1.5b below at 10 seconds. The anaerobic glycolytic/aerobic threshold, shown at 3 minutes, is the point at which the lactic acid system is exhausted and the aerobic system takes over.

> **Typical mistake**
>
> Students often explain all three energy systems when they are unsure as to which one(s) are relevant. This is not answering the question and marks could be lost!

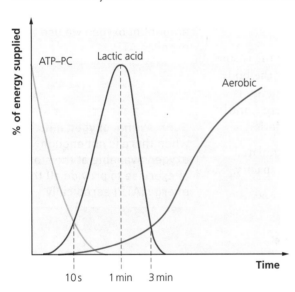

Figure 1.5b The energy continuum related to exercise duration

Differences in ATP generation between fast and slow twitch muscle fibres

Slow twitch fibres are used for low to medium intensity activity. They therefore use aerobic respiration as their main method of receiving fuel. Fast twitch fibres on the other hand are recruited for high-intensity activities such as sprinting, so anaerobic respiration is their main energy pathway.

> **Exam tip**
>
> Slow twitch fibres are aerobic and fast twitch are anaerobic.

The table below summarises the differences in ATP generation between fast and slow twitch fibres.

Slow twitch (type I)	Fast twitch (type II)
• The main pathway for ATP production is in the aerobic system. • It produces the maximum amount of ATP available from each glucose molecule (up to 36 molecules of ATP) • Production is slow but these fibres are more endurance based, so less likely to fatigue.	• The main pathway for ATP production is via the lactate anaerobic energy system (during glycolysis). • ATP production in the absence of oxygen is not efficient – only two ATP molecules produced per glucose molecule. • Production of ATP this way is fast but cannot last for long as these fibres have least resistance to muscle fatigue.

Energy transfer during long-duration/lower intensity exercise

REVISED

Exercising for long periods of time at low intensity uses the *aerobic* system as the preferred method for producing energy.

Oxygen consumption during exercise (submaximal and maximal oxygen deficit)

When we exercise, the body uses oxygen to produce energy (re-synthesise ATP). **Oxygen consumption** is the amount of oxygen we use to produce ATP and is usually referred to as VO_2.

When we start to exercise, insufficient oxygen is distributed to the tissues for all the energy to be provided aerobically, as it takes time for the body to respond to the increase in demand for oxygen. As a result, energy is provided anaerobically to satisfy the increase in demand for energy until the body can cope. This is referred to as **submaximal oxygen deficit**.

Maximal oxygen deficit is usually referred to as maximal accumulated oxygen deficit or MAOD. It gives an indication for anaerobic capacity.

The diagrams below show the difference between submaximal and maximal oxygen deficit.

> **Oxygen consumption:** the amount of oxygen we use to produce ATP.

> **Submaximal oxygen deficit:** when there is not enough oxygen available at the start of exercise to provide all the energy (ATP) aerobically.

(a) Light exercise   **(b) Heavy exercise**

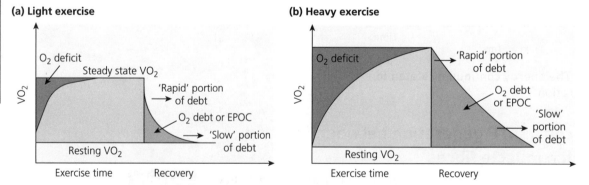

Figure 1.5c The difference between submaximal and maximal oxygen deficit

Oxygen consumption during recovery (excess post-exercise oxygen consumption, EPOC)

Recovery involves returning the body to its pre-exercise state. When a performer finishes exercise, oxygen consumption still remains quite high in comparison with oxygen consumption at rest. This is because extra oxygen needs to be taken in and used to try to help the performer recover. This breathlessness after exercise is often referred to as **excess post-exercise oxygen consumption (EPOC)**.

There are two main components to EPOC: the fast replenishment stage and the slow replenishment stage.

Fast replenishment stage

The **fast replenishment stage** (also known as the alactacid component) uses the extra oxygen that is taken in during recovery to restore ATP and phosphocreatine and to re-saturate myoglobin with oxygen. Complete restoration of phosphocreatine takes up to 3 minutes, but 50 per cent of stores can be replenished after only 30 seconds, during which time approximately 3 litres of oxygen are consumed.

Myoglobin has a high affinity for oxygen. It stores oxygen in the sarcoplasm that has diffused from the haemoglobin in the blood. After exercise, oxygen stores in the myoglobin are limited. The surplus of oxygen supplied through EPOC helps replenish these stores, taking up to 2 minutes and using approximately 0.5 litres of oxygen.

Slow replenishment stage

The oxygen consumed during the slow replenishment stage also known as the lactacid component, has several functions, outlined below.

Removal of lactic acid

Lactic acid accumulates during exercise, and during recovery it needs to be removed. Full recovery may take up to an hour or longer, depending on the intensity and duration of the exercise. Lactic acid can be removed in the following ways:

- oxidation into carbon dioxide and water in the inactive muscles and organs and used by the muscles as an energy source
- transported in the blood to the liver where it is converted to blood glucose and glycogen (**Cori cycle**)
- converted into protein
- removed in sweat and urine.

The majority of lactic acid can be oxidised in mitochondria, so performing a cool-down can accelerate its removal because exercise keeps the metabolic rate of muscles high and keeps capillaries dilated, which means oxygen can be flushed through, removing the accumulated lactic acid. The slow replenishment stage of recovery begins as soon as lactic acid appears in the muscle cell, and will continue using breathed oxygen until recovery is complete. This can take up to 5 or 6 litres of oxygen in the first half hour of recovery, removing up to 50 per cent of the lactic acid.

Maintenance of breathing and heart rates

Maintaining breathing and heart rates requires extra oxygen to provide the energy needed for the respiratory and heart muscles. This assists recovery as the extra oxygen is used to replenish ATP and phosphocreatine stores, resaturate the myoglobin and remove lactic acid, therefore returning the body back to its pre-exercise state.

> **EPOC:** the amount of oxygen consumed during recovery above that which would have been consumed at rest during the same time.
>
> **Fast replenishment stage:** the restoration of ATP and phosphocreatine stores and the re-saturation of myoglobin with oxygen.

> **Typical mistake**
>
> Students often forget that the re-saturation of myoglobin is part of the fast replenishment stage.

> **Revision activity**
>
> Summarise the key points of the fast replenishment stage.

> **Cori cycle:** the process where lactic acid is transported in the blood to the liver where it is converted to blood glucose and glycogen.

> **Revision activity**
>
> Summarise the key points of lactic acid removal.

Glycogen replenishment

The replacement of glycogen stores depends on the type of exercise undertaken and when and how much carbohydrate is consumed following exercise. It may take several days to complete the restoration of glycogen after a marathon, but in less than an hour after high-duration, short-intensity exercise a significant amount of glycogen can be restored as lactic acid and is converted back to blood glucose and glycogen in the liver via the Cori cycle. Eating a high-carbohydrate meal will accelerate glycogen restoration, as will eating within one hour following exercise.

There are two nutritional windows for optimal recovery after exercise. The first is 30 minutes after exercise, where both carbohydrates and proteins should be consumed in a 3:1 or 4:1 ratio. The second nutritional window is 1 to 3 hours after exercise, and a meal high in protein, carbohydrate and healthy fat should be consumed.

Increase in body temperature

When temperature remains high, respiratory rate rates will also remain high and this will help the performer take in more oxygen during recovery. However, extra oxygen (from the slow replenishment stage) is needed to fuel this increase in temperature until the body returns to normal.

> **Exam tip**
>
> Questions on EPOC often involve a description of the fast and slow replenishments.

Energy transfer during short-duration/ high intensity exercise

REVISED ☐

During short-duration/high-intensity exercise, energy has to be produced rapidly. The aerobic system is too complicated to produce energy rapidly, so the body needs to rely on anaerobic respiration using the ATP–PC system and the anaerobic glycolytic system. However, these systems cannot produce energy for long periods of time.

Lactate accumulation

Lactate and lactic acid are not the same thing, but the terms are often used interchangeably. Using the anaerobic glycolytic system produces the by-product lactic acid as a result of glycolysis. The higher the intensity of exercise, the more lactic acid is produced. This lactic acid quickly breaks down, releasing hydrogen ions (H^+). The remaining compound then combines with sodium ions (Na^+) or potassium ions (K^+) to form the salt lactate. As lactate accumulates in the muscles, more hydrogen ions are present and it is actually the presence of hydrogen ions that increases acidity. This slows down enzyme activity and affects the breakdown of glycogen, causing muscle fatigue. The lactate produced in the muscles diffuses into the blood and blood lactate can be measured.

Lactate threshold and onset blood lactate accumulation (OBLA)

As exercise intensity increases, the body moves from working aerobically to anaerobically. This crossing of the aerobic/anaerobic threshold is also known as the **lactate threshold** and is the point at which lactic acid rapidly accumulates in the blood (increase by 2 millimoles per litre of blood above resting levels). We are constantly producing small amounts of lactate due to red blood cell activity when working at low

> **Lactate threshold:** the point at which lactic acid rapidly accumulates in the blood.

intensity, but the levels are low and the body deals with these effectively. However, as the intensity of the exercise increases and the body is unable to produce enough oxygen to break down lactate, the levels of lactate build up/accumulate and this is known as **OBLA** (onset blood lactate accumulation).

OBLA and lactate threshold are simply different ways of measuring the same thing. OBLA is the older term and lactate threshold is a more recent American term. At rest, approximately 1–2 millimoles per litre of lactate can be found in the blood. However, during intense exercise, levels of lactate will rise dramatically and as it starts to accumulate, OBLA occurs. This is usually when the concentration of lactate is around 4 millimoles per litre. Measuring OBLA gives an indication of endurance capacity. Some individuals can work at higher levels of intensity than others before OBLA and can delay when the threshold occurs.

> **OBLA:** the point when lactate levels go above 4 millimoles per litre.

Lactate threshold is expressed as a percentage of **VO$_2$ max**. As fitness increases, the lactate threshold becomes delayed. Average performers may have a lactate threshold that is 50–60 per cent of their VO$_2$ max, whereas elite performers may have a lactate threshold that is 70, 80 or even 90 per cent of their VO$_2$ max. Training has a limited effect on VO$_2$ max because VO$_2$ max is largely genetically determined. The big difference in performance comes from the delayed lactate threshold. When we exercise, we tend to work at or just below our lactate threshold. The fitter we are, the higher our lactate threshold as a percentage of our VO$_2$ max and hence the harder we can work.

> **VO$_2$ max:** the maximum amount of oxygen that can be utilised by the muscles per minute.

Factors affecting the rate of lactate accumulation

- Exercise intensity: the higher the exercise intensity, the greater the demand for energy (ATP) and the faster OBLA occurs because when glycogen is broken down anaerobically into pyruvic acid, lactic acid is formed.
- Muscle fibre type: slow twitch fibres produce less lactate than fast twitch fibres. When slow twitch fibres use glycogen as a fuel, due to the presence of oxygen, the glycogen can be broken down much more effectively and with little lactate production.
- Rate of blood lactate removal: if the rate of lactate removal is lower than the rate of lactate production, lactate will start to accumulate in the blood until OBLA is reached.
- The respiratory exchange ratio: this is described in more detail later on in this chapter, but when the ratio has a value close to 1.0 glycogen becomes the preferred fuel and there is a greater chance of the accumulation of lactate.
- Fitness of the performer: a person who trains regularly will be in a better position to delay OBLA, as adaptations occur to trained muscles. Increased numbers of mitochondria and myoglobin, together with an increase in capillary density, improve the capacity for aerobic respiration and therefore avoid the use of the anaerobic glycolytic system.

Lactate-producing capacity and sprint/power performance

Elite sprinters and power athletes will have a much better anaerobic endurance than non-elite sprinters. This is because their body has adapted to cope with higher levels of lactate. In addition, through a process called **buffering**, they will be able to increase the rate of lactate removal and consequently have lower lactate levels. Buffering works rather like a sponge mopping up water but instead the sponge soaks up the lactate. This means the athletes will be able to work at higher intensities for longer before fatigue sets in. As well as being able to tolerate higher levels of lactate, the trained status of their working muscles will lead to adaptive responses. There will be a greater number and size of mitochondria and the associated oxidative enzymes, increased capillary density and more myoglobin.

> **Buffering:** a process which aids the removal of lactate and maintains acidity levels in the blood and muscle.

Factors affecting VO$_2$ max/aerobic power

REVISED ☐

The higher the VO$_2$ max, the greater the endurance capacity of a performer. Consequently, this enables a performer to work at higher intensity for longer as they have more oxygen going to the muscles and can utilise this oxygen in the muscles more effectively and therefore delay OBLA.

Physiological:
- increased maximum cardiac output
- increased stroke volume/ejection fraction/cardiac hypertrophy
- greater heart rate range
- less oxygen being used for heart muscle so more available to muscles
- increased levels of haemoglobin and red blood cell count
- increased stores of glycogen and triglycerides
- increased myoglobin content
- increased capillarisation around the muscles
- increased number and size of mitochondria
- increased surface area of alveoli
- increased lactate tolerance
- reduced body fat – VO$_2$ max decreases as the percentage of body fat increases
- slow twitch hypertrophy.

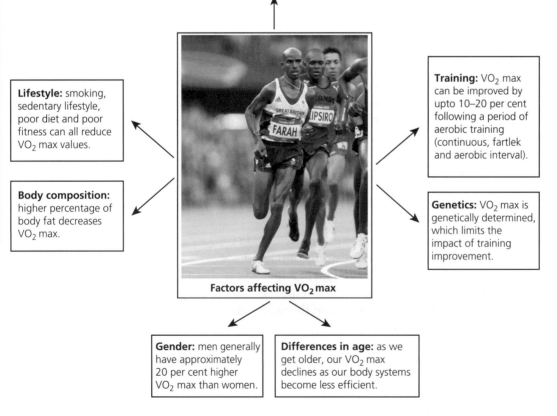

Lifestyle: smoking, sedentary lifestyle, poor diet and poor fitness can all reduce VO$_2$ max values.

Body composition: higher percentage of body fat decreases VO$_2$ max.

Training: VO$_2$ max can be improved by upto 10–20 per cent following a period of aerobic training (continuous, fartlek and aerobic interval).

Genetics: VO$_2$ max is genetically determined, which limits the impact of training improvement.

Factors affecting VO$_2$ max

Gender: men generally have approximately 20 per cent higher VO$_2$ max than women.

Differences in age: as we get older, our VO$_2$ max declines as our body systems become less efficient.

Figure 1.5d Factors affecting VO$_2$ max

Now test yourself

TESTED ☐

4 What is the relationship between VO_2 max and lactate threshold?

Answer online

Measurements of energy expenditure

REVISED ☐

You need to know the following measurements for your exam.

Indirect calorimetry

Indirect calorimetry is a technique that provides an accurate estimate of energy expenditure through gas exchange. It measures how much carbon dioxide is produced and how much oxygen is consumed at both rest and during aerobic exercise. Calculating the gas volumes also enables us to find out the main substrate being used (fat or carbohydrate). The accuracy of this test is very reliable as it gives a precise calculation of VO_2 and VO_2 max.

Lactate sampling

This is an accurate and objective measure of the level of lactate in the blood. It can also be used as a means of measuring exercise intensity (the higher the exercise intensity at which the lactate threshold occurs, the fitter the athlete is considered to be), give an idea of level of fitness and enable the performer to select relevant training zones. Regular lactate testing provides a comparison from which the coach and performer can see whether improvement has occurred. If test results show a lower lactate level at the same intensity of exercise, this should indicate that the performer has an increase in peak speed/power, increased time to exhaustion, improved recovery heart rate and finally a higher lactate threshold.

VO_2 max test

The most common test for evaluating VO_2 max is the multi-stage fitness test, more commonly called the 'bleep' test. Here the individual performs a 20-metre progressive shuttle run to a bleep, until they reach complete exhaustion. The level that is reached can be compared with a standard results table. Other tests include the Harvard step test and the Cooper 12-minute run, but all of these only give an indication or prediction of VO_2 max. A sports science laboratory can produce much more valid and reliable results using **direct gas analysis**. Tests using this method involve increasing intensities on a treadmill, **cycle ergometer** or rowing machine.

Respiratory exchange ratio (RER)

The respiratory exchange ratio (RER) is the ratio of carbon dioxide produced compared to oxygen consumed and is used as a measure of exercise intensity. It calculates energy expenditure and provides information about the use of fats and carbohydrates during exercise.

Calculating the RER will determine which energy sources are being oxidised and hence whether the performer is working aerobically or anaerobically:

- a RER value close to 1 = performer using carbohydrates
- a RER value of approximately 0.7 = performer using fats
- a RER value greater than 1 = anaerobic respiration, so more CO_2 being produced than O_2 consumed.

Direct gas analysis: measures the concentration of oxygen that is inspired and the concentration of carbon dioxide that is expired.

Cycle ergometer: a stationary bike that measures how much work is being performed.

Impact of specialist training methods on energy systems

REVISED

For your exam you need to have an understanding of the following training methods and how they impact on the different energy systems.

Altitude training

Altitude training is usually done at over 2500 metres above sea level, where the partial pressure of oxygen is lower. This means that not as much oxygen can diffuse into the blood, so haemoglobin is not as fully saturated with oxygen. This results in the lower O_2 carrying capacity of the blood. As less O_2 is therefore delivered to the working muscles, there is a reduction in aerobic performance and VO_2 max and a quicker onset of anaerobic respiration.

Advantages:

- Increase in the number of red blood cells
- Increased concentration of haemoglobin
- Increase blood viscosity
- Increased capillarisation
- Enhanced oxygen transport
- Increased lactate tolerance

Disadvantages:

- Expensive
- Altitude sickness
- Difficult to train due to the lack of oxygen
- Detraining due to the fact that training intensity has to reduce when the performer first trains at altitude due to the decreased availability of oxygen.
- Benefits can be quickly lost on return to sea level
- Psychological problems due to being away from home

High-intensity interval training (HIIT)

Interval training can be used for both aerobic and anaerobic training. It is a form of training in which periods of work are interspersed with recovery periods.

High-intensity interval training (HIIT) involves short intervals of maximum intensity exercise followed by a recovery interval of low to moderate intensity exercise, for example 4 minutes of intense exercise made up of 8 x 20 seconds maximum effort work intervals, each followed by a 10-second recovery interval. The work interval is anaerobic and the recovery aerobic. Pushing your body to the max during the work interval increases the amount of calories you burn, as it takes longer to recover from each work session. HIIT therefore improves fat burning potential, glucose metabolism and both aerobic and anaerobic endurance.

Plyometrics

Plyometrics training improves power and speed and involves high-intensity explosive activities such as hopping, bounding, depth jumping and medicine ball work using fast twitch fibres. It works on the concept that muscles can generate more force if they have previously been stretched. This is frequently called the stretch shortening cycle and consists of three phases:

> **Plyometrics:** repeated rapid stretching and contracting of muscles to increase muscle power.

- Phase 1 is the eccentric phase or pre-loading/pre-stretching phase. On landing, the muscle performs an eccentric contraction, where it lengthens under tension.
- Phase 2 is the amortisation phase. This is the time between the eccentric and concentric muscle contractions. This time needs to be as short as possible so that the energy stored from the eccentric contraction is not lost. When an eccentric contraction occurs, a lot of the energy required to stretch or lengthen the muscle is lost as heat, but some of the energy can be stored and is then available for the subsequent concentric contraction.
- Phase 3 is the concentric or muscle contraction phase which uses the stored energy to increase the force of the contraction.

Speed, agility, quickness (SAQ)

Speed refers to how fast a person can move over a specified distance or how quickly a body part can be put into motion. Agility is the ability to move and position the body quickly and effectively while under control. SAQ training aims to improve multi-directional movement through developing the neuromuscular system. Drills include zig-zag runs and foot ladders, and often a ball is introduced so passing occurs throughout the drill, making it more sport specific. As SAQ training uses activities performed with maximum force at high speed, energy is provided anaerobically.

Exam practice

1 Explain how energy is provided to allow an athlete to complete a hammer throw. [3]
2 Gymnastic floor routines can last up to 90 seconds. Explain how the majority of energy is provided for this discipline during competition. [6]
3 An athlete completes an interval training programme with short periods of high-intensity exercise followed by recovery periods lasting up to 30 seconds. What effect does this training programme have on their ATP and PC stores? [3]
4 Elite athletes may use the results from lactate sampling to ensure that their training is effective. Explain the term 'lactate sampling'. [3]
5 At the end of a team game, players may experience EPOC. Define EPOC and give the functions of the fast component of EPOC and explain how these functions are achieved. [4]

Answers and quick quizzes online

ONLINE

Summary

You should now be able to:
- identify that during short duration/high intensity exercise the anaerobic glycolytic and ATP-PC systems are used
- identify that during long duration/low intensity exercise the aerobic system is used
- explain how each of the energy systems (aerobic, ATP-PC and anaerobic glycolytic) provide energy (ATP) during exercise
- understand the energy continuum to explain which energy system is the main energy provider according to the intensity and duration of exercise
- identify the difference in ATP production depending on the fibre type used
- understand the effects of using the anaerobic glycolytic energy system through an explanation of lactate accumulation, lactate threshold and OBLA
- explain oxygen consumption during exercise and recovery through oxygen deficit and EPOC
- identify VO_2 max and explain the factors that affect it
- explain the measurements of energy expenditure to include indirect calorimetry, lactate sampling, and respiratory exchange ratio
- understand the impact of altitude training, high intensity interval training, plyometrics and speed, agility, quickness on energy systems.

2.1 Skill, skill continuums and transfer of skills

Characteristics of skill

Characteristic	Description of skilled performances
Aesthetically pleasing	The skill is good to watch.
Consistent	The skill repeatedly has a high success rate.
Efficient	The skill is produced with the least amount of energy and in the quickest time.
Fluent	The skill is performed smoothly.
Learned	The skill has been developed through practice.
Accurate	The skill is precise.
Goal directed	The skill is performed with a clear aim in mind.

Typical mistake

Students often only identify – rather than describe – the characteristics of skilled performances. Always address the command word in the question.

Exam tip

Using the mnemonic ACEFLAG to help you identify and describe the characteristics of skilled performance.

Continua

Open/closed

Type of skill	Description	Example
Open	The sporting environment changes while the skill is being performed. Performers must adapt and a high amount of decision making is involved.	A chest pass is an open skill because your team mates and opposition constantly move around the pitch as you prepare to pass the ball.
Closed	The sporting environment/playing conditions are stable, enabling the performer to repeat the same movement pattern. There are few decisions to make.	Performing a backward roll in gymnastics is closed, as the environment does not change.

Gross/fine

Type of skill	Description	Example
Gross	Large muscle groups are used to perform the skill.	A sprint start is a gross skill, as the quadriceps are used to drive out of the blocks.
Fine	Small muscles are used to perform a skill that requires precision.	A pistol shot is a fine skill because it uses the muscles of the hand to stabilise the gun for accuracy.

Self-paced/externally paced

Type of skill	Description	Example
Self-paced	The performer is in control of the speed and timing of the skill.	The hammer throw is self-paced because the performer decides when to begin the rotations and also dictates how quickly they spin.
Externally paced	The performer must adapt as they have no control over the speed and timing of the skill. It is in the control of the sporting environment.	When receiving a hockey pass from a team mate, the performer reacts to the speed and direction of the incoming ball. This makes it an externally paced skill, as the performer has no control over the speed of the incoming pass.

Highly organised/low organisation

Type of skill	Description	Example
Highly organised	The skill is difficult to break down into its subroutines/parts due to the speed at which the action is performed. Whole practice is recommended for these skills.	A sprint start is highly organised because it is performed rapidly and is therefore hard to break down into subroutines.
Low organisation	The skill can easily be broken down into its subroutines/parts. Subroutines can be practised in isolation.	Back crawl in swimming has low organisation because the subroutines, i.e. arm and leg actions, can be easily practised individually.

Simple/complex

Type of skill	Description	Example
Simple	Limited decision making is required.	A forward roll is a simple skill because there is little information to process and few decisions to make when producing the action.
Complex	Several decisions must be made.	The centre player in rugby, running with the ball, takes into account the defenders' positions before deciding which team mate to pass to during attacking play. This is a complex skill because of the large number of decisions to make before the pass can be made.

Discrete/serial/continuous

Type of skill	Description	Example
Discrete	The skill has a clear beginning and ending, and is one distinct action.	A pirouette in dance is discrete because there is an obvious start and finish.
Serial	A number of discrete skills are performed together sequentially, creating another skill.	The run-up, hop, step, jump and landing are linked and performed together as a triple jump. The individual skills are linked in a specific order and therefore it is a serial skill.
Continuous	The skill has no clear beginning or ending. The end subroutine of one skill becomes the beginning subroutine of the next. The movement is cyclical.	Cycling and swimming strokes are continuous because of their cyclical nature.

Now test yourself

TESTED

1 Give a definition of each of the 13 classifications.

Answer online

Revision activity

Draw six continua as shown below.
1 Label the extremes with the classifications.
2 Describe each classification.
3 Give a practical example for each classification.

Don't forget you will need to have three classifications on one of the continua.

Transfer of learning

REVISED

For your exam you need to be able to describe the four types of **transfer**, giving clear sporting examples to illustrate your answer. You must understand how the different types of transfer impact on the development of skills.

> **Transfer:** the effect of the learning and performance of one skill on the learning and performance of another skill.

Type of transfer	Description	Example
Positive	Learning a skill facilitates the learning of an additional skill.	Learning to throw overarm helps when learning how to serve in volleyball.
Negative	Learning a skill inhibits the learning of an additional skill.	Learning the forehand drive in tennis hinders the forehand clear in badminton.
Zero	There are no similarities between the tasks, therefore there is no effect on either skill.	Learning to tackle in rugby has no effect on a tumble turn.
Bilateral	Learning and performing a skill on one side of the body is then transferred to the opposite side.	Learning how to perform snooker shots with one hand can then be transferred to the other hand.

Opportunities to highlight where positive transfer takes place should be sought out, as it enables performers to develop a greater range of skills across sports. In order to encourage positive transfer, the coach should:
- ensure the performer has overlearned the first skill before introducing the second/more advanced skill
- make the practice environment as close to game situation as possible, for example in a football free kick practice session use real defenders instead of free kick mannequins

- give praise/positive reinforcement when positive transfer takes place
- avoid teaching skills close together that might appear the same but have a distinct difference, for example tennis and badminton skills, as this increases the likelihood of negative transfer occurring.

Typical mistake

Students often repeat the question, e.g. negative transfer is when there is a negative effect on a skill. Use words such as 'hinders' or 'inhibits' to describe what negative transfer is.

Revision activity

Create a revision card for each type of transfer. On one side write the type and on the other side write the description and an example. Ask a friend to test you!

Now test yourself

TESTED ☐

2 Describe positive, negative, zero and bilateral transfer.

Answer online

Exam practice

1 Which of the following accurately describes the characteristics of a skilled performance? [1]
   (a) Consistent, genetic, aesthetically pleasing and goal directed
   (b) Consistent, genetic, long-lasting and goal directed
   (c) Consistent, learned, aesthetically pleasing and fluent
   (d) Consistent, learned, goal directed and enduring
2 Classify the triple jump on the following continua. Justify your answers. [4]
   - Gross/fine
   - Open/closed
   - Discrete/serial/continuous
   - Self-paced/externally paced
3 Explain bilateral transfer and give a sporting example to illustrate where this might take place. [2]

Answers and quick quizzes online

ONLINE ☐

Summary

You should now be able to:
- identify and describe the characteristics of skill
- use the six continua to classify skills in sport and justify your answers
- support your classifications and justifications with clear examples
- describe the four types of transfer
- illustrate your understanding of transfer with clear examples
- explain how transfer has an impact on skills as they are developed.

2.2 Impact of skill classification on structure of practice for learning

Methods of presenting practice

REVISED

Method	When to use	Advantages	Disadvantages	Examples
Whole The skill is presented in its entirety and not broken down into parts/ subroutines.	Skill is: ● highly organised ● continuous/ cyclic ● simple ● discrete ● fast/ballistic ● not dangerous Performer is: ● autonomous	● Kinaesthesis is developed ● Fluency between subroutines is maintained ● Not time consuming ● Creates a clear mental image ● Easily transferred into full game ● Aids understanding	● Not ideal for cognitive performers ● Can cause information overload and fatigue ● Must be physically capable of producing the full skill	● Golf swing ● Tennis serve ● Cycling ● Forward roll
Whole–part– whole The learner attempts the full skill, then one (or each) subroutine is practised in isolation before being integrated back into the entire skill.	Skill is: ● complex ● fast/ballistic Performer is: ● cognitive and grooving individual parts ● autonomous and concentrating on a specific weakness	● Kinaesthesis is maintained in the whole ● Weak parts/ subroutines can be improved ● Fluency between subroutines is maintained in the whole ● Confidence and motivation increase as success is seen in each part	● Time consuming ● Cannot use with highly organised skills ● Kinaesthesis/ fluency can be negatively affected if the part is not integrated adequately and quickly	Front crawl Whole: ● introduce the full stroke; allow the performer to experience it entirely ● note that arm action is weak Part: ● practise arm action in isolation with the aid of a pull buoy/floats until grooved Whole: ● practise the stroke as one again, now with improved arm action
Progressive part ('chaining') The first subroutine/ part is taught and practised until perfected. The rest of the parts are then added sequentially until the whole of the skill can be performed.	Skill is: ● low organisation ● serial ● complex ● dangerous Performer is: ● cognitive	● Focusing on just one part of the skill reduces the chance of overload and fatigue ● Aids understanding of each part ● Confidence and motivation increase as success is seen in each part ● Danger is reduced	● Very time consuming ● Cannot use with highly organised skills ● Fluency between subroutines can be negatively affected ● Kinaesthesis/ feel for whole skill not experienced until the very end	Triple jump: ● teach hop – practise until grooved ● teach step – practise until grooved ● practise hop and step together ● teach jump – practise until grooved ● practise hop, step and jump together

TESTED ☐

1 What are the advantages and disadvantages of whole practice?

Answer online

Revision activity

Copy the table above onto card and cut the cells into boxes. Shuffle the pieces of card and place them in a pile face down. Turn each card over, read it and place it under the correct heading for each type of practice.

Types of practice

REVISED ☐

Type	When to use	Advantages	Disadvantages	Examples
Massed Continuous practice without rest periods	Skill is: ● discrete ● closed ● self-paced ● simple Performer is: ● highly motivated ● autonomous ● physically fit	● Grooves/ overlearns skills so they become habitual ● Motor programmes are formed ● Improves fitness	● Causes fatigue ● Performer may not be physically capable of undertaking the practice ● No time for feedback	Badminton player attempting to perfect their short serve, or a trampolinist continuously practising seat drops to make it habitual
Distributed Practice with rest periods included	Skill is: ● continuous ● complex ● serial ● low organisation ● dangerous/ tiring ● externally paced ● open Performer is: ● cognitive ● unfit ● lacking motivation	● More effective than massed practice ● Allows time for physical recovery ● Allows time for mental practice ● Coach can give feedback ● Motivational	● Time consuming ● Can cause negative transfer	Steeplechaser physically runs the race on the track followed by a rest period; they will mentally rehearse the performance, seeing the stride pattern, clearing the hurdles and water barrier in their mind
Variable Practising skills and drills in a constantly changing environment	Skill is: ● open ● externally paced ● complex Performer is: ● cognitive ● lacking motivation	● Develops schema (see pages 69–70) ● Increases motivation ● Performer gains experience in a range of situations ● Positive transfer from training to game	● Time consuming ● Can cause fatigue ● Possibility of information overload ● Can cause negative transfer	When practising 3 vs 2 attacking play in rugby, performers will develop their passing technique and positional play, which can be directly transferred into a game situation

Type	When to use	Advantages	Disadvantages	Examples
Mental Going over a skill in the mind without moving: ● internal – seeing performance from 'within' through own eyes and being aware of emotions/anxiety etc. ● external – seeing performance from outside as a spectator	Skill is: ● complex ● serial Performer is: ● cognitive – to build a clear mental image of the basics of the skill ● autonomous – to focus on key strategies/tactics	● Produces a clear mental image ● Performers can see themselves being successful ● Can rehearse strategies/tactics ● Increases confidence ● Reduces anxiety ● Muscles are stimulated ● Reaction time improves	● Difficult for cognitive performers to complete effectively ● Mental image must be accurate ● Difficult if environment is not quiet	Triple jumper about to take final jump in a competition may visualise the stages of the jump in their mind before actually beginning

Now test yourself

TESTED

2 What is variable practice and what are the advantages and disadvantages of using this method?

Answer online

Exam practice

1 As a coach, for what types of skills would you choose to use varied practice? Use a practical example to illustrate your answer. [4]
2 Mental practice is used increasingly as part of an athlete's training programme. What are the benefits of using this method? [4]

Answers and quick quizzes online

ONLINE

Summary

You should now have clear knowledge and understanding of:
● how skills are presented
● how practices are structured
● the most effective method to use with performers considering their experience
● the most effective method to use when learning and developing different skills
● the advantages and disadvantages of each method.

You should be able to:
● give a clear practical example to illustrate how you would use each method.

2.3 Principles and theories of learning and performance

Stages of learning and how feedback differs between the different stages of learning

1 Cognitive stage

Description
- The performer begins to create a clear mental image of what the skill is supposed to look like.
- An accurate demonstration is necessary, which the performer will copy.
- Mental rehearsal of the skill is required.
- Many mistakes are made.
- The performer uses trial and error, learning to work out the correct method.
- Movements appear uncoordinated and jerky.
- The performer has to think about the skill: all their attention is placed on working out the main components of the skill.
- Motor programmes are not yet formed.

Feedback
- The performer is reliant on extrinsic feedback from the coach to direct performance and highlight weaknesses.
- Feedback should be positive so that the performer will persevere with the learning process.
- Some knowledge of results can be used, so that successful actions are repeated and unsuccessful actions are modified.

Example

A hockey player who is initially learning to dribble will be very slow. Their movements will be jerky and they often lose the ball as a result of hitting it too hard. Their head will be down as they watch the ball intently. As they do not yet know how it is supposed to feel, they rely on their coach for feedback. The coach will give various demonstrations and the learner will watch and work out each subroutine. They should constantly mentally rehearse dribbling in this phase.

2 Associative stage

Description
- The performer must continue to practise.
- The performer models their current actions on those of skilled athletes.
- Some performers never progress beyond this stage.
- The performer becomes more proficient, making fewer mistakes.
- Movement appears smoother and more co-ordinated.
- The performer can begin to focus their attention on the finer aspects of the skill.
- Motor programmes are developing and will be stored in the long-term memory.
- Demonstrations, positive feedback and mental rehearsal are still required to aid learning.

Feedback
- The performer begins to develop kinaesthesis and uses intrinsic feedback to correct movement. They will know how the movement is supposed to feel.
- Extrinsic feedback is still used to refine actions.
- The performer begins to use knowledge of performance.

Example

A gymnast on a beam will have practised and mastered the basic skills and will now be able to execute more complex movements. They can now use intrinsic feedback, as they are beginning to become aware of how the movement should feel. They can now look up and forward rather than down at their feet.

3 Autonomous stage

Description
- Movements are fluent, efficient and have become habitual due to extensive practice.
- Skills are executed automatically, without consciously thinking about subroutines.
- Motor programmes are fully formed and stored in the long-term memory.
- The performer can concentrate on fine detail, tactics and advanced strategies.
- It is still important to practise and mentally rehearse in order to stay at this level.

Feedback
- The performer uses intrinsic feedback to correct their own mistakes by means of kinaesthesis.
- Extrinsic feedback can be negative to aid error correction.
- The performer uses knowledge of performance to understand why the action was successful or unsuccessful.

Example

A basketball player will be able to dribble the ball fluently and consistently without having to look down at the ball. They are able to scan the court for passing options without concentrating on controlling the ball, as it is being controlled automatically. They can correct errors they make immediately, without assistance from the coach.

Now test yourself

TESTED ☐

1 How does feedback differ when moving from the cognitive to the associative stage of learning?

Answer online

Typical mistake

Students often confuse stages of learning with theories of learning. Read the questions very carefully!

Revision activity

Complete the table below. Give a clear example from *your* sport in each stage.

Name of stage	1.	2.	3.
Characteristics			
Feedback used			
Example			

Learning plateaus

REVISED ☐

A learning plateau is a period during performance when there are no signs of improvement; the performer does not appear to be getting any better at doing the task. This can be illustrated by a graph called a learning curve.

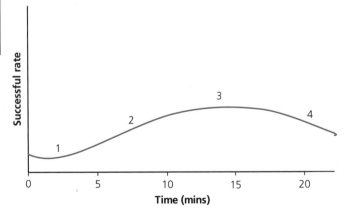

Figure 2.3 a A typical learning curve showing the rate of improvement when attempting a closed skill over a 20-minute period

The learning curve illustrates the stages a performer goes though when learning a new closed skill.

Stage 1 – the performer is in the cognitive phase of learning, therefore their success rate will be low. They will be slow and jerky when performing. They are trying to work out the parts of the skill and are developing an understanding.

Stage 2 – as the performer practises, there is a sharp increase in their success rate as they begin to grasp the skill. They enter the associative phase of learning and begin to look more fluid when performing. Motivation levels will be high as they recognise they are being successful.

Stage 3 – the performer reaches a plateau, where they are no longer progressing with the skill. Performance levels are maintained with no further improvement shown.

Stage 4 – the performer has a dip in their success rate. There is a lack of motivation and they may be experiencing drive reduction. To re-motivate them, they will require a new task or challenge.

Causes of and solutions to the plateau effect

Causes	Solutions
Loss of motivation/boredom	● Set new tasks/challenges ● Use variable practice ● Offer tangible rewards
Mental/physical fatigue	● Allow the performer to rest ● Use distributed practice
Limit of ability reached	Allow the performer to compete against others of similar ability
Poor coaching	● Try a variety of coaching methods ● Try an alternative coach
Incorrect goals set	Set goals using the SMARTER principle

Now test yourself   TESTED ☐

2 What are the main causes of the learing plateau? Give a solution for each cause.

Answer online

Revision activity

Draw the learning curve graph. Identify the key points on the curve and describe what is happening at each stage.

Cognitive theories: insight learning (Gestalt)   REVISED ☐

Gestaltists believe that we learn skills through experiencing the whole task/skill, rather than isolated parts/subroutines. They believe that part learning is not effective and that by learning the skill as a whole, kinaesthesis and the flow of the skill are maintained, and the performer gains a greater understanding of the task with which they are faced.

This is a cognitive theory, which suggests that the performer has to think about what to do but uses their experiences and prior knowledge to help with the situation in hand. They use their insight and adapt to the sporting situation with which they are faced, even in completely new situations. The coach may pose questions which the performer has to answer. Insight learning allows performers to be creative and to develop their own strategies and tactics, without having to rely on the coach. This creates independent thinkers and is much better than being told what to do. Performers' intrinsic motivation will also improve, as they know that they have successfully worked out what to do on their own. For example, in a 2 vs 1 situation in rugby, the attacking player who is the ball carrier evaluates the full situation and works out that she can pass, kick, take the tackle or dummy a pass and run for the try line. Remembering a previous match where she was successful, she decides once again to dummy. The full back follows the pass towards the second attacker, leaving space to run in the try.

Now test yourself

TESTED

3 Explain why Gestaltists believe that part learning is not as efficient as whole learning.

Answer online

Behaviourism: operant conditioning (Skinner)

REVISED

Learning happens by making and strengthening a link/association between a stimulus and a response. This is known as an S–R bond. Once this link/bond is made, it increases the likelihood of the desired response happening. S–R bonds are formed by using reinforcement. Skinner suggested that reinforced actions are strengthened and that incorrect actions can be weakened.

When learning skills using operant conditioning, the coach should:
- allow the performer to use trial and error, e.g. try various methods of serving in tennis
- manipulate the environment to ensure the successful/desired response occurs, e.g. placing cones in the service box as a target for the performer to hit, starting with them close to the net to make the task easier and gradually moving them further back or removing them
- offer a satisfier (e.g. positive reinforcement) when the correct response is shown so the response will be repeated, e.g. when they perform the serve correctly give them lots of praise and positive reinforcement so they will repeat the action
- offer an annoyer (e.g. punishment) when an incorrect response is shown so that the response will not be repeated, e.g. a lap of the court for every serve 'out'.

As a result of this, behaviour is shaped.

Positive reinforcement, negative reinforcement and punishment are used to shape behaviour and form S–R bonds:
- Positive reinforcement is endorsing a performer's action when it is *correct*, so that they repeat that action in the future. For example, when a footballer defends a corner well the coach praises them, in the hope they will repeat it in similar situations in the future.
- Negative reinforcement is saying nothing when a *correct* action is shown, after a period of criticism about a performance. For example, a netball coach constantly criticises the GA for missing shots. When the GA scores a goal, the coach says nothing. The GA recognises that she has not been criticised and repeats the correct shooting action.
- Punishment is a method of reducing or eliminating undesirable actions. This can include extra training, substitution, fines or bans if necessary, for example a basketball player is instructed to complete 'suicide runs' as a result of being late for training.

Now test yourself

4 Define positive reinforcement, negative reinforcement and punishment.

Answer online

TESTED

Social learning: observational learning (Bandura)

Bandura suggested that we learn by watching and replicating the actions of other 'model' performers, whom we respect and admire. These 'models' are known as significant others. They may include our family members, coaches, teachers, peers or role models in the media.

Learners are more likely to copy:
- significant others
- models that have similar characteristics, e.g. age/gender
- actions that are successful
- actions that are reinforced.

Bandura suggested that performers can learn new skills by engaging with four key processes:

Model	1. Attention	2. Retention	3. Motor (re) production	4. Motivation	Matching performance
	• Coach ensures performer concentrates on model • Coach points out key cues in demonstration • Model should be attractive, e.g. use a role model • Model should be accurate	• Coach ensures performer remembers demonstration/mental image • Demonstration should be repeated • A clear mental image should be created through visualisation or mental rehearsal	• Performer must be physically and mentally able to copy the model demonstration	• Performer must have determination to copy and learn skill • Coach could generate this by offering praise or rewards	

Now test yourself

5 Describe the attention and motor (re)production processes in Bandura's model.

Answer online

Constructivism: social development theory (Vygotsky)

Vygotsky suggested that learning is a social process and that social interaction plays a key role in an individual's development. In a sporting context, this means that we learn skills from people around us with whom we interact. There are three key aspects to this theory.

1 Role of social interaction

Vygotsky suggests that social learning comes before development. Initially we learn from other people on a social level. This is called inter-psychological learning. For example, you begin to learn how to do a handstand by watching your older sister performing and by receiving advice and feedback from more knowledgeable others (MKOs – see below). Second, the individual begins to think about how to do that handstand on their own and construct actions based on what they have learned from others. This is called intra-psychological learning.

2 More knowledgeable other (MKO)

This is a person, normally a coach or teacher, who has a greater understanding of the task than you do. They give you technical advice and feedback on how to produce the skill. For example, the coach informs you where to place your hands in the handstand. This advice or feedback also be gained from online video clips/social media.

3 Zone of proximal development

This describes what the learner needs to do next to learn a skill. There are three stages, which outline what the learner can:

- achieve independently without assistance, e.g. can get up into a handstand position and shuffle hands when trying to achieve a balanced position
- achieve with help from the MKO, e.g. can get up into a handstand position and balance if the coach uses manual guidance (see page 60) to support her (scaffolding is used to allow learners to develop skills they will then use on their own in the future)
- not do at this moment in time, e.g. cannot yet properly balance and hold a static handstand position.

Coaches should ensure that learners are provided with a range of experience in their zone of proximal development, as this will motivate and encourage them to advance their individual learning.

> **Revision activity**
>
> This section is theory heavy. Read the chapter out loud and record yourself using a voice recorder/voice recorder app. Listen to it repeatedly.

Now test yourself

TESTED

6 What is an MKO and why are they so important when learning skills in sport?

Answer online

Exam practice

1 Bandura suggested that there are four key processes to learning. Identify the correct processes. [1]
 A: demonstration, selection, motivation, replication
 B: attention, retention, motor production, motivation
 C: attention, determination, practice, motivation
 D: model, rehearsal, reward, imitation
2 A coach notices that one of her performers is not progressing in terms of her skill development. Name this phase. How would you combat this to ensure the performer continues to progress? [4]

Answers and quick quizzes online

ONLINE

Summary

You should now be able to:
- clearly describe the characteristics of the three stages of learning
- give clear examples of each stage
- explain which types of feedback are most effective for each stage
- draw and fully label a graph showing a typical learning curve
- give reasons for the learning plateau
- give solutions to the learning plateau
- explain the key concepts of each of the four theories of learning
- show how skills can be learned by using the approach suggested in each of the theories.

2.4 Use of guidance and feedback

Methods of guidance

REVISED

There are four methods of guidance used to assist the effective learning of skills.

Visual guidance

Description	• Any method where performer sees the correct way to perform the skill • Could be a demonstration, coaching videos, clips on social media/websites or a coaching manual • Effective for cognitive performers and should be readily used at this stage of learning • Performer should be given time to repeatedly practise and mentally rehearse following the demonstration. • Performer should focus on the key aspects of the skill; Coach should highlight the key aspects of the skill • Coach can also change or modify the display, e.g. placing a chalked square on the tennis court for performer to aim for during serves
Advantages	• Illustrates exactly what a skill should look like • Helps to build a clear mental picture of how the skill should be performed • Used effectively in conjunction with verbal guidance • Highlights weaknesses
Disadvantages	• Demonstration must be accurate • Performer must be able to match the demonstration given • Too much information given at once could induce overload
Example	A coach introduces the overhead clear to performers by demonstrating the technique himself and also by showing them a video. He also chalks a circle in the back section of a court, which gives performers a target to aim for.

Verbal guidance

Description	• Coach instructs, explains and directs performer to the key points of the skill by telling them what to do and how to do it • Useful for more advanced performers, i.e. autonomous stage of learning • Used to give tactical, strategic or technical information that a cognitive performer may not understand • Information should be kept brief and meaningful
Advantages	• Can be given immediately during performance • Very useful for open skills where performer needs to make decisions and adapt quickly • Used effectively in conjunction with visual guidance
Disadvantages	• May be a chance of information overload if too many instructions are given together • Lengthy explanations may cause performer to lose concentration • Cognitive performers may not understand specific technical instructions
Example	A rugby coach instructs his players to run a 'miss pass' set play. This would be useless to cognitive performers who would not understand the terminology.

Manual guidance

Description	Coach uses their own body to physically support or manipulate performer's body, or to force a response
Advantages	<ul><li>Effective for cognitive performers</li><li>Useful in dangerous tasks, as it improves safety during performance</li><li>Reduces fear/anxiety and therefore builds confidence</li><li>Whole skill can be attempted</li><li>Allows performer to develop the kinaesthesis or feeling of the movement</li></ul>
Disadvantages	<ul><li>However, performer may become reliant on the support/aid</li><li>It could create incorrect kinaesthesis – the 'feeling' might not be correct</li><li>Bad habits might be instilled</li><li>Performer may become demotivated as they feel that they are not performing the skill by themselves</li><li>Physical contact or proximity of coach may make performer feel uncomfortable</li></ul>
Examples	During a vault, the coach would support the gymnast's back and assist them to travel over the vault. A golf coach may stand behind the performer and, with their hands on top, force the performer through the golf drive.

Mechanical guidance

Description	Any equipment, apparatus or device used to aid and shape movement
Advantages	<ul><li>Effective for cognitive performers</li><li>Useful in dangerous tasks, as it improves safety during performance</li><li>Reduces fear/anxiety and therefore builds confidence</li><li>Whole skill can be attempted</li><li>Allows performer to develop the kinaesthesis or feeling of the movement</li></ul>
Disadvantage	<ul><li>However, performer may become reliant on the support/aid</li><li>It could create incorrect kinaesthesis – the 'feeling' might not be correct</li><li>Bad habits might be instilled</li><li>Performer may become demotivated as they feel that they are not performing the skill by themselves</li></ul>
Examples	A trampoline coach uses a rig and harness to teach the front somersault for the first time. The performer is able to experience the feeling of the whole movement safely. A swimming coach uses swimming floats/armbands with his young swimming group.

Now test yourself

TESTED ☐

1 What are the advantages and disadvantages of verbal guidance?

Answer online

Revision activity

Create a revision card for each type of guidance. On one side write the type and on the other side write the description, two advantages, two disadvantages and an example. Ask your friend to test you!

Purposes and types of feedback

Purposes of feedback

- Reinforces correct actions
- Corrects errors
- Eliminates bad habits
- Acts as a motivator
- Builds confidence.

Type of feedback	Description and uses
Knowledge of performance (KP)	Information about why the skill/action was successful/unsuccessful, including technique and quality of action
Knowledge of results (KR)	Information about whether or not the skill/action was successful (if so, repeat) or unsuccessful (if so, adjust next time)
Positive	Information about what was correct, so that it will be repeated in the future
Negative	Information about incorrect actions, so that they are not repeated and errors are corrected
Intrinsic	From within using kinaesthesis, used to 'feel' if the action was correct or not; can be positive/negative
Extrinsic	From an outside source, used to reinforce correct actions and correct errors; can be positive/negative

Now test yourself

2 Define and give an example of negative feedback and knowledge of results.

Answer online

Typical mistake

Students often repeat the question, e.g. negative feedback is giving the performer negative information. Do not use the question word in your answer but instead describe what each type of feedback is.

Exam practice

1 Explain how a coach could utilise knowledge of performance feedback and visual guidance to assist a performer in the autonomous stage of learning. Use examples to support your answer. [4]

Answer and quick quizzes online

Summary

You should now have clear knowledge and understanding of:
- the four methods of guidance
- the six types of feedback
- the most effective methods of guidance and types of feedback to use with performers considering their experience

- the most effective methods of guidance and types of feedback to use when learning and developing different skills
- the advantages and disadvantages of each method of guidance.

You should be able to:
- give a clear practical example to illustrate how you would use each method of guidance or type of feedback.

2.5 Information processing

Stages of information processing

Information processing refers to the ways in which a performer is able to receive information from the sporting environment, rationalise that information and decide what to do with it, before putting a skill into action. Information processing has four main stages:

1 Input: the senses of sight (vision), hearing (audition), touch, balance and kinaesthesis are used to gather cues from the sporting environment (display). The performer uses their perception to interpret the information and judge which of the environmental cues are required and which can be disregarded. The cues are filtered into relevant and irrelevant by a process known as selective attention. The performer focuses on the relevant stimuli and ignores the irrelevant noise.

2 Decision making: a decision is made on what course of action to take. The memory system (see page 65) is engaged and previous experiences are reflected on. The relevant motor programme is retrieved and sent to the muscles in readiness to produce the skill.

3 Output: the skill is produced.

4 Feedback: the performer receives information about the skill. See page 61 for types of feedback that can be utilised.

Whiting's information-processing model

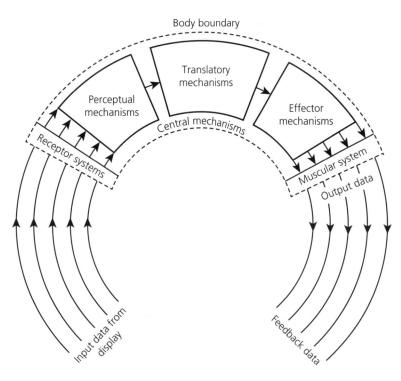

Figure 2.5a **Whiting's information-processing model; Whiting 1969,** *Acquiring Ball Skill*

Environment

The environment contains all the information needed to perform a skill/action.

Display

This is the information available to the performer. Some of this information will be relevant and some will be irrelevant. For example, a rugby player will have their team mates, opponents, ball, pitch markings, posts, referee, linesmen, crowd and coach in their display.

Receptor systems

We use the following senses to receive sensory information from the display:
- vision, e.g. seeing the ball and opponents
- audition, e.g. hearing the shouts from the coach concerning tactics or the crowd calling 'man on'
- proprioception, which tells us about the position of our body.

Proprioception consists of:
- touch, e.g. feeling of equipment on the skin
- kinaesthesis – the internal muscle feeling which gives us information about whether the movement felt correct or not
- equilibrium – information about whether the body is balanced.

Perceptual mechanisms

A judgement is made regarding the incoming information received by the sense organs. Perception includes the DCR process (detection – receive cues; comparison – cues compared with those already stored in the memory system; recognition – understand what response is required based on the stored memories).

Selective attention occurs, which means that the relevant information, such as the ball, opponents and team mates, is focused on, whereas the irrelevant information, such as the crowd, linesman etc., is filtered out. Only the relevant information is acted upon while the irrelevant information is disregarded.

Selective attention is important as it:
- aids concentration
- improves reaction time
- filters out any distractions
- controls arousal levels
- reduces the chance of information overload in the short-term memory (STM).

For example, you detect a high ball through vision and judge the incoming speed of it travelling towards you. You compare it to stored memories and recognise that you have received a high ball before. Using selective attention, you focus on the ball only and disregard the crowd etc. You now decide on a plan of action or an appropriate response – for example, I must turn sideways and jump to receive the high ball.

Translatory mechanisms

Using the information from the perceptual mechanisms, a decision is then made on what action should be taken, with the help of previous experiences stored in the memory. The correct response is selected in the form of a motor programme – for example, select the motor programme for receiving a high ball.

Effector mechanisms

Once the motor programme/plan of action is selected, impulses are sent to the relevant working muscles in order to carry out the movement. For example, impulses are sent to the quadriceps in the legs to prepare to jump for the ball and to the biceps in the arms to get ready to receive the ball.

Muscular system

The muscles receive these impulses and are ready to jump and catch. For example, the biceps brachii receive the impulse and begin to contract.

Output data

The movement/action is performed, for example jumping to receive the high ball.

Feedback data

Once the motor programme has been put into action, information about the movement is received. This could be intrinsic feedback from within the performer using proprioception, for example knowing that I have caught the ball correctly as it 'feels' right in my muscles, knowing through touch that the ball is in my hands and feeling balanced as I have landed on two feet. Or it could be extrinsic feedback from an outside source, for example the coach shouts 'good jump, great catch' or the crowd cheers.

Now test yourself

TESTED

1 What are the functions of the perceptual mechanisms and the effector mechanisms?

Answer online

Typical mistake

Students do not identify the part of the model they are describing. Make it clear to the examiner – they cannot award the mark if it is unclear.

Revision activity

Complete the table below. Describe each part of Whiting's model and give an example from *your* sport.

Aspect of model	Description	Example
Environment		
Display		
Receptor systems		
Perceptual mechanisms		
Translatory mechanisms		
Effector mechanisms		
Muscular system		
Output data		
Feedback data		

Memory system

The memory system is an integral part of information processing. It stores and retrieves information, makes comparisons with previous movement experiences and selects which motor programme to retrieve in order to produce movement.

The diagram below illustrates one memory system suggested by Baddeley and Hitch (1978).

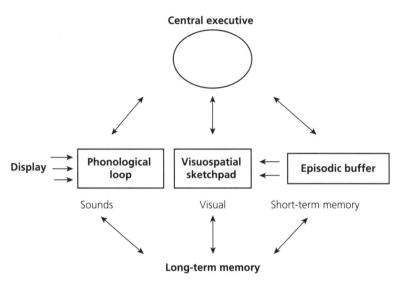

Figure 2.5b The working memory model

This model has a supervisory system called the central executive and three 'slave' systems. The central executive maintains overall control. It links with the long-term memory, focuses and switches attention if required, but has limited capacity. It identifies which information goes to which subsystem, as they perform different functions:

- The phonological loop deals with auditory information, for example it processes the call from your team mate. It is a temporary storage system, which creates a memory trace that is sent to the long-term memory (LTM) to trigger the motor programme. The memory trace will fade away if it is not rehearsed. For example, you repeatedly say out loud the moves in your trampoline ten-bounce routine so that you do not forget the order.
- The visuospatial sketchpad holds visual and spatial information temporarily, for example images of set plays and where you would be during the action. It also stores kinaesthetic information about how the movement feels.
- The episodic buffer stores three/four chunks or 'episodes'. It allows different parts of the working memory system to talk to each other and produces sequences of information to send to the LTM, which initiates the motor programme. It also gathers perceptual information, for example about the flight of the ball as you receive a cross, the sound of the 'man on' call from the coach and also how the limbs and muscles feel as you move to receive the pass.

Now test yourself

2 What are the functions of the central executive and episodic buffer?

Answer online

Functions and characteristics of the working memory and long-term memory

- The working memory receives the relevant information that has been filtered away from the irrelevant information by selective attention.
- The working memory has a limited capacity; it can store 7 +/− 2 items for up to approximately 30 seconds.
- If a skill is practised/rehearsed, it can be transferred and stored in the LTM and stored as a motor programme.
- The working memory produces a memory trace of the current skill, which is compared to information stored in the LTM.
- The LTM then sends the motor programme to the working memory to use in the current sporting situation.
- The LTM has an unlimited capacity and stores information for an unlimited time.
- Once the LTM sends the motor programme to the working memory, it initiates the motor programme.

> **Revision activity**
>
> Create a mind map for the:
> - central executive
> - phonological loop
> - visuospatial sketchpad
> - episodic buffer.

Ensuring effective storage

1 Chunking: small groups of information should be put together and memorised as one. This expands the capacity of the working memory. For example, instead of learning a trampoline sequence as individual movements, the coach could 'chunk' three or four movements together. However, coaches should avoid giving too much information, as the working memory can easily become overloaded.

2 Mental rehearsal/imagery: visualising the skill or going over it mentally enables learners to remember what is needed to perform the skill more easily. This is why demonstrations are imperative.

3 Reinforcement/rewards: if learners receive positive feedback or reinforcement, or are rewarded with praise after a correct response, they are more likely to remember the information.

4 Enjoyable/fun experiences: if the learner has a positive experience that is presented to them in a new or distinctive way that they find interesting, they are more likely to remember the information.

5 Practice/rehearsal: repetition overlearns or 'grooves' a skill. This will help to create a motor programme and enable it to be stored in the LTM.

6 Linking/association with past experiences: relate the new information to that already stored. For example, when learning to serve in tennis, link it to the basic overarm throw which the performer will have previously experienced. (See positive transfer, page 48.)

7 Chaining: information should be presented in an organised manner. For example, when learning a tumble sequence in gymnastics, the elements should be presented together in order to make it easy for the learner to remember.

8 Meaningful: information is more likely to be remembered if the learner understands its relevance to them and their performance. Coaches should explain explicitly to performers.

> **Revision activity**
>
> Use the mnemonic below to help you recall the strategies for ensuring effective storage of information.
>
> **C**hoose to
> **M**ake
> **R**emembering
> **E**asy
> **P**ractising
> **L**ots
> **C**reates
> **M**emories

Now test yourself

TESTED ☐

3 What are the characteristics and functions of the working memory?

Answer online

Responding to stimuli

Key terms and definitions

Term	Definition
Reaction time	This is the time from the onset of the stimulus to the onset of the response.
	It can be either:
	simple reaction time, where there is one stimulus and one response, so the reaction time will be very short, e.g. in a swimming race the stimulus is the starter signal and the only response is to dive in
	choice reaction time, where there are several stimuli and several possible responses, so reaction time will be slower, e.g. in football in open play you may have several team mates calling for a pass and several responses in terms of whom you pass to, type of pass etc.
Movement time	This is the time from the onset of movement to completion of the task.
Response time	This is reaction time plus movement time. It is the time taken from the onset of the stimulus to completion of the task.

For example, in a 100-metre race:
- reaction time is the time from when the performer first hears the gun sound to when they begin to push on the blocks
- movement time is the time from when the performer pushes on the blocks to when they cross the finish line
- response time is the time from when the performer first hears the gun sound to when they cross the finish line.

> **Typical mistake**
>
> Remember, if reaction time or response time improves, the time is *decreased*.

Now test yourself

TESTED ☐

4 Define reaction time, movement time and response time.

Answer online

Hick's law

Hick's law describes the impact of choice reaction time on performance. It states that as the number of choices increases, so does the time it takes to react. In other words, the more choices there are, the slower the reaction time. It is illustrated in the graph below.

Note that is it is not a linear relationship. Reaction time does not increase proportionately with the number of choices.

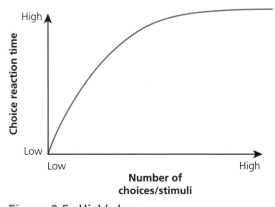

Figure 2.5c Hick's law

Strategies to improve the response time of a performer

- Practice: the more you respond to a stimulus, the faster your reactions become.
- Selective attention: if you focus and concentrate just on the relevant information, your reactions will be quicker.
- Mental rehearsal: this is going over the performance in your mind. As discussed earlier, the muscles involved in the movement will be stimulated; this is almost as good as physical practice.
- Experience: actually participating in the activity gives you valuable insight and awareness of stimuli being presented, meaning you can detect them more quickly and respond faster.
- Improve fitness levels: the fitter you are, the quicker you can respond.
- Warm up: if the body and mind are prepared, you can respond quicker.
- Gain optimum arousal: if you are at the peak of your arousal, you will respond quicker.
- Detect cues early: analyse your opponents play, for example body/limb position and line out calls, in order to anticipate what they intend to do next.
- Try anticipation: anticipation is predicting that a movement will happen before it occurs, for example correctly judging that the centre player in netball will pass back to the wing defence from the centre pass as their body is slightly turned.

Anticipation

Anticipation can be

- temporal: this is predicting when the action will be performed; for example, in netball a centre player hearing the whistle can assume that the wing attack will run into the centre third to receive the pass immediately
- spatial: this is predicting what action is going to be performed and where; for example, seeing a rugby player adjust their grip on the ball you predict they are going to kick over the top of the full back rather than pass.

If a performer anticipates correctly, their response time will be very quick and they will have more time to perform the skill. However, if they anticipate incorrectly, response time can increase vastly and the psychological refractory period may occur (see page 69).

(see page 69)

Now test yourself

TESTED ☐

5 Define anticipation and explain the difference between temporal and spatial anticipation.

Answer online

Single channel hypothesis

According to the single channel hypothesis, while we can detect many stimuli at once, we can only *process* one piece of information at a time. Any further stimuli must wait, as a 'bottleneck' occurs. If we are in the middle of processing one stimulus and a second arrives, it must wait until we have finished processing the first before it can be dealt with. Just as Hick's law states, the more stimuli presented, the slower the reaction time.

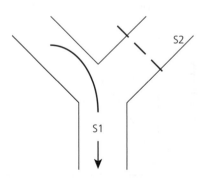

Figure 2.5d The single channel hypothesis: only one stimulus can be processed at a time

Psychological refractory period

As explained above, the single channel hypothesis suggests that we can only process one stimulus at once. However, in the sporting arena, two or more stimuli can arrive in quick succession for processing. This causes a delay in processing and the performer may physically freeze while they seek to clarify and process the correct stimuli.

This delay in processing causes our reaction time to increase and is known as the psychological refractory period.

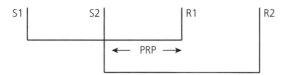

Figure 2.5e The psychological refractory period

We can use this in sport to try to intentionally slow down our opposition. In rugby, for example, you may be approaching a defender with the ball in your hands and feign a pass to the left. This is the first stimulus and they begin moving in that direction. However, you decide to dummy and quickly run past them without releasing the pass. This is the second stimulus; however, they must process the first stimulus of the left pass. The time period where they may actually freeze before changing direction (as the second stimulus has arrived before the first has been processed) is the psychological refractory period.

> **Revision activity**
>
> Write a list of questions and answers for Hick's law, single channel hypothesis and the psychological refractory period. Test a friend!

Schmidt's schema theory

When playing sports like netball and basketball, we make several chest passes in a game, but it is highly unlikely that we make *exactly* the same pass twice. Each chest pass is unique in its speed, height, direction, force, position of team mates and opponents etc. but the basic movement pattern is the same.

Schmidt suggested that the brain is unable to store and retrieve every individual pass separately in the long-term memory. Instead he suggested that we store schema. A schema is a generalised motor programme that allows the performer to adapt their skills and transfer experiences of one skill to another. This accounts for why some performers seem to be effective in many sports. The performer may have taken their knowledge and skills from one sport, adapted them, then transferred them into the current situation, even if they have never tried to play that sport/perform that specific skill before.

The parameters/considerations for every movement will be different, for example environmental position, duration of movement, muscles used to produce the action etc. Therefore, the performer's experiences draw together information within the schema from four areas, known as memory items, as shown in the following table.

> **Typical mistake**
>
> Students often abbreviate this to PRP and therefore miss the mark. Make sure you write it out fully.

RECALL SCHEMA – stores information about and initiates the movement		
1. Initial conditions	This involves gathering information about whether you have been in this situation or a similar situation before. Information about the environment and your body is collated.	Example: I am a centre player in netball. I have the ball in my hands and I am on the edge of the shooting circle. The goal shooter is unmarked to my left. I remember being in a similar situation before, both in training and previous games.
2. Response specifications	Based on the initial conditions, you decide what movement to perform.	Example: I will send a short, flat, fast pass to the goal shooter, as she is quite near, before her defender recovers her position.
RECOGNITION SCHEMA – controls and evaluates the movement		
3. Sensory consequences	This involves gathering information about the movement using intrinsic feedback or kinaesthesis.	Example: as I pass the netball, I feel my elbows bend and I know that as it left my hands it felt correct. I placed enough power and height on the pass.
4. Response outcome	This involves gathering information concerning the result of the movement. Was it successful or unsuccessful?	Example: the pass was successfully received by the goal shooter, and she went on to score a goal.

Developing schemas

- Ensure that practice is variable to build a range of experience.
- Ensure practised skills are transferable from training to the game situation.
- Give feedback to continuously help to improve skills.
- Give praise and positive reinforcement.
- Practise a range of skills until they are well learned.

Now test yourself

TESTED ☐

6 What are the functions of recall schemas and recognition schemas?

Answer online

Revision activity

Review the information on schema included in the table above, then cover it up. Complete the table below and then check your answers. Using a different colour pen, add any information that you missed out.

R _ _ _ _ _ SCHEMA - stores information about and initiates the movement		
1.	This involves...	Example:
2.	Based on the initial conditions...	Example:
R _ _ _ _ _ _ _ _ _ SCHEMA - controls and evaluates the movement		
3.	This involves...	Example:
4.	This involves...	Example:

Exam practice

1 What is selective attention and how does it benefit the performer? [4]
2 Explain how a player can improve their response time. [4]

Answers and quick quizzes online

ONLINE ☐

Summary

You should now be able to:

- outline the basic stages of information processing
- explain each stage of Whiting's informing-processing model and support your explanation with practical examples
- explain the functions and characteristics of Baddeley and Hitch's working memory model
- identify and describe methods to aid the storage of information
- describe the importance of selective attention to working memory
- define reaction time, movement time and response time using practical examples
- draw and label an illustration of Hick's law
- identify and describe strategies to improve response time
- describe the psychological refractory period with a practical example
- explain the functions of both recall and recognition schema and their associated memory items using practical examples.

3.1 Sport in pre-industrial Britain (pre-1780)

Sport is often said to reflect the society of the time. This is certainly true of sport in pre-industrial Britain (i.e. pre-1780).

Characteristics of life in pre-industrial Britain

Pre-industrial society had a number of features/characteristics (sometimes referred to as 'socio-cultural' factors in exam questions), including the following:

- Communications and transport were limited, with life lived in a local area.
- There was widespread illiteracy: the lower classes were uneducated, with little ability to read or write.
- Cruel or violent existences were the norm for the lower classes, whereas the upper class lived in comfort/luxury.
- There was very limited free time for the lower classes, as work was based on the land; free time was dictated by the agricultural calendar/ seasons.
- Class divisions clearly existed; there was a two-tier divided society in existence (upper class and lower class) based on a **feudal system**.
- The majority of the population lived in the countryside/rural areas.

> **Feudal system:** broadly defined, a way of structuring society around a relationship derived from the holding of land in exchange for service or labour.

Characteristics of popular recreation as a reflection of pre-industrial Britain

The table below illustrates the links between socio-cultural features/ characteristics of pre-industrial Britain and **popular recreation** activities of the time.

> **Popular recreation:** the sports and pastimes associated with the lower classes in pre-industrial Britain.

Socio-cultural features/characteristics of pre-industrial Britain	Features/characteristics of popular recreation
Limited communications/transport	Sport was restricted geographically to the areas and communities where people lived.
Widespread illiteracy	Sports had simple, basic rules that were set locally. There was a lack of codification and limited organisation.
Harsh society	Sport was violent, aggressive and unruly in nature and male dominated, with wagering/gambling on the outcome.
Little free time due to agricultural/ seasonal work and very long working hours	Mob football was only played occasionally/annually or as part of a festival (e.g. on Holy Days).
Two-tier/feudal system	There was a clear division/separation between activities played by the lower classes (e.g. mob games) and those played by the upper classes (e.g. real tennis).
Majority of the population lived in the countryside/rural areas	Mob football was played in the countryside/rural areas where people lived, using the natural resources they had available (e.g. a pig's bladder for the ball).

Popular recreation activities such as mob football became increasingly unpopular with the local authorities as the nineteenth century progressed. They were eventually banned for a variety of different reasons including the following:

- They were violent or unruly in nature.
- They led to injury or death in extreme cases.
- They led to damage of property.
- They involved gambling/wagering.
- They were linked to alcohol consumption/drunken behaviour.

Now test yourself

TESTED

1 Explain the characteristics of pre-industrial mob football.

Answer online

Typical mistake

Exam questions on the characteristics of mob football with the command word 'explain' require you to explain the links with socio-cultural factors. To score marks, you would need to say, for example, that mob football was violent and reflected a harsh and cruel society where violence was common (not just that mob football was violent and aggressive).

Characteristics of real tennis

REVISED

Real tennis (also called 'Royal Tennis' or 'the sport of kings') was another activity played in pre-industrial Britain. However, it did not reflect the typical popular recreation characteristics of many activities at the time and was more typical of rational recreation (i.e. a more structured/organised/civilised activity). The characteristics of real tennis include the following:

- It was an exclusive activity, courtly and royal in nature, played by the upper-class males of the two-tier society evident at the time (e.g. by Henry VIII, who had a real tennis court at Hampton Court).
- The upper classes were educated and highly literate, so complex rules could be written down for the sport as the players could readily understand and apply them (i.e. it was codified).
- The upper classes played real tennis to a high moral code, so it lacked violence and was instead played in a civilised manner, with opponents mutually respectful of one another.
- With plenty of leisure time, the upper classes were able to play real tennis on a regular basis, developing their skills/techniques to a high level in many cases.
- It was played in expensive, purpose-built facilities, using expensive specialist equipment, e.g. racquets.
- The upper classes also had the ability to travel to play real tennis, so it was non-local in nature.
- Real tennis was a skilful game with difficult technical demands, which enabled the upper classes to show their 'superiority' over the lower classes. Wagering (i.e. betting) was common on the outcome of matches.

Revision activity

Summarise the characteristics of real tennis in a spider diagram to give you a visual image of key information that you can then apply to questions on key features of real tennis.

It is important that you can compare and contrast the characteristics of mob football for the lower classes with real tennis for the upper classes, as in the table below.

	Mob football	Real tennis
Participation	Played by the lower classes	Played by the upper classes
Rules	Few/simple/locally agreed	Complex/written
Conduct	Violent/unruly	Non-violent/civilised
When played	Occasional/annual/linked to festival occasions	Regularly
Facilities/equipment	Played in the natural environment, using natural resources available	Played in purpose-built facilities, using specialist equipment

Now test yourself

TESTED

2 Identify the ways in which real tennis was different from popular recreation activities, e.g. mob football.

Answer online

Exam practice

1 Popular recreation was often cruel, violent and male dominated. Identify other characteristics of popular recreation activities such as mob football. [3]
2 Explain two characteristics of real tennis in eighteenth-century Britain. [4]

Answers and quick quizzes online

ONLINE

Summary

You should now be able to:
● identify the characteristics of pre-industrial Britain and explain how these influenced popular recreation activities of the time.

3.2 Sport in industrial and post-industrial Britain (1780–1900)

In this section, the main focus is on how sport reflected a rapidly changing society as it moved from being agriculturally/rurally based to one very much dominated by factory life in a machine-based/urban environment.

As Britain changed into an industrially based society, sports and pastimes developed in a number of different ways, reflecting such societal changes. These activities were termed 'rational recreation'. Rational suggests that a level of order, logic and structure began to be applied to sports such as football, reflecting a more ordered society.

Characteristics of rational recreation

REVISED

Rational recreation involved the development of well-ordered, organised and controlled sport for the masses. It was characterised by features such as:

- Respectability: sport was non-violent in nature and the emphasis was on sportsmanship/fair play.
- Regional/national/regular play: sport was competitive, with winners and losers decided by competitions, which were played regionally, nationally and internationally. Watching Saturday-afternoon football was particularly popular among the masses of working-class people during their time off work.
- Stringent administration and codification: strict and complex written rules were set down by national governing bodies (NGBs) for the conduct of sports.
- Referees/officials: these were present to enforce the newly developed rules in sporting contests.
- Purpose-built facilities: sport took place in specially constructed grounds, pitches or tracks, often set around urban areas with large populations to draw on for spectators (as there was less space available in urban areas).
- Skills/tactics based: players had positional roles in which they became 'specialist'; performers trained to improve their tactical awareness as well as their techniques and fitness levels to increase their chances of winning.

> **Revision activity**
>
> Draw a table comparing pre-industrial socio-cultural factors relating to popular recreation with post-industrial factors relating to rational recreation.

Social and cultural influences on the development of rational recreation

REVISED

Industrial Revolution

The **Industrial Revolution** was a key period in British history, which witnessed massive changes in the way people lived. For example, it led to more of the population being concentrated in towns and cities and working in factories, as opposed to living in the countryside and working off the land.

> **Industrial Revolution:** deemed to have occurred during the mid-eighteenth to the mid-nineteenth centuries. This period marked a change in Britain from a feudal, rural society into an industrialised, machine-based, capitalist society, controlled by a powerful urban middle class.

Negative effects of the Industrial Revolution on sports and pastimes

The influence of the Industrial Revolution on the development of rationalised sports and pastimes changed over the course of the nineteenth century. During the first half of the nineteenth century, the initial effects were often negative, as outlined below:

- Migration of the lower classes into urban areas looking for work in the new factories being built: this led to a lack of space to play traditional mob games and overcrowding.
- Lack of leisure time: the shift from 'seasonal' to 'machine' time led to long 12-hour working days, six days a week; the Sabbath (i.e. Sunday) was a religious observance 'day of rest'.
- Lack of income: low wages and poverty were evident, with little spare income for leisure pursuits.
- Poor health: along with poor working and living conditions that led to pollution, and a lack of hygiene, this also meant little energy to play sport.
- Loss of rights: restrictions were placed on mob games and blood sports by changes in criminal laws.
- A lack of public provision: there was no access to private facilities and no personal equipment for the lower classes.

> **Exam tip**
>
> You can remember the initial negative effects of industrialisation on sport and pastimes by using the 'HITFOR' acronym:
>
> H = poor **health and hygiene**
>
> I = lack of **income**
>
> T = lack of **time**
>
> F = **facility** provision was lacking
>
> O = **overcrowding** and lack of space
>
> R = loss of **rights**

Positive effects of the Industrial Revolution on sports and pastimes

In the second half of the nineteenth century, some improvements had a positive effect, as outlined below:

- Health and hygiene improved as a result of gradual improvements in living conditions and local council provision of public baths to improve cleanliness and help stop the spread of disease, enabling more energy/ willingness to participate in sport.
- There was a gradual increase in wages and more time for sport due to the Factory Acts and Saturday half-days being provided to the workers (i.e. a gradual decrease in working hours).
- A new middle class developed (i.e. self-made men who took advantage of the new business opportunities available in the newly industrialised Britain). This changed ways of behaving and playing sport. It became more acceptable and respectable and was played to a high moral code; they developed strict rules, leagues and competitions; they provided facilities/public parks via their involvement in the local council; they gave more time off work, broken time payments etc.
- The influence of ex-public schoolboys via setting up teams and providing facilities to participate in.
- The values of athleticism (i.e. physical endeavour with moral integrity – always trying hard and working to the best of your ability but taking part in the spirit of fair play) spread to the lower classes.

- **Industrial patronage** led to provision for recreation and sport – factory teams were set up, sporting facilities were provided and excursions to the seaside were organised. This decreased absenteeism and encouraged loyalty in the workforce.
- Improvements in transport and communications via the development of roads and steam trains influenced the distances spectators and players could travel, and leagues were established. Fixtures and results could be published in newspapers.
- It became cheaper to travel, so participation in sport and the spectating of sport became more accessible.

Now test yourself   TESTED ☐

1 Identify the ways in which the leisure opportunities for the working classes improved as a result of industrialisation.

Answer online

Urbanisation

Urbanisation in the industrial period had a huge impact on the development of many of the sports we play today. The following is a summary of the key features of urbanisation that contributed to the development of sport in this period:
- Lack of space: in cities, unlike in the countryside, space was at a premium. This led to the development of purpose-built facilities to play sport (e.g. football grounds).
- Large working-class populations: urbanisation meant a large working-class population that needed entertaining, resulting in mass spectator numbers at football and rugby matches for the first time.
- Loss of traditional sports: many traditional working-class sports, such as mob games, were banned in a civilised urban society, so there was a need for new sports to emerge.
- Change in working conditions: initially, the working classes worked long hours in the factories, and had limited free time, income or energy to devote to sport. As this situation improved, sports attendance and participation among the working classes went up.

Transport revolution

The following is a summary of the key ways in which the development of the railways contributed to the development of sport in the industrial period:
- Movement of teams/spectators: the development of the railways and steam trains enabled faster and further travel for players and fans alike, leading to nationwide fixtures developing on a regular basis.
- Improved access to different parts of the country: nationwide train travel enabled sport to develop from local to regional to national, with leagues forming, involving clubs from across the country (e.g. Football League in 1888 with 12 founder members from the North/Midlands).
- Cheaper train travel: train travel became relatively cheap and affordable, with an Act of Parliament making third-class travel cheaper, which led to the working classes following their teams home and away.
- Improved access to the countryside: activities such as rambling became popular as rural areas were reachable and affordable via train travel.

Industrial patronage: kind factory owners becoming 'patrons of sport' for the working classes by providing support for them to participate in various ways.

Urbanisation: large numbers of people migrating/moving from rural areas into towns and cities, seeking regular work in the factories.

Now test yourself

2 Identify the positive impact of developments in transport on sporting opportunities for the working classes.

Answer online

TESTED ☐

Communications

Urban industrial society was associated with a gradual improvement in educational provision for the working classes in the second half of the nineteenth century, which led to improvements in their reading and writing abilities. Rules could therefore be developed, as more people could understand them.

'Communications' (e.g. via newspapers) improved as society became more literate. Such developments in the printed media increased the knowledge and awareness of sport in a number of different ways (e.g. when fixtures were taking place involving a local team; increased knowledge of results of matches). It led to the emergence of sporting heroes and role models, as people could read match reports and relate to their favourite players scoring goals and/or helping to win matches due to their high levels of skill.

Influence of the Church

Changing views of the Church during Victorian times (i.e. the late nineteenth century) also helped to promote sport and recreation among local communities, as approval was given to rational recreation.

Reasons why the Church promoted sport included:
- It encouraged social control (i.e. improved behaviour) through 'civilised' activities, diverting people away from 'less socially acceptable activities' such as drinking and gambling. Church facilities such as halls provided venues for 'improving the morality' of the working classes. Ex-public schoolboys promoted **'Muscular Christianity'** – this involved the actions of churchmen who engaged their communities proactively by attempting to eradicate the excesses of working-class behaviour such as gambling and drinking, in favour of more healthy and positive pursuits.
- It was viewed as a good way of promoting Christian values. The development of the YMCA promoted the healthy body/healthy mind link. The clergy viewed sport as a good way to increase church attendance and help swell their congregations!

> **Muscular Christianity:** a Christian movement that emerged in mid-nineteenth century England and was characterised by a belief in manliness, the moral and physical beauty of athleticism, teamwork, discipline and self-sacrifice.

It is also important to consider how the Church helped provide more opportunities for sporting involvement:
- The approval and active involvement of the clergy gave encouragement for the working classes to participate in rationalised sporting activities such as association football.
- The Church organised teams, set up clubs and organised competitions. Many modern-day football clubs have their origins traceable to church organisations (e.g. Aston Villa via Villa Cross Methodist Church).
- The Church provided facilities to play sport in their church halls and on their playing fields. A number of church groups formed, with sporting involvement a key part of their programmes of activities, e.g. the Boys' Brigade, the Scouts, the YMCA etc.

Now test yourself

TESTED ☐

3 Identify how the Church encouraged the post-industrial game of football.

Answer online

Emergence of the middle class in a three-tier society

The following is a summary of key ways in which members of the middle class supported the development of sport:

- Codification: this was the development of strict rules, as ex-public school boys and university old boys played a key role in the formation of many national governing bodies (NGBs) of sport. They controlled sport and became key organisers via their administration experience, which enabled them to form and run clubs and NGBs (e.g. the Football Association set up in 1863, the Rugby Football Union set up in 1871 and the Lawn Tennis Association established in 1888). Members of the middle class took prominent leadership roles in such organisations.
- Competitions: leagues and competitions were developed via middle-class involvement in public schools/universities/clubs/NGBs/factory teams/church teams.
- Public provision: public facilities (e.g. parks and public baths) were developed by middle-class **philanthropists**, factory owners and the Church; members of the middle class were able to pass government Acts in their role as local politicians.
- Increased leisure time: middle-class factory owners gradually gave their workers more leisure time (e.g. a Saturday half-day), which allowed more time to watch or participate in sport.
- Move to 'professionalism': the middle class helped in the development of early commercial/professional sport (e.g. acting as agents, promoters in athletics; as factory owners setting up factory teams and paying broken time payments in football).

> **Philanthropists:** kind, generous, middle-class individuals who had a social conscience and were keen to try to provide a better life for the working classes.

British Empire

Sport was seen as a very good and powerful way of instilling moral values into people across the world and of binding the various people of the British Empire together. Young men (nineteenth-century ex-public school boys and university old boys) educated to become leaders of the British Empire spread the playing of games in a number of different ways:

- As teachers they developed teams and taught traditional sporting values in schools throughout the Empire.
- As industrialists/factory owners they set up teams and gave time off to play competitive sport nationally and internationally.
- As clergy they developed church teams or became missionaries and took sport abroad (good for social control/morality etc.).
- As officers in the British army they used sport with the armed services and spread sport throughout the Empire.
- As diplomats they travelled the world and took sport with them (e.g. rugby and cricket).
- They formed the national governing bodies of sport (e.g. the Rugby Football Union) which codified sports and established leagues and competitions which eventually spread internationally as well as nationally.

Public provision and its influence on the development and spread of rational recreation

The development of public baths in urban and industrial areas positively influenced the opportunities for working-class rational recreation. Poor living conditions, disease and pollution were the harsh side-effects of industrialisation. To try to combat this, and improve the health and hygiene of the working classes, local authorities felt a civic responsibility to apply for grants to provide public washing facilities and improve their status as a town (e.g. via the Wash Houses Act of 1846).

Increased **public provision** was made in the second half of the nineteenth century for public bath houses, with first- and second-class facilities to reflect the social class of a visitor. Plunge baths were developed for swimming/recreational use. Such involvement in positive physical activity was seen as a means of social control of the working classes, keeping them away from drinking and violence. It also helped improve productivity at work, as workers became healthier and less prone to serious diseases and infection.

> **Public provision:** local council provision of facilities (e.g. sport/recreational) for the masses.

Now test yourself

TESTED

4 Give reasons why local authorities in the nineteenth century started to provide recreational and sporting activities for their local communities.

Answer online

Development of national governing bodies (NGBs)

During the mid- to late-nineteenth century, lots of NGBs began to develop in England (e.g. the Football Association in 1863):

- Sport was becoming increasingly popular with more widespread playing of sport.
- More teams and clubs were forming.
- Leagues and competitions were required for these teams to compete in.
- More national and international fixtures were being organised.
- Nationally agreed rules and **codification** for different sports were required (e.g. association football); a single set of rules was required in order to enable 'fair competition'.
- Maintenance of the 'amateur ideal' to deal with professionalism and early commercialisation of sport and the desire to maintain control of sport among the middle/upper classes, e.g. 'exclusivity', where the middle and upper classes were able to set rules of eligibility to exclude the working classes from joining in (and potentially beating them!). In rugby union, no payments for players were allowed, which in effect excluded the working classes from playing it for a living.

> **Codification:** the gradual organisation and definition of rules (e.g. for the actual playing of a sport, as well as the conduct and behaviour of participants).

Amateurism and professionalism

REVISED

Participation in sport over time has been viewed as being played according to two very different codes. First, there is the **amateur** code, which focuses on sport as being purely for enjoyment; second, there is the **professional** code, which places far more emphasis on winning.

> **Amateur:** someone who plays sport for the love of it and receives no financial gain.
>
> **Professional:** someone who plays sport for financial gain.

Typical mistake

Amateurism is often taken today to mean low-level, poor performance, but in the nineteenth century the opposite was true and the amateur sports performer was very much admired and respected.

The upper classes were so wealthy that they could afford not to work and play sport whenever they wanted. The working classes, on the other hand, had to make money from sport or they could not afford to play.

The gentleman amateur in nineteenth-century Britain: C.B. Fry, England international footballer/cricketer; World Record holder in the long jump	The working-class professional in nineteenth-century Britain: Jimmy Forrest, Blackburn Rovers Footballer and first professional to play for England vs Wales in 1884
Came from a public school/university background (Repton and Oxford University)	Came from a state education background
Had high status/social position in society and sport (upper and middle class); he was a politician and diplomat	Had low status/social position in society and sport (working class)
Had wealth and did not need 'financial compensation' to participate in sport	Had very little wealth/was poor with limited income – therefore needed 'financial compensation' to participate in sport
Had lots of free time available to participate in sport	Had very little free time available to participate in sport due to long working hours
Viewed sports participation as good for character building	Viewed sport as a 'way out' of poverty; earning money from sport was seen as an avenue of social mobility
Played lots of sports – viewed as an 'all-rounder', e.g. an England footballer/cricketer and long jump record holder; training was frowned upon as this would constitute professionalism and he preferred to use his natural talents	Specialised in a single sport (association football); commitment to training to improve fitness/skill levels
Played sport to a high moral code with an emphasis on participation/fair play/appreciating the value of rule-regulated activity	Played sport with a 'low level of morality' with an emphasis on winning/gamesmanship/cheating; viewed as 'corruptible' and open to bribes

Key features of early twentieth-century amateurs

At the start of the twentieth century, amateurs maintained their prominence in sport in a number of ways. This included their positions at the top of national governing bodies, which influenced access for the working classes into amateur sports such as rugby union. The amateurs were therefore still the best performers, playing with high morality and emphasising sportsmanship in their participation.

- High status: amateurs held high status in sport and society.
- Controllers of sport: the middle and upper classes controlled sport, excluding (e.g. financially) working classes from 'amateur sports'.
- Top performers: it was more likely that top performers would come from the middle or upper classes.
- Highly moral: amateurs had sufficient income and leisure time to play sport for the love of it, receiving no payment. They emphasised fair play and sportsmanship.

Key features of modern-day 'amateurs'

As the twentieth century progressed, amateurs began to lose some of their status and power in sport. Society slowly began to become concerned with equality of opportunity, with achievements based more on merit and personal performance standards:

- Modern-day 'amateurs' of the late twentieth and early twenty-first centuries tend to be of lower status (professionals are now of higher status).
- Some high-level performers are still not professional (e.g. gymnasts).
- There has been a blurring of amateur and professional distinctions, with less likelihood of exclusions, as society has become more egalitarian (i.e. based on equality) and achievement is based on merit.

- Performance at the top level in most sports is now open to all.
- Some amateurs receive finance to pay for training expenses (e.g. National Lottery/Sports Aid money). It could be argued that this enables them to train as full-time athletes in modern-day sport and they do not gain financially from Lottery funding. Does this mean they are still amateurs?

'Positives' of modern-day 'amateurism'

- The amateur code is still evident in British sport, e.g. via fair play and sportsmanship.
- It is still viewed positively and promoted in a number of ways, e.g. Fair Play awards in football, shaking of hands prior to and at the end of sporting contests and through the Olympics with the Olympic ideals based on principles of amateurism.
- Sports such as rugby union maintained their amateurism until late into the twentieth century and still have codes of conduct based on such principles, e.g. calling the referee 'Sir'.

Modern-day professionalism

Many factors are responsible for the growth of professional sport and the increased status of professional performers from the twentieth century through to the modern day:

- All classes can compete; social class is no longer a barrier to participation or success. Social mobility is far more possible now than it was in nineteenth-century Britain.
- People are now respected for their talents and efforts in reaching the top.
- There are high rewards for professionals through media and sponsorship (e.g. for footballers and tennis players).
- Celebrity status, more media coverage and investment in sport have all led to vast increases in financial rewards available for sportsmen and women, as large numbers of sports have become able to support professional performers, e.g. in golf, tennis and football. Many professionals are very wealthy and are able to afford big houses, expensive cars etc. Such materialism is highly valued by many in modern-day society.
- Money invested into sports enables events and the sports themselves to operate and survive commercially; there has been a general increase in commercial sport and the sponsorship of sport.
- Professionals have more time to train (i.e. many are full-time sports professionals), leading to higher standards of performance than amateurs in the same sport.
- Positive role models act as motivators for others to achieve in professional sport.

Rationalisation and development of lawn tennis

Lawn tennis was a middle-class invention, as the middle classes aspired to be like the upper classes in society but were excluded from or could not play real tennis. Hence, with the help of Major Walter Clompton Wingfield who patented his game of tennis on 23 February 1874, they devised their own form of tennis. It had set rules and suited their middle-class suburban housing, with lawned gardens as appropriate venues for tennis courts. Walls and hedges ensured privacy from the lower classes, who were initially excluded from participation.

> **Lawn tennis:** a sport played with racquets and a ball, originally called 'Sphairistike' and played on an hourglass-shaped court before its name and court shape were quickly replaced.

By 1877, the All England Croquet Club had been renamed the All England Croquet and Lawn Tennis Club. As a rational sporting activity mainly for the middle classes, lawn tennis was first introduced at Wimbledon in 1877, joining croquet as another sport.

Lawn tennis was viewed as an important activity in the emancipation of women, with female participation first allowed in 1884, helping to overcome suppression and negative stereotypes. Positive female role models inspired participation, for example Lotti Dodd who won five ladies' singles titles in the late nineteenth century and was an outstanding all-round sportswoman. The first female winner of Wimbledon was Miss Maud Watson.

The game of lawn tennis aided women as it could be played in the seclusion and privacy of their own gardens. They could play the game as a 'minimum exercise activity', dressed in a modest and reserved way, with their bodies fully covered by high-necked, long-sleeved dresses. As lawn tennis was 'not too vigorous', women were not expected to sweat, which was seen as unladylike. They could play the game with both males and females as part of social gatherings, improving their health at the same time.

Now test yourself

TESTED

5 Identify the factors which led to tennis increasing women's participation in physical activity in the late nineteenth century.

Answer online

The following is a summary of the key features of lawn tennis as it developed in the industrial/post-industrial era:

- Middle-class invention: it was a middle-class development/invention as an affordable alternative to real tennis, which set the middle classes apart from the working classes and led to private clubs developing for participation.
- Played by the middle classes: it was played in middle-class suburban gardens on lawns big enough to house private tennis courts.
- Organised by the middle classes: the middle classes had the organisational experience necessary to form their own private clubs.
- Use of specialist equipment: the middle classes had sufficient finance to purchase their own equipment. Wingfield sold a 'kit' as a portable product necessary to play the game of tennis. It cost five guineas (21 shillings or £1.05) and included a net, balls, racquets and poles for the net.
- Use of standardised rules: Wingfield's 'kit' also contained a rulebook, which helped standardise the game, with lawn tennis always played to the same rules.
- Played by males and females: tennis allowed respectable social and gender mixing; it was a good, civilised 'social game' which both sexes could play with a smart dress code to adhere to.
- **Public provision:** it eventually spread to the working classes via public parks.

Wenlock Olympian Games

In 1850, the Wenlock Agricultural Reading Society (WARS) resolved to form a class called the Olympian Class. This was set up to promote moral, physical and intellectual improvements, especially in the lower-class people of Wenlock. Participation in outdoor recreation challenges was an important means of promoting such improvement, with prizes offered for successful participants to encourage taking part.

The secretary of the class and the driving force behind the Wenlock Olympian Games was Dr William Penny Brookes, who was inspired to create such an event because of his work as a doctor and surgeon in the borough town of Much Wenlock in Shropshire.

In the first games, held in October 1850, there was a mixture of athletics and traditional country sports, including quoits, football, cricket, running, the hurdles and cycling on penny farthings. In the early games, there were also some fun events, including the blindfolded wheelbarrow race and an 'old woman's race', with a pound of tea for the winner! Pageantry and celebration were important parts of the games from the start. For example, a band led the procession of flag bearers, officials and competitors as they marched to the event.

By 1867, the programme featured a range of early athletic events, many of which were later developed into track and field athletic events (e.g. under-10 boys 60 yards; under-14 boys 100 yards; a mile foot race; running high leap/long leap; putting the stone/hammer throwing).

Baron Pierre de Coubertin visited the Olympian Society in 1890, which held a special festival in his honour. De Coubertin was inspired by Dr Brookes and went on to establish the (IOC) International Olympic Committee and reform the modern Olympic Games in Athens in 1896.

Rationalisation and development of track and field athletics

The industrialisation of society led to the end of rural fairs. They were replaced by urban fairs, as people migrated in large numbers to towns and cities looking for work. Athletics events became popular in such towns and cities, with purpose-built tracks and facilities in most major cities by the mid-nineteenth century. Walking and running races took place over set distances on race courses. Large numbers of people attended athletics events, with up to 25,000 spectators at meetings as the nineteenth century progressed. Wagering was common in athletics, as it was in its early days of pedestrianism/foot racing. Class divisions were also still evident as it became a 'rationalised' activity. Upper- and middle-class amateurs ran for enjoyment or to test themselves, while the lower classes ran to make money and were deemed 'professionals'.

An 'exclusion clause' (excluding the working classes/manual workers) attempted to separate modern athletics from the old professional/corrupt form. In 1866, the Amateur Athletic Club (AAC) was formed by ex-public school and ex-university men who were gentleman amateurs and did not allow mechanics, artisans or labourers to join (i.e. they excluded the working classes, or those earning money, from running from membership of the AAC). They brought respectability to athletics, emphasising endeavour, fair play, courage and no wagering.

The Amateur Athletic Association (AAA), established on 24 April 1880, withdrew the exclusion clause and opened up the sport to everyone. A professional became defined as somebody who ran for money as opposed to someone from the working classes.

Track and field athletics was not deemed to be an acceptable activity for women, as it was thought unladylike and did not have an appropriate dress code. The Women's AAA was not founded until 1922, with female participants not allowed into the Olympics until Amsterdam 1928. Even then, women were not allowed to race in events above 800 metres, as they were seen as 'too strenuous'.

Rationalisation and development of association football

REVISED

A variety of reasons can be given to explain the growth and development of association football from the mid-nineteenth century through to the present day. In terms of the post-industrial revolution period through to the second half of the nineteenth century, these included the following:

- Urbanisation: large numbers of people living in one place offered a large captive audience for football. The lack of space in urban areas led to purpose-built, specialist facilities for playing football, with terraces to house the high spectator demand.
- More free time/increased leisure time: as workers spent less time in the factories, more time was available for them to watch and play sport. Saturday afternoon at 3 p.m. became the traditional time for 'association football' matches.
- More disposable income: improved standards of living via higher wages gave workers enough money to pay entrance/gate money and afford transport to matches, as national fixtures began to spread football nationwide.
- Improved transport: the development of trains, in particular, enabled fans to travel to watch 'away' fixtures and increased the regularity of matches, with the resultant need for organised leagues/cup competitions. The FA Cup was first played for in the 1871–72 season.
- Increased professionalism: the opportunities to play football professionally as a job gradually increased, e.g. via broken time payments which enabled workers to take time off work to play football but still be paid their wage. Professional football, first recognised by the FA in 1885, was looked upon as a 'good job', as it was a chance to escape the factory system of work and urban deprivation that accompanied it.
- Social class links: middle-class influence and approval gave association football more respectability, with its emphasis on high morality and sporting etiquette. This was challenged relatively quickly by the working classes who made it 'the people's game', with larger numbers both playing and watching association football as the Football League commenced from 1888 onwards.
- Increased organisation: football quickly became highly structured and standardised when in 1863 ex-public schoolboys set up the Football Association (FA). National rules and codification meant the game was far more controlled with less violence, which reflected an increasingly civilised society. Referees controlled the games to further improve the behaviour of the players. Football quickly expanded, with lots of teams being set up via factories and churches.

Exam practice

1 Discuss the impact of the Industrial Revolution on leisure opportunities for the working classes. [8]
2 Which of the following best describes a professional performer? [1]
   (a) Someone who plays sport for the love of it
   (b) Someone who receives direct payment for their participation in sporting activities
   (c) Someone who does not get paid for competing in sport
   (d) Someone who plays sport emphasising sportsmanship and fair play
3 Explain two characteristics of lawn tennis in nineteenth-century Britain. [4]

Answers and quick quizzes online

ONLINE

Summary

You should now be able to:
- identify the characteristics of industrial and post-industrial Britain and how these influenced the development of sporting activities such as Association Football, lawn tennis and track and field athletics through to the late nineteenth century
- understand and explain a range of socio-cultural factors in industrial and post-industrial Britain which impacted on the development of rational recreation/sport, e.g. the industrial, urban and transport/

communications revolutions; the role of the middle classes, factory owners, Church and local authorities in supporting sporting developments at home and abroad
- understand the reasons for the development of national governing bodies of sport in the nineteenth century
- understand the changing status of the amateur and the professional sports performer from the late eighteenth century through to the modern day.

3.3 Sport in Britain after the Second World War (1950 to present)

Development of modern-day Association Football

Football became Britain's major sporting activity as the twentieth century progressed, with attendance and gate receipts soaring. However, the wages of the players did not reflect this increased income until later in the second half of the twentieth century, due to the setting of a maximum wage which constrained earnings. In 1900, the maximum wage was set at £4 a week and it was very slow to increase. Indeed, a footballer's wages did not significantly increase until Professional Footballers' Association chairman Jimmy Hill successfully fought for the abolition of the maximum wage in 1961 and Johnny Haynes became the first £100-a-week footballer.

More recently in the late twentieth and twenty-first centuries, football has undergone a massive increase in commercialisation linked to far more media coverage via TV and the internet. Top players such as Messi and Ronaldo are known the world over with pop star/role model status. Their salary scales have increased massively, with the **Bosman ruling** giving 'freedom of contract' to players and huge transfer fees being paid, particularly to a player who is 'out of contract'.

> **Bosman ruling:** a European Court of Justice decision made on 15 December 1995 concerning freedom of movement for workers. It allowed the free movement of labour in the European Union. It effectively allowed footballers within the EU to move at the end of their contract to another club without a transfer fee being paid.

Emergence of elite female footballers in modern-day sport

In the UK, football has become increasingly available to women. Key moments in the history of women's football in England are as follows:

- **1966** England's successful hosting of the World Cup led to a resurgence of interest in women's football.
- **1969** The Women's Football Association (WFA) was formed to promote the women's game at a national level, including the development of league structures.
- **1971** The WFA organised the first national competition, the Mitre Trophy, which is now the Women's FA Cup; the Football Association's 50-year ban on women's football being played on league grounds was lifted.
- **1972** The WFA launched an official England national team.
- **1991** The WFA set up the Women's Premier League.
- **1993** The FA began its direct involvement in women's football.
- **2001/02** Premier League club Newport Ladies FC was the first to broadcast its match highlights via OnDemand TV.
- **2004** The BBC broadcast the Women's FA Cup final to an audience of more than 2 million.
- **2008–12** The FA published a plan for a four-year strategy for women's football, which included 20 English women footballers gaining central contracts, initially earning £16,000 a year then £20,000 in 2012; the Women's Super League (WSL) was launched in 2011, initially as an eight-team summer competition; the TV rights to this were sold as a

four-year package to a 'pay-per-view' channel, restricting increased exposure and potentially more sponsorship deals than if the coverage had been available via free-to-air channels such as the BBC.

- **2012** A Team GB women's team participated for the first time at the Olympics in London 2012, creating considerable momentum to harness and move the women's game forward.
- **2013–18** The FA published a plan called 'Game Changer', which included a plan for the development of the women's national teams. It also included an increased media focus to promote the game via live coverage of the WSL on BT Sport and internationals on the BBC. The WSL announced a switch back to the winter season to move it in line with other leagues in Europe and improve the chances of the national team, as well as increase attendance at games and participation in the sport at all levels.

Socio-cultural factors positively influencing women's participation in association football

A number of socio-cultural factors have led to an increase in opportunities for women to participate and progress through to elite level in football in modern-day society. These include:

- Equal opportunities: more sports are generally available to and socially acceptable for women, including football. The Sex Discrimination Act has led to less sexual discrimination in sport on the basis of gender. The war effort from women also led to the breaking down of myths and stereotypes about the physical capabilities of women.
- There is increased media coverage of women's football. BT Sport provides live coverage of the Women's Super League (WSL); women's football is part of EA Sports FIFA 16 Game. This has generated more sponsorship via partners such as Continental, Nike, SSE and Vauxhall.
- There are more female role models in football, for example performers, coaches and officials.
- There is more provision via school PE programmes, in National Curriculum PE lessons as well as via extra-curricular opportunities.
- There is increased approval/encouragement resource investment via the FA. For example, the women's national teams at various levels are fully supported by the FA; the Women's FA Cup Final was held at Wembley for the first time in 2015.
- More clubs are forming, at local, as well as professional, levels (e.g. WSL 1 and 2).
- There is increased participation via more funding into the game, at grass roots level as well as at elite level.
- Women have more free time, as the traditional domestic responsibility role has decreased for women.

As the twenty-first century has progressed, women's football has become increasingly prominent across the world. The Union of European Football Associations (UEFA) has set up competitions such as the Women's EURO and UEFA Champions League, which have gained in media exposure. In England, women's football enjoyed a post-World Cup boom following the success of the team in finishing third overall in Canada. The 2015 World Cup itself was an expanded tournament, with 24 teams competing and all of England's matches televised live on the BBC. The success can be traced in part to the setting up of the Women's Super League, as mentioned above, which has provided women with more opportunities to play professionally and they can earn up to £50,000 a year when combining club wages with FA central contracts of £23,000.

Factors affecting the emergence of elite female officials in football

The story of the emergence of elite female officials in football is not quite so encouraging. At the end of the twentieth century, a very limited number of female officials were progressing through to the Football League. The first female ever to officiate in the Football League and then Premier League, both as an assistant referee, was Wendy Toms. Progress following on from this breakthrough has been slow.

While relatively small in number in relation to their male counterparts, the fact that the FA reports an increasing number of female referees at different levels of the game provides optimism, with ambassadors and elite role models (e.g. Sian Massey) in refereeing for young girls to aspire to.

Indeed, the Game Changer FA plan for women's football in England reports that the number of qualified female referees increased from 636 in 2008 to 1,035 in 2012. A number of possible reasons can be given to account for such a reported increase in women refereeing elite-level football matches:

- FA approval/active involvement in women's football in a variety of roles, including officiating (e.g. via FA development and recruitment programmes which have targeted female referees and the creation of the 'Women's Referee Development Pathway')
- the FA National Referee Strategy (NRS) included new frameworks and structures in 2016/17, such as separate classifications for men's and women's football and a specific focus on female referee recruitment and retention; as part of the NRS, county FAs were set targets on female referee recruitment and retention.
- use of positive role models/mentors to encourage women to become football referees through to the highest level
- FA Respect campaign aiming to improve player conduct and behaviour towards all referees, including women, to try to increase recruitment and retention
- general increase in equality in society and recognition of women's ability to officiate football matches at the highest levels of the game; legal support/ legislation in place against sexism (e.g. the Sex Discrimination Act).

While the Game Changer statistics for qualified female referees point to increased numbers from 2008 to 2012, in general recruitment and retention of female referees continues to face a number of barriers, including:

- physical/psychological intimidation (e.g. hostile attitudes from male players swearing/physically threatening referees)
- lack of adherence to FA Respect protocol
- personal factors – allegations of sexism and marginalisation in the predominantly 'male world' of football
- organisational factors, which in reality means there is a lack of support/ training/feedback on performance within the system for female referees
- a lack of female role models at the elite level of football refereeing.

Now test yourself

1 Outline the factors which are negatively impacting on women's involvement as officials in association football.

Answer online

Development of modern-day lawn tennis

Modern-day tennis spread around the world during the twentieth century, with tournaments in the USA, France and Australia taking place alongside Wimbledon as the four 'majors'. Players soon realised they could earn considerable amounts of money from their tennis skills, and professional tours and tournaments were established as early as the 1920s to enable them to do so. However, the rest of tennis, including the four 'majors', remained strictly amateur, with professionals excluded from participation. It was not until 1968 that commercial pressures and rumours of some amateurs taking money illegally (colloquially known as 'shamateurism') led to the abandonment of the distinction between amateur and professional, inaugurating the **open era**, in which all players could compete in all tournaments.

> **Open era:** when professional tennis players were allowed to compete alongside amateurs and earn money.

With the beginning of the open era, the establishment of an international professional tennis circuit and revenues from the sale of TV rights, the popularity of the game has spread worldwide and the sport has tried to shed its English middle-class image. Tennis in the UK is still perceived by many to be a middle-class preserve. This may be because it developed later than other sports, or it may be due to the fact that joining a tennis club has always appeared difficult or off-putting, with the requirement to stick to rigid dress codes. The image of the sport as a means to gather socially rather than as a competitive opportunity has been hard to shed.

The open era witnessed distinct inequalities in the amount of prize money offered to men and women. The 1968 Wimbledon Championship awarded £2,000 to Rod Laver, the men's singles winner, with only £750 given to Billie Jean King, the women's champion. Representatives from the Women's Tennis Association (WTA), including Billie Jean King, fought for equal recognition and prize money, with equality achieved in 2007 at Wimbledon when both winners earned £700,000. By 2015 it had risen to £1,760,000 each for the respective men's and ladies' singles champions.

Emergence of elite female tennis players in modern-day sport

The work of the WTA (which is now a global leader in women's professional sport) illustrates how tennis can be viewed as one of a few sports in which female professional performers have played a significant part. As part of the battle fighting pay differentials in tennis tournaments such as Wimbledon, a number of women decided to create their own tour away from the men's.

The WTA therefore developed its own professional circuit in the late twentieth century, providing ground-breaking opportunities for women to play at the top level, eventually earning millions of pounds through tournament earnings and sponsorship deals. Billie Jean King became the first female athlete to earn £100,000 in a single year, with Chris Evert generating over $1,000,000 in career earnings by the mid-1970s. The WTA also stated that in 2015, more than 2,500 elite players competed for $129 million in prize money at the 55 WTA events and four Grand Slams available in tennis. Lots of potential role models for girls, as well as large sponsorship deals, continue in the early twenty-first century via worldwide media coverage of women's elite tennis tournaments.

Development of moden-day track and field athletics

As the twentieth century progressed, in the immediate post–Second World War period, interest in athletics was stimulated when the Olympics took place in London in 1948. However, while the rest of the world found ways to get round the strict amateur rules of international athletics, Britain left its athletes to manage as best they could.

'Trust funds' were eventually established, which enabled athletes to safeguard their eligibility to take part in amateur competitions but still allowed them to receive financial rewards as an athlete. The governing body for athletics kept control of the sport by insisting that it should channel or authorise all payments. Payments from the fund for day-to-day living expenses were allowed and the balance became available to the athlete on retirement. Such arrangements enabled a group of male and female athletes to go around the world and compete in a programme of championships and grand prix events, with both appearance money as well as prize money for winning.

Today, there are no trust funds as payments can be made directly to athletes and/or their agents within rules which were laid down by the International Amateur Athletics Association (IAAA), which is now called the International Association of Athletics Federations (IAAF).

At the end of the twentieth century and into the early twenty-first century, the IAAF established and organised a number of major international athletics competitions for male and female athletes where they could earn considerable amounts of money. For example, in 2010 a new global competition structure headed by the IAAF Diamond League was unveiled. It involves 14 one-day invitational track and field meetings in the USA, Europe, the Middle East and Asia. Large spectator numbers, both live and via global media coverage, ensure athletes can generate healthy incomes via prize money and sponsorship deals with large multi-nationals such as Nike and Adidas.

Emergence of elite female athletes in modern-day sport

Treatment of women in athletics remained 'indifferent' at best through to the late twentieth century. Women were still excluded from a number of events in the Olympics. The marathon was not open to women until the Los Angeles Olympics in 1984. The triple jump and hammer were only introduced for women in Atlanta 1996 and Sydney 2000 respectively.

Fortunately, the negative myths (e.g. impact on women's child-bearing capacity) and stereotypes about the capabilities of elite-level female athletes are being challenged, and competitions such as the Diamond League enable female as well as male athletes to earn millions from their talents.

Now test yourself

TESTED

2 Why was women's involvement in elite-level marathon running delayed until towards the end of the twentieth century?

Answer online

Commercialism, media and sponsorship

There is massive **media** interest in certain 'high-profile' sports – television companies pay huge amounts of money for the rights to show a sporting event, such as football on Sky Sports and BT Sport, as sport has a positive image. **Sponsorship** deals result from television exposure. Merchandising too relates to media exposure – clothing and equipment companies such as Nike and Adidas have become strong rivals in sponsoring teams and individuals in order to aid their merchandising.

Media: an organised means of communication by which large numbers of different people can be reached quickly.

Commercialism: the process of attempting to gain money from an activity, e.g. sport.

Sponsorship: when a company pays for it's products to be publicly displayed or advertised, usually as an attempt to increase the sales of it's goods.

'Golden triangle'

Figure 3.3a The 'golden triangle'

Sport, the media, business and sponsorship are all strongly interlinked and mutually dependent – the 'golden triangle'. Each element of the triangle relies on the others. For instance, without media coverage, sports are less attractive to sponsors who want their business or product to be publicised to as many people as possible. The media use sport to gain viewers, listeners and readers. In turn, businesses and sponsors use the media to advertise their products and services: organisations often pay substantial sums to sport and the media for advertisements.

Characteristics of commercial sport

Commercial sport (especially association football, tennis and athletics) has close links with:

- professional sport – it is high quality and has high skill levels
- sponsorship and business – they go hand-in-hand
- entertainment – watching sport is part of a mass-entertainment industry; viewing needs to fit into a relatively short timescale
- contracts, e.g. involving sales of merchandise and bidding for television rights
- athletes as commodities, e.g. as an asset to companies through product endorsement, which brings increased sales/profits; athletes become well-known role models
- widespread media coverage, and interest in high-profile sports that are visually appealing and have high skill levels, well-matched competition and simple/understandable rules.

Now test yourself

TESTED ☐

3 Identify the characteristics of a sport which make it attractive for TV coverage.

Answer online

Effects of commercialisation on sport

Some sports have changed as a result of commercial and media interest:

- Rules and scoring systems have been changed or introduced to speed up the action and prevent spectator boredom, e.g. the multi-ball system at football matches cuts down on time-wasting.
- Breaks are extended/provided in play so that sponsors can advertise their products and services.
- Competition formats have changed, e.g. Twenty20 cricket is a major revenue-earner due to spectator, television and commercial interests.
- Sports played by women receive less coverage, which can negatively affect participation and funding. There are fewer female role models and there is less money to re-invest in sport at grassroots and professional levels.
- The increased use of technology through the media has led to a more personal experience for the viewer, e.g. HD coverage of sport.

Media

There are a number of different types of media involved in covering sport. These include TV, newspapers, radio, the internet and social media.

TV can be viewed as the most powerful aspect of the media – the buying and selling of TV broadcasting rights is a very important part of twenty-first century sport as it has 'gone global'!

Globalisation in sport is seen via:

- the sponsorship of events (e.g. Coca-Cola as a 'universal sponsor')
- the way players are recruited to play for teams/compete in events in countries other than their own
- the spreading of different sports to 'new nations', e.g. the 1994 soccer World Cup which was successfully hosted in the USA
- increasing pressure on athletes to perform at their best; this may lead some to use illegal substances to maintain high performance levels and benefit from the accompanying rewards that success brings in a number of high-profile sports.

> **Globalisation:** the process whereby nations are increasingly being linked together and people are becoming more interdependent via improvements in communication and travel.

Impact of social media on sport

In the last few years, social media have changed the behaviour of both sports performers and sports fans. Top sports performers are involved in social media in a big way and usually create lots of excitement via their social media communications as opposed to other media channels such as newspapers. More and more fans prefer getting their sports news from Twitter and Facebook rather than from TV or national news websites.

There are a number of big players in the world of social media, including Twitter, Facebook, Instagram, BlogSpot and WordPress. In addition, YouTube is increasingly being used by many athletes to help them achieve their goals (e.g. posting videos of edited highlights to attract university scholarships/coaches).

The power and reach provided by social media to sports performers have changed sport at all levels, for example enabling top-level sports performers to build up very large and engaged fan bases in a very short space of time. Social media have empowered athletes at every level to engage with a much wider audience than was possible a few years ago. However, while this has a number of positives, sevrral elite performers have got into trouble for their postings on social media. Sports performers now need to be trained to understand the responsibilities and liability that go with such global social media communication.

Exam practice

1 Which factors have been responsible for the advancement in opportunities for women in sport (e.g. tennis/athletics/football) since the end of the Second World War? [8]
2 Describe the main factors responsible for the increased commercialisation of sports such as football in the twenty-first century. [6]

Answers and quick quizzes online

ONLINE

Summary

You should now be able to:
- explain the changing role of women in sport and factors affecting their emergence in modern-day elite sport via a consideration of their involvement in football, tennis and athletics
- understand how the 'golden triangle' influences the development of sport in modern-day society, particularly in relation to football, tennis and athletics.

3.4 Sociological theory applied to equal opportunities

The syllabus requires you to know and be able to define a number of key sociological terms and to explain how they relate to equality of opportunity in sport.

Society

A human **society** is a group of people involved in persistent interpersonal relationships. It is often a large social grouping, sharing the same geographical territory and typically subject to the same political authority and dominant cultural expectations. A society can therefore be viewed as the sum total of all the relationships in a given space (e.g. within a specific country or nation state).

Success in sport on a global scale is often viewed as an important measure of the relative status of a society or nation in the world. For example, national identity and national pride are often achieved as a result of success at events such as the Olympics (e.g. in Britain through Team GB's third position on the medal table at London 2012 and second position in Rio 2016, with the Olympic and Paralympic heroes receiving the adulation of the British public at home-coming parades in Manchester and London in October 2016).

> **Revision activity**
>
> Create a table of the key sociological terms on the syllabus and their definitions so you are clear on their meanings.

> **Society:** an organised group of people associated for some specific purpose or with a shared common interest.

Socialisation

Socialisation is a lifelong process whereby members of a society learn its norms, values, ideas, practices and roles in order to take their place in that society. It can be divided into two main parts: primary and secondary socialisation.

Primary socialisation

This refers to socialisation during the early years of childhood which takes place mainly within the immediate family (i.e. the mother, father, brothers and sisters). A key process involved at this stage is the **internalisation** of a society's culture, whereby individuals absorb and accept its shared norms and values.

The nature of living in a society is such that people are constantly communicating within a social group among family and close friends. Much of the early basic socialisation occurs as a young child, when families and early friends teach basic values and accepted behaviour patterns. Play is a good way to learn how to share, interact and practise becoming an adult.

For many families, physical exercise provides a time when they come together, whether it be a shared involvement in an activity such as cycling or a family commitment to one (or more) member of the family who has devoted themselves to regular involvement in sporting competition.

> **Socialisation:** a lifelong process whereby members of a society learn its norms, values, ideas, practices and roles in order to take their place in that society.
>
> **Internalisation:** the learning of values or attitudes that are incorporated within yourself.

Secondary socialisation

This occurs during the later years (i.e. as teenagers and adults), when the family is less involved and other 'agencies' deliberately set up for the socialisation process begin to exert more and more influence (e.g. peer groups, friends, schools).

School is an important part of social development. For example, it can help with the socialisation process by teaching important moral skills such as co-operation, teamwork and learning to take responsibility for one's own actions.

Gender socialisation involves the learning of behaviour and attitudes historically considered appropriate for a given sex. 'Boys learn to be boys' and 'girls learn to be girls' via the many different agents of socialisation, including family, friends, school, college and the mass media. Participation in sport/physical activity can help create a 'social identity' (e.g. such participation can socialise boys and girls into traditional gender roles of masculinity and femininity).

Now test yourself
TESTED

1 Define the following terms: 'socialisation', 'primary socialisation' and 'secondary socialisation'.

Answer online

Social processes
REVISED

Social processes involve different forms of social interaction which occur again and again and are the means by which 'culture' and 'social organisations' are either preserved or changed. It refers to some of the general and recurrent forms that social interaction may take; it involves ways in which individuals and groups interact, adjust and readjust to establish relationships and patterns of behaviour on an ongoing basis. Examples of social processes include integration, co-operation and conflict.

> **Social processes:** forms of social interaction between individuals and groups which occur again and again.

Social control

Social control is a concept that refers to the way in which people's thoughts, feelings, appearance and behaviour are regulated in social systems.

Society is made up of various **institutions**, with the family viewed as the most basic unit. These institutions work together for the benefit of society, undertaking a variety of social processes to ensure socialisation into society, maintaining order and social control.

However, in society there are various social processes at work which act as constraints and potentially limit the opportunities to become involved in sport. Historically, our society has been male dominated, with restrictions placed on women engaging in sport. Nowadays, the constraints are less pronounced, although milder forms of social control exist in the form of what is deemed to be gender-appropriate behaviour.

For example, mild disapproval from their husband or male partner might persuade women to limit their physical activity to what they view as

> **Social control:** a concept that refers to the way in which people's thoughts, feelings, appearance and behaviour are regulated in social systems.
>
> **Institutions:** an established organisations founded for a religious, educational, professional or social purpose.

'respectable' and therefore 'socially acceptable'. So they might choose badminton over rugby or aerobics over boxing if under the influence of social control. Social control from peers or the media to 'look feminine' and maintain a slim appearance could also rule out certain sports requiring muscular development which is seen as 'unfeminine', for example weightlifting, boxing and rugby.

Social pressures mean that sometimes women are made to feel guilty about leaving a young baby and therefore tend to give up previous active leisure pursuits once their child has been born. A lack of free time compared to men and lower disposable income can also act as agents of social control and decrease the opportunities for women to get involved in regular healthy sporting activity, as illustrated by data on sport's participation. Sport England's Active People Survey (8Q3–9Q2) discovered that 40.6 per cent of men compared to 30.7 per cent of women took part in sport at least once a week.

Social change

The data above confirm that sports participation inequalities exist when comparing women to men. It is difficult for any social group to bring about change without having strong influence in the decision-making groups (e.g. local councils, national governing bodies etc.). **Social change** occurs when institutions readjust to meet 'new needs' of groups in society such as women, for example leisure providers such as local councils offering more crèche facilities to minimise/lessen the negative effects of traditional childcare responsibilities and/or feelings of guilt at leaving young children while mothers participate in sporting activity.

In addition to gender inequalities, certain ethnic groups such as Indians and Pakistanis have faced constraints on their participation in sport. Some of these have been viewed as emerging from within the family unit itself (e.g. via cultural norms valuing educational achievement over sporting participation, as well as limiting women's participation due to clothing restrictions).

Social change can therefore be viewed as an alteration in the social order of a society. Sporting activities can be used in specialist programmes to try to bring about social change in a positive way.

In terms of gender, Sport England launched 'This Girl Can' as a high-profile campaign to try to bring about social changes in the way women's participation in sport and physical activity is viewed.

'Kick it Out' is a campaign designed to bring about social change in relation to ethnicity by increasing awareness of racial issues within society. It uses positive role models/high-profile sports performers to educate/re-educate individuals in society about appropriate behaviour in attempting to bring about social change and reduce the incidence of racism in sport/society in general.

> **Social change:** an alteration in the social order of a society, i.e. significant changes in social behaviours and/or cultural values over time leading to long-term effects.

Now test yourself

TESTED

2 Define the term 'social change'.

Answer online

Social issues – causes and consequences of inequality

REVISED

Many people dream of a society where all members are equal and there is no ranking of people in terms of prestige, power, wealth etc. It is obvious to us all that such a society is likely to remain a dream and all human societies have some form of social **inequality**, with power, prestige and wealth unequally divided.

Social inequality is a modern-day **social issue**. It occurs when resources in a society are unevenly distributed among categories of people who are identifiable via socially defined characteristics such as ethnic/racial and gender identities.

Related to this is economic inequality on the basis of unequal distribution of income or wealth. This is a frequently studied type of social inequality, with major implications for all aspects of life, including participation in sport.

Sex- and gender-based prejudice and discrimination (i.e. sexism) are major social issues which contribute to social inequality, as they give rise to role divisions, ultimately leading to fewer women in positions of power and decision making, whether in the world of sport or more generally in political activities within society. Women's participation in work has been increasing globally (e.g. in professional sport) but their earnings still tend to be lower than those of their male counterparts and they face inequality in terms of political influence and their role in most major religions.

In sport, there are a number of possible causes of inequality, which include:
- lack of money/high costs of participating
- lack of confidence/self-esteem
- lack of role models to aspire to (in terms of participants/coaches/leaders of sports organisations in positions of responsibility)
- myths or stereotypes in some sections of society about the capabilities of women, ethnic minorities and disabled people.

As far as sport and physical activity are concerned, there are a number of negative consequences of such inequalities. They result in lower participation rates in sport among a number of groups/sections of society, including people with disabilities, women, those from ethnic minority groups, the unemployed and elderly people.

> **Inequality:** the unfair situation where resources or opportunities are distributed unevenly within a society.
>
> **Social issues:** problem/conflict which affects a considerable number of people in society (e.g. gender or disability discrimination, drug abuse and low activity patterns linked to health/obesity problems).

Social structures and social stratification

REVISED

A number of different social structures exist which have an impact (positive or negative) on an individual and their overall life chances. As an example linked to participation in sport, the type of school you go to (e.g. state vs private) can affect the activities you get to try out, as well as the amount of time devoted to sport, the quality of teaching/coaching received to develop your talents and the quality of facilities you train in.

Social stratification is a type of social inequality. It is the division of a society into different levels (i.e. strata) on the basis of a social characteristic such as wealth or social status. Social differences are divided into different layers (i.e. upper, middle and lower classes) when the relative possession or non-possession of a social characteristic becomes the distributing principle for individuals within a system of unequal rewards.

> **Social stratification:** a type of social inequality where society is divided into different levels on the basis of a social characteristic, such as wealth or social status.

Modern-day societies use individual wealth as a means of stratification, which gives individuals a relative social position. The importance of stratification is that those at the top of the system have greater access to resources than those at the bottom.

In some ways, participation in sport means individuals can leave behind their normal lives and adopt a new athletic identity in a sporting context. This (temporarily) replaces the inequalities of everyday life with a situation where everyone is equal.

However, the idea that sport provides equality of opportunity can be viewed as problematic, as the very nature of sport emphasises competition and dominance. Furthemore, the realities of the 'real world' and people's relative position in the social class hierarchy do affect their involvement in sport. For example, disposable income can influence the type of activity undertaken, the type of club joined, the equipment used and so on. Equestrian and other horse-related activities tend to be relatively expensive and require high income levels linked to the upper classes in society. Activities associated more with the middle classes include rugby union and tennis, leaving Rugby League and darts as more traditional lower-class pastimes.

The social stratification system continues to be visible in sport, with a number of sections or groups of society identified by Sport England as under-represented in terms of sports involvement, e.g. low social class groups and individuals with a disability.

When looking at the organisation and structure of society, it is clear that some individuals and groups have traditionally held the positions of power. In the UK, those in such positions have tended to be white males from the middle classes. This leads to the social stratification of society being reflected in sport, with a hierarchy evident that gives power and influence to those at the top. For many years, **social class** variations in sports participation have been highlighted by research and data produced by Sport England.

Social class/stratification and schools

While National Curriculum PE aims to offer all young people a broad and balanced programme, it is evident that some young people may be disadvantaged as a result of social inequality.

Children from low-income families tend to have poorer health than other children, and this may undermine their physical abilities and/or skill levels. These children also have less money to spend on sports equipment, additional specialist coaching etc. Schools themselves may magnify social class differences (e.g. public schools and state schools situated in more affluent areas often have better sports facilities than schools located in working-class areas).

Social class and sports clubs

Involvement in extra-curricular activities may be negatively affected by working-class expectations on children to carry out domestic responsibilities (e.g. looking after younger children in the family, doing household chores etc.). Economic inequalities are also likely to impact on membership of sports clubs, increasing the likelihood of more middle- and upper-class children joining clubs compared to working-class children.

Social class: a term used to define social inequalities, i.e. certain groups have more access to wealth and power than others. Factors which contribute to social class include a person's job, family background, education and income.

This can be illustrated via the Sport England Active People Survey data on tennis participation among the 16+ age group, which for many occurs within tennis clubs. In terms of social class, the data show higher rates of participation in tennis among the highest socio-economic groups. While 202,500 adults from National Statistics Socio-economic Classification (NS-SEC) levels 1–4 (managerial/skilled professions) participated in tennis at least once a week, only 64,100 adults from NS-SEC levels 5–8 (non-skilled/manual professions) did so.

Now test yourself

TESTED

3 Identify how participation in sport and other physical activity can be increased among individuals in the working classes.

Answer online

Social action theory and its influence on physical activity and sport

REVISED

Social action theory accepts that sport is produced and developed at a particular time through the relationships and social networks of people who share similar views. The links between these people and their social interdependence are the key ideas of such a theory.

Sports involvement and **progression** are therefore determined by the relationships between people based on the different amounts of power they have in society. The way these relationships are built up and why they change is an open-ended process.

Sport has therefore developed in a complex way alongside aspects of society such as class structure, education and family. Social action theory stresses the fact that people can intervene in social processes and change them.

Social action theory: a way of viewing socialisation, emphasising the proactive role of people in shaping social life (i.e. social action).

Progression: the process of gradually developing towards a more advanced state.

Interactionist approach

Social action theory is sometimes called 'interactionist theory'. In sociology, the interactionist approach is the study of how individuals behave within a society. It is a theoretical perspective that stems from social processes that occur when humans interact, for example co-operation and conflict.

Interactionism works from the individual towards society. It stresses that people have an active role in shaping society. The ways we communicate and interact (e.g. via language and gesture) are emphasised. Although it is accepted that society does have some control over individuals, there is always the opportunity for creative action. Through social interactions and the use of language, people negotiate the various social roles they are expected to play.

Social action theory/the interactionist approach views sport and physical activity as an essential part of society's make-up. Sport can have an impact on the social and cultural fabric of society, and society can have an impact on sport.

Answers and quick quizzes at **www.hoddereducation.co.uk/myrevisionnotes**

There are a number of ways in which sport can have an impact on society, for example by:

- highlighting inequalities that exist between different social class groups (e.g. via the types of sports undertaken being linked to wealth/upbringing)
- influencing our ideas/beliefs about masculinity and femininity
- influencing our ideas/beliefs about race/ethnicity (e.g. negatively through racist chanting at football matches aimed at players)
- influencing our ideas about ability and disability (e.g. positively through the achievements of Paralympic athletes such as Dame Sarah Storey)
- contributing to our sense of national pride/social integration (e.g. via media images of successful Team GB athletes receiving their medals at the Olympics)
- targeting social problems such as unemployment, crime, disengaged communities and inequalities; sport can help increase understanding and appreciation of cultural differences and prejudices, limiting the social exclusion felt by minority groups (e.g. StreetGames/Doorstep Sport/Community Football Leagues act as an incentive to integrate and interact with others without necessarily realising the wider concept of what they are doing; they also provied a sense of belonging and increased self-worth).

Key terms for the study of equality in physical activity and sport

REVISED

There are a number of key terms you need to understand when studying **equal opportunities** in physical activity and sport.

Embedded in British law, equal opportunities is a term used to emphasise inclusiveness and the importance of treating all people fairly/similarly, unhampered by artificial barriers, **discrimination**, **prejudice** or preference.

Now test yourself

TESTED

4 Define the term 'equal opportunities'.

Answer online

The explanation of equal opportunities given above identifies discrimination and prejudice as important factors which can determine whether equality of opportunity is present within a society. In addition, negative **stereotypes** can also adversely affect an individual's chances of taking part in sport or a certain type of sport (e.g. sport is for men and not for women; boxing/rugby is for men and not for women). However, sport can also be used to break down traditional gender stereotypes and ideologies of masculinity and femininity, e.g. when women take part in traditionally male sports such as boxing, rugby and football (i.e. they participate in 'male perceived sports').

Sport's interpretation of equal opportunities can be explained with reference to Sport England's equality and diversity policy, which involves a commitment to:

- develop a culture that enables and values everyone's full involvement
- create an environment in which everyone has opportunities to play, compete, officiate, coach, volunteer and run community sport
- overcome potential barriers for those wishing to play sport, particularly if they are from groups who are currently under-represented in sport.

Equal opportunities: treating people fairly; giving people the same chance (e.g. in relation to gender).

Discrimination: the unfair treatment of a person or minority group; distinguishing and acting on a prejudice.

Prejudice: an unfavourable opinion of an individual or group, often based on inadequate facts (e.g. dislike of people from a specific race, religion or culture).

Stereotype: a standardised image/belief shared by society; a simple generalisation about all members of a group which allows others to categorise and treat them accordingly.

Discrimination involves the unfair treatment of a person or minority group based on a stereotype/prejudice and can be divided into:

- overt discrimination: visible/obvious (e.g. verbal racist abuse of a player)
- covert discrimination: hidden/less obvious (e.g. non-selection of an individual as captain because of their race).

Now test yourself

TESTED

5 The participation of ethnic minorities in sport can be negatively affected by discrimination. Explain what is meant by the term 'discrimination'.

Answer online

Typical mistake

Answers often repeat words/phrases already given when a question asks for a definition of a term. So if, for example, you are asked to define equal opportunities you should avoid 'equal' and use an alternative such as 'the same'.

Exam tip

Avoid giving general answers where questions are asking for specific examples or explanations of barriers to participation among a target group (e.g. link gender to non-aggressive stereotypes which can negatively impact on participation).

Barriers to participation and possible solutions for under-represented groups

REVISED

Sport England's data on sports participation have shown some improvements since it started its regular bi-annual Active People Survey in 2005–6.

In the figures released in June 2015, adult numbers taking part in sport had risen by 1.4 million compared to 2005–6, but most adults were still reported as not taking part in sport (58 per cent). The fact that over half of all adults in England play no sport at all is a worrying statistic for those trying to encourage participation.

It is still therefore important to be able to identify various barriers to participation for sections of society under-represented in sport, as well as seeking to provide solutions to try to overcome those barriers.

The table below outlines general barriers to participation and possible solutions.

Barriers	Solutions
Lack of time	Add physical activity to a daily routine, e.g. walk or cycle to work/school
Negative social influences; poor PE experiences	Invite family and friends to exercise with you; join a group where physical activity plays an important part, e.g. a youth club offering activities such as the Duke of Edinburgh Award
Lack of motivation	Invite a friend to exercise with you on a regular basis; join an exercise class
Lack of skill	Select activities requiring few or no skills, e.g. walking/jogging
Lack of resources/high costs of participation	Select activities which require few facilities/limited equipment, e.g. walking, jogging, skipping
Family obligations/domestic responsibilities	Exercise with the children, e.g. go for a walk or swim

You need to be aware of three main target groups, i.e. sections of society specifically aimed at due to their relative lack of involvement in sport/physical activity. These are people with disabilities, individuals from ethnic minorities and women/teenage girls.

Disability

Generally speaking, people with disabilities have a low level of participation in sport. Data from the Sport England Active People Survey (APS) for 2011–12 (APS7) illustrate that 1,739,000 people with a disability regularly played sport during this time period, compared to 1,419,000 when the survey first started gathering data in 2005–6. While this is a welcomed improvement in disabled participation, it still means that only 18.5 per cent (around 1 in 5) of people with a disability in England play sport regularly, compared to 39.2 per cent (around 1 in 2.5) of non-disabled people.

Disabilities may be physical, sensory or mental, with all of these potentially negatively affecting participation in sport in some way. Society often discriminates against disabled people participating in sport:
- Overt discrimination is highly visible and could occur when verbal abuse is aimed at individuals with a disability participating in sport.
- Covert discrimination is harder to uncover and might occur when individuals at a sports club vote for their annual captain and their negative stereotypes influence them against voting for a disabled candidate.

Disability sport is sometimes participated in at the same time as able-bodied sport (i.e. it is integrated). Alternatively, disability sport can occur completely separately from able-bodied sport (i.e. it is segregated).

Barriers

Common barriers to people with disabilities taking part in sport include:
- negative self-image or lack of confidence
- relatively low income levels; high costs of participation such as membership fees and transport costs
- lack of access into and around facilities, e.g. facility front desk is too high for disabled individuals to communicate with, doorways are too narrow, ramps do not exist within areas of a facility etc.
- lack of organised programmes
- low levels of media coverage/few role models to aspire to; lack of information available
- lack of specialist coaches/clubs/competitions; lack of adaptive/accessible equipment
- myths/stereotypes about the capabilities of people with a disability; lower societal expectations; safety concerns – disability participation has traditionally been considered dangerous.

Solutions

Solutions to decrease the effects of such barriers include:
- providing more opportunities for success; helping talented athletes reach the highest levels possible, e.g. the Paralympics
- increased investment in disabled sport – subsidising it and making it more affordable
- providing transport to facilities and improved access into/around facilities, e.g. via local authority sport and leisure departments using specialist architects when planning facilities so that they meet the needs of disabled people

- improved technology, e.g. prosthetics/wheelchairs
- increased media coverage and promoting role models to relate and aspire to
- training of more specialist coaches; setting up more clubs for people with a disability
- educating people on the myths/stereotypes about the capabilities of disabled people and challenging inappropriate attitudes
- designing activities specifically for individuals with disabilities, e.g. goalball and boccia for the visually impaired, or modifying existing activities to enable involvement in them, e.g. wheelchair tennis and basketball etc.
- specialist organisations such as the English Federation for Disability Sport (EFDS) and Sport England working to support and co-ordinate the development of sporting opportunities for people with disabilities.

> **Exam tip**
>
> When identifying barriers to participation in relation to disability, it is important to link coaching to a shortage of specially trained leaders/coaches, and to link activities to failure to modify/adapt them. In other words, link points being made to the specific target group in focus.

Ethnicity

Britain is a multi-cultural, multi-racial, egalitarian (i.e. equal) society. Equal opportunities to participate in sport should exist for all racial or **ethnic groups** in society. Such equality is not yet a reality due to many factors, including **racism**.

Racism is illegal but still exists in society (and therefore in sport, as a reflection of society). It stems from prejudice linked with the power of one racial group in society over another. This can lead to discrimination, i.e. unfair treatment/acting on a prejudice, for example exclusion of an individual from participation on the basis of their **race**/ethnicity, skin colour, language or cultural observances.

Examples of racism in sport include:

- **stacking** – a term used as an illustration of possible racism in sport particularly in relation to explaining the lack of team captains from ethnic minorities; it is based on the stereotypical assumption that ethnic minority individuals are more valued for their athletic prowess compared to their decision-making or leadership capabilities
- **channelling** – ethnic minorities may also be channelled (i.e. pushed) away from certain sports into others, based on stereotypical assumptions about them (e.g. Asians channelled away from football into cricket).

As a society, it is important that we encourage diversity in sport and physical activity as it encourages social inclusion and better health, as well as improving standards of performance. However, there are still worrying statistics which illustrate the fact that ethnic diversity in sport and physical activity is not necessarily being achieved. Research reported by Sporting Equals in 2015 suggests that more than 50 per cent of people from black and minority ethnic (BME) communities do not participate in sport or physical activity.

> **Ethnic groups:** people who have racial, religious or linguistic traits in common.
>
> **Racism:** a set of beliefs or ideas based on the assumption that races have distinct hereditary characteristics that give some races an intrinsic superiority over others; it may lead to physical or verbal abuse.
>
> **Race:** the physical characteristics of an individual.
>
> **Stacking:** the disproportionate concentration of ethnic minorities in certain positions in a sports team, which tends to be based on the stereotype that they are more valuable for their physicality than their decision-making and communication skills.
>
> **Channelling:** ethnic minorities may be pushed into certain sports, and even certain positions within a team, based on assumptions about them.

Barriers

Possible barriers to ethnic groups participating in sport/physical activity include:

- conflict with religious/cultural observances (e.g. a particular concern with Muslim women)
- a higher value placed on education as opposed to sporting participation; discouragement via family and friends
- fear of racism/racist abuse, prejudice or discrimination

- fewer role models to aspire to, particularly in coaching/managerial positions (e.g. in football there are very few black footballers who break into and maintain management positions at Premier League/Football League clubs)
- fear of rejection/low levels of self-esteem
- stereotyping/attempts at channelling ethnic minorities into certain sports and away from others
- language barriers for some ethnic minority groups.

NB Not all ethnic groups are the same and not all ethnic groups will face precisely the same forms of discrimination and challenges.

Solutions

Possible solutions to overcome these barriers include:
- training more ethnic minority coaches, teachers and sports leaders and educating them on the effects of stereotyping
- ensuring there is single-sex provision if required, e.g. for Muslim women, to overcome any cultural barriers
- publicising and punishing severely any racist abuse (e.g. as the FA did when the then Liverpool player Suarez racially abused his Manchester United counterpart Evra)
- ensuring provision in PE programmes is appropriate for all ethnic preferences, e.g. ensuring kit rules and showering procedures are reflective of cultural norms
- organising campaigns against racism in sport.

Kick it Out is football's equality and inclusion organisation, which is working through the football, educational and community sectors to challenge discrimination and campaign for change.

> **Now test yourself**   TESTED ☐
>
> 6 Identify barriers to sports participation which still exist for ethnic minority groups in twenty-first century Britain.
>
> Answer online

Gender – the under-representation of women in sport

Women should have the same opportunity as their male counterparts to participate and excel in their chosen sports. However, more men participate in sport than women. Sport England's June 2015 Active People data illustrate such a point: 40.6 per cent of men play sport at least once a week compared to 30.7 per cent of women.

Barriers

Barriers to women participating in sport include:
- stereotypical myths, e.g. the belief that women lack the aggression necessary for sports where this is key, e.g. rugby
- far less media coverage of women's sport compared to men's
- fewer attainable role models for women to aspire to, e.g. as performers, coaches, officials, or in positions of power making decisions on national governing bodies
- pressure on women to be thin as opposed to healthy; the media promote a thin, decorative and passive ideal of the female body, which is at odds with an 'active' body

> **Exam tip**
>
> Equality of opportunity questions often use the command word 'discuss'. Be prepared to provide arguments that illustrate there has been evidence of increased equality and arguments that illustrate that there hasn't.

- fewer sponsorship opportunities/opportunities to become full-time sports performers
- negative impact of school PE programmes, e.g. rules on showering/kit; lack of appealing choice of activities
- lack of fitness, low levels of self-confidence and body image issues
- lack of income/leisure time due to work, traditional childcare and/or domestic responsibilities
- channelling into 'female appropriate' sports, with fewer leagues/competitions/clubs available for women to participate in.

Solutions

Possible solutions to overcome these barriers include:
- introducing/enforcing laws which make sex discrimination unlawful, e.g. the Sex Discrimination Act 1975
- encouraging greater social acceptance of women having jobs/careers with more disposable income, giving increased financial independence
- encouraging shared domestic/childcare responsibilities, creating more leisure time for women to devote to sport; improving childcare provision
- increasing media coverage of women's sport; giving women's international sport the recognition it deserves; providing more positive/attainable role models to aspire to
- increasing sponsorship for women's sport
- providing education to refute/reject stereotypical myths
- improving PE provision, e.g. via Women in Sport's 'Changing the Game for Girls'
- providing more opportunities for women to join sports clubs/participate in the activities they enjoy
- encouraging the use of social media to connect women playing sport; friendships with like-minded individuals will hopefully increase motivation/interest
- supporting the work of organisations such as Sport England, as well as specialist organisations such as Women in Sport (formerly the Women's Sport and Fitness Foundation, WSFF).

Based on the Active People Survey April 2011–12, women's participation in football was found to be 252,000 compared to 215,000 taking part in netball, its closest rival in the 'team sport' category.

A number of socio-cultural reasons can explain this:
- increased opportunities in society in general/increase in leisure time and disposable income
- increased media coverage of women's football, giving more female role models with whom to identify
- more opportunities for girls to play football in school PE programmes
- more football clubs to join in the area in which they live
- the rejection of stereotypes affecting female participation in contact activities such as football
- more opportunities to play the game professionally in England, e.g. via formation of the FA
- creation of the Women's Super League (WSL) as part of a five-year FA strategy 'Game Changer', which is building on the successes of the 2012 Olympics and 2015 World Cup to turn women's football into the second largest team sport in the country, behind only men's football, by 2018.

Exam tip

In this section of the syllabus, it is important to develop your ability to understand and correctly interpret and analyse data and graphs relating to participation in physical activity and sport and relate them to barriers/solutions as appropriate.

Benefits of raising participation in physical activity and sport

Regular participation in physical activity and/or sport is an important part of a healthy lifestyle.

Health benefits

Research commissioned by Sport England into the costs of physical inactivity showed that NHS providers in England spent more than £900 million in 2009/10 treating people with diseases which could have been prevented if more people were physically active.

Regular participation in physical activity and/or sport can help protect individuals from a range of health problems. Benefits include:
- decreased risk of developing heart disease/suffering a stroke
- avoidance of high/low blood pressure
- decreased risk of type 2 diabetes
- maintaining a healthy weight/decreased risk of obesity
- strengthening of bones and decreased risk of osteoporosis
- improved psychological/mental health and stress management; decreased risk of conditions such as anxiety/depression/emotional disturbance
- decreased risk of some cancers (e.g. colon cancer and breast cancer).

Now test yourself

TESTED

7 Sport England estimates that taking part in regular sport can save up to £6,900 on health care costs per person per annum. Identify the health benefits to society of raising participation in sport/ physical activity.

Answer online

Regular participation in physical activity and/or sport can also help improve an individual's level of fitness and is likely to result in:
- improved posture/body shape/body tone as a result of weight loss
- improved cardiovascular fitness/muscular strength/muscular endurance
- improved flexibility/agility/balance/co-ordination
- improved speed/power/reaction time.

Continuous activities, such as long-distance cycling and running, lead to improved stamina/endurance.

Social benefits

Regular participation in physical activity and/or sport can help individuals socially:
- Exercise causes the body to release chemicals such as serotonin and endorphins, which have a calming effect and help a person to feel happier/better about themselves. When individuals, feel better about themselves they are more likely to benefit emotionally and socially, e.g. via a more positive outlook on life.
- Improved sleep patterns result from participation in regular exercise, which can enhance a person's mood and their relationships.
- The boost in a person's mood can also help improve skills of concentration, which allow a clearer focus on social relationships.

- As an individual's social and emotional health improves, confidence and self-esteem are likely to increase, and involvement in sport/exercise classes becomes increasingly likely.
- Physical activity/sport introduces us to new people who share a common interest and helps develop new friendships/relationships; this many lead to an increased sense of community integration/morale.
- Physical activity is a positive use of free time which can help keep individuals out of trouble and decrease criminality.

Inter-relationship between Sport England and local and national partners to increase participation

REVISED

Sport England has an overall mission reflected in its new strategy 'Towards an Active Nation' (2016–21). It works with a range of partners locally and nationally to try to achieve its ambition of increasing participation in sport/physical activity. At the heart of its new strategy are five main outcomes. These aim to increase:

1 physical well-being
2 mental well-being
3 individual development
4 social and community development
5 economic development.

Sport England is committed to providing sporting opportunities for all and putting in place schemes and initiatives which attempt to overcome barriers for those wishing to play sport, particularly if they are from groups currently under-represented in sport. It is an organisation focused on helping people and communities across the country create a 'sporting habit for life'.

To help achieve its new strategy of creating an 'active nation', Sport England has identified the following key principles of its work through to 2021:

- focusing more money and resources on tackling inactivity
- investing more in children and young people from the age of 5 (building positive attitudes in young people towards sport/physical activity)
- helping those who are active now to carry on participating (including investment in talented sporting individuals), as well as focusing investment on encouraging inactive people to become active
- helping the sport/active leisure sector to become more welcoming and inclusive (e.g. especially to groups under-represented in sport)
- helping to deliver a more joined-up experience of sport and physical activity for customers (e.g. via stronger local collaboration)
- encouraging innovation and sharing of best practice.

One of Sport England's key roles is to help its partners, locally and nationally, to deliver sporting opportunities to as many people as possible and particularly to groups who experience specific issues that may prevent them participating regularly in sport.

> **Revision activity**
>
> Create a spider diagram identifying the key principles of Sport England's latest strategy.

Local partners

Sport England places a key emphasis on local delivery in terms of meeting its objectives, and works with a range of local partners to try to ensure sport is accessible across every region in the country. It invests in 49 **county sport partnerships (CSPs)** spread across the country so that programmes can be delivered regionally/locally to meet specific local needs.

CSPs work with a number of sport/physical activity providers, including local authorities, health organisations, national governing bodies, sports clubs and schools/education providers – all with a commitment to increasing participation across their network. One example is Oxfordshire's CSP, which set a target to make Oxfordshire the most physically active county in England by 2017.

Sport England also offers support and expertise to local authorities to help them develop sport in their area, designing and implementing schemes and initiatives specific to their needs and requirements.

Its local outreach teams work across the different regions, offering support and advice as and when necessary at a local level (e.g. to the Suffolk Fit Villages project aiming to make it the most active county in the country).

National partners

Sport England works directly with a number of nationally funded partners, including the following:

- The English Federation of Disability Sport (EFDS) is a national charity dedicated to increasing participation in sport and physical activity among disabled people.
- Sporting Equals is an organisation which exists to actively promote ethnic diversity across sport and physical activity. In 2013, Sport England invested £1 million into Sporting Equals to help more black and minority ethnic (BME) communities get into sport. Sporting Equals works closely with a number of local and national providers of sporting opportunities, such as NGBs and local authorities.
- Women in Sport is the new name for the Womens Sport and Fitness Foundation (WSFF). It aims to make being active more attractive to women and teenage girls by trying to break down the barriers which are putting them off participating in sport/physical activity.
- StreetGames is a national charity dedicated to developing sport in disadvantaged communities, making it accessible to all, regardless of social circumstances. In terms of social class, StreetGames is working to create networks at national and local levels (e.g. nationally with NGBs and locally with local authorities and local sports clubs) to strengthen the commitment to 'doorstep sport', i.e. providing access to sports in local communities where people live. To try to overcome some of the issues surrounding participation of the lower socio-economic groups in society, StreetGames provides affordable, low-cost activities within the neighbourhood of communities, so travel is less of an issue. Informal, multi-sport sessions take place at times convenient to targeted participants to make participation more likely.

Disability sport

Sport England is working with the EFDS to challenge and change low levels of disability participation in sport, helping disabled people to view taking part in sport as a viable lifestyle choice.

> **County sport partnerships (CSPs):** national networks of local agencies working together to increase participation in sport and physical activity.

- In 2015, out of the £150 million of Lottery funding from Places People Play, Sport England ringfenced £10.2 million to improve the sport on offer for disabled people.
- Inclusive Sport was another initiative designed to build on Sport England's investments to improve the expertise offered by the disability sport sector to other organisations that want to get disabled people playing sport. The Inclusive Sport programme was aimed at increasing the number of disabled young people (aged 14+) and adults regularly playing sport, as part of Sport England's wider commitment to increasing regular sport participation by disabled people.
- Get Equipped is a funding scheme aimed at providing disabled people with the specialist equipment required to engage in sporting activity.

Participation by disabled people is a key strategic outcome for Sport England's work with NGBs.

Gender

Sport England is working hard with local and national partners, including CSPs, NGBs and Women in Sport, to get more women playing more sport. These initiatives include the following:

- Sport England is making women's sport a major priority financially across the board in the 46 core sport NGBs in which it is investing millions of pounds; in 2015 it invested £2.3 million into I Will If You Will – a year-long pioneering behavioural change pilot in the local authority of Bury to help understand how to get more women playing sport.
- Sport England has also invested millions of pounds into Women in Sport via the WSFF, to help sports bodies attract more women and teenage girls to do sport more regularly.
- Millions more went into 20 Active Women projects across different local authorities, to encourage women in disadvantaged communities and women with young children to be more physically active and tackle the gender gap in sport.
- In 2015 it introduced This Girl Can in a wave of media publicity. Essentially this is a scheme designed to overcome barriers to increase participation in sports among women and girls.

Ultimately, Sport England and its various partners all aim to make a sustainable difference to the inclusion of under-represented communities in sport and physical activity, in order to improve the long-term opportunities and health outcomes of those communities.

Investment in national governing bodies (NGBs)

National governing bodies submitted **Whole Sport Plans** to Sport England to operate from 2013–17, detailing how they would invest money to help increase the number of young people playing their own sport once a week and how to nurture talent. British Rowing identified a number of different approaches designed to get more people into their sport, e.g. 'Rowability' – a rebranding of 'Adaptive Rowing' to develop partnerships with disability organisations and establish five new recognised delivery centres.

Whole Sport Plan: a business plan/document submitted to Sport England outlining each national governing body's strategies to grow sport participation and enhance talent over the four-year period the plan is in operation.

Exam practice

1 Which of the following best describes an agent of primary socialisation? [1]
   (a) Brothers and sisters
   (b) Teachers
   (c) Sports coaches
   (d) Peer groups
2 Using an example, define the term 'social issues'. [2]
3 How do stereotyping and discrimination cause lower sport participation rates among women? [4]
4 Identify the benefits to the individual of participating in club sport. [3]
5 Sport England's Active People Survey (APS) data from 2005–06 showed that 15.1 per cent of disabled people in England played sport regularly, compared to 37.8 per cent of non-disabled people.

   In 2011–12 the data revealed that 18.5 per cent of disabled people compared to 39.2 per cent of non-disabled people were regular active participants in sport.

   Discuss the information above in relation to participation in sport among disabled people in England. [15]
6 The AoC Sport 2016 College Sport Survey revealed that student participation in college-organised activities involved 37 per cent female participants compared to 63 per cent male participants (up from 34 per cent in 2015).

   Discuss the participation patterns illustrated by the data above. [6]

Answers and quick quizzes online

ONLINE

Summary

You should now be able to:
- define a number of key sociological terms (eg society, socialisation, social processes, social issues, social structures/stratification, social control and social change) and assess their impact on equality of opportunity in sport and society
- understand how social action theory applies to social issues in physical activity and sport
- understand and explain the barriers to participation in sport and physical activity and ways in which such barriers can be overcome

- in relation to under-represented groups in sport (eg disability, ethnicity, gender)
- define the terms equal opportunities, discrimination, stereotyping and prejudice and explain their impact on participation in physical activity
- identify and explain the benefits to individuals and society of raising participation
- explain the inter-relationship between Sport England and its local and national partners in relation to increasing participation of under-represented groups in sport at grass roots level

4.1 Diet and nutrition and their effect on physical activity and performance

A balanced diet is essential for optimum performance in all sporting activities.

Carbohydrates

There are two types of carbohydrates:
- Simple carbohydrates are the quickest source of energy and easily digested by the body. They are found in fruits as well as in processed foods and anything with refined sugar added.
- Complex carbohydrates are found in nearly all plant-based foods, and usually take longer for the body to digest. They are most commonly found in bread, pasta, rice and vegetables.

Carbohydrates are the principal source of energy used by the body. They are also the main fuel for high-intensity or anaerobic work. Carbohydrate in food is digested and converted into glucose and enters the bloodstream. The glucose is stored in the muscles and liver as glycogen, but these stores are limited so regular refuelling is necessary.

> **Exam tip**
>
> Carbohydrates are the principal source of energy for both low-intensity (aerobic) and high-intensity (anaerobic) exercise. They are the only food source that can be broken down anaerobically.

Fats

There are different types of fats.

Saturated fats

These can be found in both sweet and savoury foods, but most come from animal sources. Too much saturated fat leads to excessive weight gain, which will reduce stamina, limit flexibility and lead to health problems such as coronary heart disease, **atherosclerosis**, diabetes and high blood pressure.

Cholesterol

Cholesterol is a type of fat found in the blood. Too much saturated fat leads to high cholesterol levels. Cholesterol is made predominantly in the liver and is carried by the blood as **low-density lipoprotein (LDL)** and **high-density lipoprotein (HDL)**. Too much LDL can lead to fatty deposits developing in the arteries, which can have a negative effect on blood flow. HDL, on the other hand, takes cholesterol away from the parts of the body where it has accumulated to the liver, where it is disposed of.

Trans-fats

Trans-fats are artificial hydrogenated fats and can be found in meat and dairy products. Most are made from an industrial process that allows food to have a longer shelf life. Trans-fat can lead to high levels of blood cholesterol, heart disease and diabetes.

However, not all fats are bad. Replacing saturated and trans-fat with unsaturated fats is important, as fat is a major source of energy in the body. Fats are used for low-intensity, aerobic work such as jogging and cannot be used for high-intensity exercise where oxygen is in limited supply, as they require oxygen to be broken down. Fats are also a carrier for the fat-soluble vitamins A, D, E and K.

> **Atherosclerosis:** where arteries become clogged with fatty substances.
>
> **Low-density lipoproteins (LDL):** these transport cholesterol in the blood to the tissues and are classed as 'bad' cholesterol since they are linked to an increased risk of heart disease.
>
> **High-density lipoproteins (HDL):** these transport excess cholesterol in the blood back to the liver where it is broken down and are classed as 'good' cholesterol since they lower the risk of developing heart disease.

> **Exam tip**
>
> Fats are an energy source for long-duration, low-intensity exercise.

Answers and quick quizzes at **www.hoddereducation.co.uk/myrevisionnotes**

Now test yourself

TESTED ☐

1 Describe the importance of carbohydrates and fats for a games player.

Answer online

Proteins

REVISED ☐

These are a combination of many chemicals called amino acids. They are important for muscle growth and repair and to make enzymes, hormones and haemoglobin.

Proteins are a minor source of energy and tend to be used more by power athletes, who have a greater need to repair and develop muscle tissue.

Exam tip

Proteins are necessary for muscle growth and repair.

Revision activity

Create a table to summarise the exercise-related role of carbohydrates, fats and proteins.

Vitamins

REVISED ☐

Vitamins keep an individual healthy with a good immune system. This allows a performer to train maximally and recover quickly. The following table lists the vitamins you need to know for your exam and summarises the exercise-related function of each.

Vitamin	Source	Exercise-related functions
C (ascorbic acid)	Green vegetables and fruit	• Protects cells and keeps them healthy • Required for the breakdown of carnitine, which is a molecule essential for the transport of fatty acids into the mitochondria (mitochondria convert food sources, such as fats, into energy in the body, therefore vitamin C is also indirectly responsible for this process) • Helps in the maintenance of bones, teeth, gums and connective tissue such as ligaments
D	Most vitamin D is made by our body under the skin when it is exposed to sunlight; to a lesser extent it can come from oily fish and dairy produce	• Has a role in the absorption of calcium, which keeps bones and teeth healthy • Helps with phosphocreatine recovery in the mitochondria
Vitamin B complex includes several important vitamins		
B1 (thiamin)	Yeast, egg, liver, wholegrain bread, nuts, red meat and cereals	• Works with other B-group vitamins to help break down and release energy from food • Keeps the nervous system healthy
B2 (riboflavin)	Dairy products, liver, vegetables, eggs, cereals and fruit	• Works with other B-group vitamins to help break down and release energy from food • Keeps the skin, eyes and nervous system healthy
B6	Meat, fish, eggs, bread, vegetables and cereals	• Helps form haemoglobin • Helps the body to use and store energy from protein and carbohydrate in food
B12 (folate)	Red meat, dairy products and fish	• Makes red blood cells and keeps the nervous system healthy • Releases energy from food

Now test yourself

2 Explain the importance of vitamin B6 for an elite performer.

Answer online

Minerals

For your exam you need to know the importance of calcium, sodium and iron. The following table summarises their exercise-related functions.

Mineral	Exercise-related functions
Calcium	This is needed for strong bones and teeth and is also necessary for efficient nerve and muscle contraction, which is important during exercise.
Sodium	This helps regulate fluid levels in the body. However, too much sodium is linked to an increase in blood pressure, which can increase the risk of a stroke or heart attack.
Iron	This is involved in the formation of haemoglobin in red blood cells, which helps transport oxygen and therefore improves stamina. A lack of iron can lead to anaemia.

Now test yourself

3 Explain the importance of calcium for a sports performer.

Answer online

Fibre

Good sources of fibre are wholemeal bread and pasta, potatoes, nuts, seeds, fruit, vegetables and pulses. Fibre is important during exercise as it can slow down the time it takes the body to break down food, which results in a slower, more sustained release of energy. Dietary fibre causes bulk in the small intestine, helping to prevent constipation and aiding digestion.

Water

Water makes up to 60 per cent of a person's body weight and is essential for good health. It transports nutrients, hormones and waste products around the body and is the main component of many cells, playing an important part in regulating body temperature. When you take part in exercise, energy is required, and some of that energy is released as heat. Water will keep you from overheating. The evaporation of sweat helps to cool you down, but this means water is lost during the cooling down process. A lack of water pre-, during or post-exercise can cause **dehydration** and this can result in:

- an increase in blood viscosity, reducing blood flow to working muscles and the skin
- reduced sweating to prevent water loss, which results in an increase in core temperature
- muscle fatigue and headaches
- reduction in the exchange of waste products/transportation of nutrients
- increased heart rate, resulting in a lower cardiac output
- decreased performance/reaction time/decision making.

Dehydration: occurs when the body is losing more fluid than it is taking in.

Exam tip

It is possible that you may need to discuss or evaluate the importance of each of the food groups during exercise.

Effects of dietary supplements/manipulation on the performer

Glycogen loading

Glycogen loading is a form of dietary manipulation to increase glycogen stores over and above that which can normally be stored (supercompensation). An increase in water intake will also aid glycogen storage.

Glycogen loading is used by endurance performers. You need to know the following three methods for your exam:

- Method one: six days before competition performer eats a diet high in protein for three days and exercises at relatively high intensity to burn off any existing carbohydrate stores, followed by three days of a diet high in carbohydrates and some light training. The theory is that by totally depleting glycogen stores they can then be increased by up to two times the original amount (supercompensation) and can prevent a performer from 'hitting the wall'.
- Method two: day before competition three minutes of high intensity exercise opens a 'carbo window'. Replenishing glycogen stores during the first 20-minute window after exercise can enhance performance the next day. In the 20 minutes immediately after exercise the body is most able restore lost glycogen. The 'carbo window' closes after two hours.
- Method three: non-depletion protocol – training intensity reduced the week before competition. Then three days before competition a high carbohydrate diet is followed with light intensity exercise.

The effects of glycogen loading are outlined in the following table.

Positive effects	Negative effects
<ul><li>Increases glycogen storage</li><li>Increases glycogen stores in the muscle</li><li>Delays fatigue</li><li>Increases endurance capacity</li></ul>	During the carbo-loading phase:<ul><li>water retention which results in bloating</li><li>heavy legs</li><li>problems with digestion</li><li>weight increase</li></ul>During the depletion phase:<ul><li>irritability</li><li>need to alter the training programme through lack of energy</li></ul>

Creatine monohydrate

This is a supplement used to increase the amount of phosphocreatine stored in the muscles. Phosphocreatine is used to fuel the ATP–PC system, which provides energy. Increasing the amount of creatine in the muscles will allow this energy system to last longer. It can also help improve recovery times. Athletes in explosive events, such as sprints, jumps and throws, are likely to experience the most benefits, as they can perform at higher intensity for longer.

The effects of taking creatine monohydrate are outlined in the following table.

> **Exam tip**
>
> Remember the ATP–PC system is an energy system that provides quick bursts of energy and is used for high-intensity exercise but it can only last for up to 10 seconds.

Positive effects	Negative effects
<ul><li>Aims to provide ATP (energy)</li><li>Replenishes phosphocreatine stores</li><li>Allows the ATP–PC system to last longer</li><li>Improves muscle mass</li></ul>	<ul><li>Possible side effects include muscle cramps, diarrhoea, water retention, bloating and vomiting</li><li>Hinders aerobic performance</li><li>Mixed evidence to show benefits</li></ul>

Sodium bicarbonate

Sodium bicarbonate is an antacid. It can increase the **buffering** capacity of the blood, so it can neutralise the negative effects of **lactic acid** and **hydrogen ions** that are produced in the muscles during high-intensity activity.

The concept behind drinking a solution of sodium bicarbonate or 'soda loading' is that it reduces the acidity within the muscle cells in order to delay fatigue and allows the performer to continue exercise at a very high intensity for longer.

The effects of taking sodium bicarbonate are outlined in the following table.

> **Buffering:** the ability of the blood to compensate for the build-up of lactic acid or hydrogen ions to maintain the pH level.
>
> **Lactic acid:** a by-product of anaerobic respiration. As it accumulates, it causes fatigue.
>
> **Hydrogen ions:** responsible for the acidity of the blood.

Positive effects	Negative effects
● Reduces acidity in the muscle cells ● Delays fatigue ● Increases the buffering capacity of the blood	● Possible side effects include vomiting, pain, cramping, diarrhoea and feeling bloated

Caffeine

Caffeine is a naturally occurring stimulant, which can increase mental alertness and reduce fatigue. It is also thought to improve the mobilisation of fatty acids in the body, thereby sparing muscle glycogen stores. It is used by endurance performers who predominantly rely on the aerobic system, since fats are the preferred fuel for low-intensity, long-endurance exercise. Caffeine can be found in coffee, tea, cola, chocolate, energy bars with caffeine and caffeinated gels.

The effects of taking caffeine are outlined in the following table.

Positive effects	Negative effects
● Stimulant/increases mental alertness ● Reduces effects of fatigue ● Allows fats to be used as energy source/delays use of glycogen stores ● Improves decision making/reaction time ● May benefit aerobic performance/endurance athletes	● Loss of fine control ● Against rules of most sports when consumed in large quantities ● Possible side effects include dehydration, insomnia, muscle cramps, stomach cramps, vomiting, irregular heartbeat and diarrhoea

> **Revision activity**
>
> Create your own table and summarise the positive and negative effects of glycogen loading, creatine monohydrate, sodium bicarbonate and caffeine.

Exam practice

1 Describe one method of glycogen loading and outline the benefits to an elite performer. [5]
2 What problems will an athlete face if they dehydrate? [4]
3 Explain why an elite performer may choose to take sodium bicarbonate. [4]
4 Evaluate the importance of sodium in an athlete's diet. [2]

Answers and quick quizzes online

ONLINE

Summary

You should now be able to:
● identify the seven classes of food as: carbohydrates, fats, proteins, vitamins, minerals, fibre and water

● identify the exercise-related functions of each of these classes of food
● identify the positive and negative effects of glycogen loading, creatine monohydrate, sodium bicarbonate and caffeine on the performer.

4.2 Preparation and training methods in relation to maintaining physical activity and performance

Key data terms for laboratory conditions and field tests

Quantitative and qualitative

Quantitative data contains factual information and numerical values. **Qualitative data** is subjective, as it looks at feelings, opinions and emotions.

When drawing conclusions from fitness testing, the results can be analysed quantitatively and qualitatively. Quantitative analysis compares the scores to other people or standardised tables, and qualitative analysis makes judgements on these scores.

Objective

Objective data is based upon facts and is measurable. In fitness testing, objective tests involve a measurement and are therefore more likely to be accurate.

Subjective

Subjective data is based upon personal opinions, assumptions, interpretations and beliefs.

Validity

When testing a performer, it is important to ensure that the test is valid and set up in such a way as to produce reliable results. To assess the **validity** of a fitness test, the following questions are important:

● Is the research method relevant and does it do exactly what it sets out to do?
● Is the test sport-specific?

Reliability

Reliability means that a test produces results that are consistent and can be repeated with the same outcome. To ensure a test is reliable, the following considerations need to be taken into account:

● tester should be experienced
● equipment should be standardised
● sequencing of tests is important
● repetition of tests should be possible to avoid human error.

Warm-up

The warm-up helps prepare the body for exercise and should always be carried out before the start of any training session:

● The first stage of any warm-up is to perform some kind of cardiovascular exercise such as jogging, gently increasing your heart rate.

> **Quantitative data:** data that contains facts or numbers.
>
> **Qualitative data:** data that is descriptive and looks at the way people think or feel.

> **Exam tip**
>
> Quantity requires a number; quality requires an opinion.

> **Exam tip**
>
> Make sure you can give examples of fitness tests that use measurements, for example the Wingate test or multi-stage fitness test.

> **Objective data:** fact(s).
>
> **Subjective data:** opinion.
>
> **Validity:** when the test actually measures what it sets out to measure.
>
> **Reliability:** the test can be repeated accurately.

> **Revision activity**
>
> Identify several fitness tests and try to decide on their validity and reliability.

- The second stage includes stretching/flexibility exercises, especially with the joints and muscles that will be most active during the training session. The type of stretching used will depend on the activity.
- The third stage of a warm-up should involve the movement patterns that are to be carried out, for example practising shooting in basketball or netball and dribbling in hockey or football.

Static stretching

Static stretching is stretching while not moving and can be active or passive. Active static stretching involves the performer working on one joint, pushing it beyond its point of resistance, and lengthening the muscles and connective tissue surrounding it. Passive static stretching is when a stretch occurs with the help of an external force, such as a partner, another part of your body, gravity or a wall.

> **Static stretching:** when the muscle is held in a stationary position for 30 seconds or more.

Figure 4.2a **A passive static stretch**

Ballistic stretching

Ballistic stretching involves performing a stretch with swinging or bouncing movements, to push a body part even further. It is important that this type of stretching should only be performed by an individual who is extremely flexible, such as a gymnast or dancer, who will try to push their body beyond the limits of their range of movement in comparison to a games player.

> **Ballistic stretching:** performing a stretch with swinging or bouncing movements to push a body part even further.

Whatever the stretch, it is important that it is started slowly, is sport-specific and, if it is painful, the stretch is stopped. In addition, stretches should be balanced between agonists and antagonists, and if the stretch is static it should be held for approximately 30 seconds.

Now test yourself

TESTED ☐

1 Define static and ballistic stretching and explain how to complete them safely.

Answer online

Physiological effects and benefits of a warm-up

A warm-up can have the following physiological effects:
- It reduces the possibility of injury by increasing the elasticity of muscle tissue.
- The release of adrenalin will increase heart rate and dilate capillaries. This allows more oxygen to be delivered to the skeletal muscles.
- Muscle temperature increases and this will first enable oxygen to dissociate more easily from haemoglobin and, second, allow for an increase in enzyme activity, making energy readily available through better chemical reactions.

- An increase in the speed of nerve impulse conduction allows us to be more alert, improving reaction time.
- It allows efficient movement at joints through an increased production of synovial fluid.
- It allows for rehearsal of movement, so the performer is practising the same skills they use in their activity.
- It facilitates mental rehearsal, stress or anxiety reduction and psychological preparation.
- It supplies an adequate blood flow to the heart to increase its efficiency.

Cool-down

REVISED

A cool-down takes place at the end of exercise. It consists of some form of light exercise to keep heart rate elevated.

Physiological effects and benefits of a cool-down

A cool-down can have the following physiological effects:
- It keeps the skeletal muscle pump working.
- It maintains venous return.
- It prevents blood pooling in the veins.
- It limits the effect of DOMS (delayed onset of muscle soreness).
- It removes lactic acid.
- It reduces heart rate and body temperature.

> **Exam tip**
>
> Questions usually ask for an explanation of either a warm-up or a cool-down and the physiological benefits of performing them.

Principles of training

REVISED

For your exam you need to be able to identify the following principles of training and also apply them.

Specificity

Specificity is important to make sure the training you do is relevant for your chosen activity. You need to consider whether you are using the same energy system, muscle fibre type, skills and movements. The intensity and duration of the training should also be similar to your activity.

Progressive overload

This is where the performer gradually trains harder throughout their training programme as their body adapts. A performer who wishes to improve their power, for example, will be lifting heavier weights at the end of their training programme compared to the start. This is because the muscles will be overloaded every few weeks as the amount of weight lifted is increased. It is important to not overload too much too soon. Doing it more gradually will reduce the risk of injury.

Reversibility

This is often referred to as detraining. If training stops, then the adaptations that have occurred as a result of the training programme deteriorate.

Recovery

Rest days are needed to allow the body to recover from training. Research suggests that the 3:1 ratio should be used, where the performer trains hard for three days and then rests for one.

> **Revision activity**
>
> Remember 'SPORR' for the principles of training:
>
> **S**pecificity
> **P**rogression
> **O**verload
> **R**eversibility
> **R**ecovery

FITT principles

In order to improve performance, it is important to apply the FITT principles:

- F stands for frequency, so you need to increase the number of training sessions, increase the work period or number of sets, and decrease the number of rest periods.
- I is for intensity, so to improve you must train harder. To implement this you may use heart rate/Borg scale/one rep max to help.
- T is the time spent training, so this needs to gradually increase and rest periods need to decrease.
- T stands for the type of exercise. Using different forms of exercise maintains motivation, but the type chosen needs to be relevant to your activity. For example, if an improvement in stamina is the aim of a training programme, there are a variety of different types of training that can be used to maintain motivation, such as continuous training, circuit training and fartlek training. However, if you are a games player you need to make sure that these types of training involve running (as opposed to cycling), so that you are exercising your muscles in a similar way to how you use them in the game.

Now test yourself

TESTED

2 Explain how time and type principles can be applied to a training programme.

Answer online

Periodisation

Elite performers need to programme their training year very carefully so they can improve performance but also reduce the risk of injury.

Periodisation is a key word when planning a training programme. It involves dividing the year into blocks or sections where specific training occurs.

Periodisation comprises three cycles: macrocycle, mesocycle and microcycle.

> **Periodisation:** dividing the training year into specific sections for a specific purpose.

Macrocycle

A **macrocycle** is the 'big' period, which involves long-term planning. In rugby it may be the length of the season, while for an athlete it could be four years as they build up to the Olympics. A macrocycle is made up of three distinct periods:

1 The preparation period involves general conditioning and the development of fitness levels.
2 The competition period is where the performer refines skills and techniques, as well as maintaining fitness levels.
3 The transition period is the rest and recovery stage. This phase allows the athlete to recharge physically and mentally and ensures an injury-free start to the forthcoming season.

> **Macrocycle:** long-term planning phase.

Mesocycle

A **mesocycle** is usually a 4–12 week period of training with a particular focus. A sprinter, for example, will focus on power, reaction time and speed, whereas an endurance performer will focus more on strength endurance and cardio-respiratory endurance.

> **Mesocycle:** usually a 4–12 week period of training with a particular focus such as power.

Microcycle

A **microcycle** is a description of one week or a few days of training that is repeated throughout the length of the mesocycle.

Now test yourself

TESTED

3 Explain what is meant by macrocycle, mesocycle and microcycle.

Answer online

Tapering and peaking

Tapering is where there is a reduction in the volume and/or intensity of training prior to a major competition. This usually occurs a few days beforehand but can depend on the event or type of competition. Planning and organising training in this way prepares the athlete both physically and mentally for the big event and allows **peaking** to occur.

Training methods to improve physical fitness and health

REVISED

Continuous training

Continuous training works on developing aerobic endurance. It involves low-intensity exercise for long periods of time without rest intervals, such as jogging, swimming and cycling. As a result, improvements in the cardiovascular and respiratory systems take place, which increases the ability to take up, transport and use oxygen more effectively.

Fartlek training

The word 'fartlek' is Swedish and means speed-play. This is a slightly different method of continuous training, where the pace of the run is varied to stress both the aerobic energy system due to its continuous nature and the anaerobic energy system through the high-intensity bursts of exercise. This is a much more demanding type of training and will improve an individual's stamina and recovery times.

Interval training

Interval training is predominantly used by elite athletes to improve anaerobic power. It is a form of training in which periods or intervals of high-intensity work are followed with recovery periods. This method of training is very versatile, as it can be adapted to suit a variety of anaerobic needs.

When planning an interval training session, it is important to take the following into account:
- duration of the work interval
- intensity or speed of the work interval
- duration of the recovery period
- number of work intervals and recovery periods.

Circuit training

In circuit training, the athlete performs a series of exercises at a set of stations. When planning a circuit, it is important to decide on the number and variety of stations, the number of repetitions or amount of time spent at each station and the length of the rest interval. The resistance used is the athlete's body weight, and the layout of each exercise should ensure that the same body part is not exercised continuously to allow for recovery. A circuit can be designed to cover any aspect of fitness but tends to be used for muscular endurance.

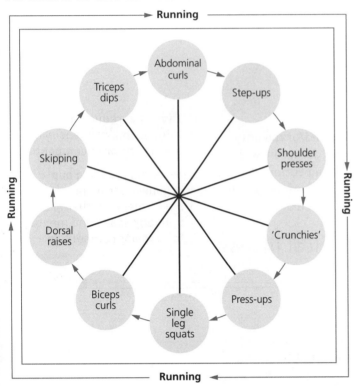

Figure 4.2b An example of a circuit

Weight training

Weight training can be used by everyone to develop muscular strength. It involves doing a series of resistance exercises through the use of free weights or fixed-weight machines, which tend to be described in terms of **sets** and **repetitions**.

A repetition is the number of times you do a particular weight exercise and a set is the number of cycles of repetitions that you do, for example a performer may squat ten times. This means they have done one set of ten repetitions.

The number of sets and repetitions that are performed and the amount of weight lifted will depend on the type of strength being improved. Before a programme can be designed, it is important to determine the maximum amount of weight that a performer can lift with one repetition (**1 rep max**). Then, if maximum strength is the goal, it will be necessary to lift high weights with low repetitions. If muscular endurance is the goal, it will be necessary to perform more repetitions of lighter weights, for example three sets of ten repetitions at approximately 50 per cent of maximum strength.

The choice of exercise should relate to the muscle groups used in sport, both the agonists and antagonists (specificity). The exercises are usually classed into four groups:
- shoulders and arms, e.g. bench press, curls and pull down
- trunk and back, e.g. sit-up and back hyper-extension
- legs, e.g. squat, calf raise and leg press
- all body exercises, e.g. power clean, snatch and dead lift.

> **Sets:** the number of cycles of repetitions (reps).
>
> **Repetitions:** the number of times you do an exercise, often referred to as reps.
>
> **1 rep max (1RM):** the maximum amount a performer can lift in one repetition.

Proprioceptive neuromuscular facilitation (PNF)

Proprioceptive neuromuscular facilitation (PNF) is an advanced stretching technique. It is a form of passive stretching, where the stretch position is held by something other than the agonist muscles, for example a partner or a wall. PNF is considered to be one of the most effective forms of flexibility training for increasing range of movement. How it works is discussed in more detail in the revision notes for the neuromuscular system (Chapter 1.3).

Now test yourself

TESTED ☐

4 Which methods of training could be used to improve (a) muscular endurance and (b) anaerobic power?

Answer online

Exam practice

1 Explain how frequency and intensity can be applied to a training programme. [4]
2 Describe the main parts of a cool-down that should end a session and the benefits of that cool-down. [5]
3 What do you understand by the terms 'objectivity' and 'subjectivity'? [2]

Answers and quick quizzes online

ONLINE ☐

Summary

You should now be able to:
- understand the terms 'quantitative', 'qualitative', 'objective', 'subjective', 'validity' and 'reliability' for laboratory conditions and field tests
- explain the physiological benefits of a warm-up and cool-down
- explain the principles of training as SPORR and FITT
- understand and be able to apply the principles of periodisation
- explain how interval, continuous, fartlek, circuits, weights and PNF training can improve physical fitness.

4.3 Injury prevention and the rehabilitation of injury

Types of injury

There are two types of sports injury, **acute** and **chronic**:
- An acute injury occurs suddenly during exercise or competition, for example a sprained ankle or torn ligament. Pain is felt straight away and is often severe.
- A chronic injury occurs after playing sport or doing exercise for a long time. This type of injury develops slowly and can last a long time. It is often ignored by performers, which makes the injury worse, causing more problems.

> **Acute injury:** sudden injury caused by a specific impact or traumatic event, where a sharp pain is felt immediately.
>
> **Chronic injury:** injury that occurs after playing sport or doing exercise for a long time; often referred to as an overuse injury.

Acute injuries

For your exam you need knowledge of fractures, dislocations, strains and sprains.

Fractures	A fracture is a break or crack in a bone. A bone can fracture in different ways: • A simple or closed fracture is a clean break to a bone that does not penetrate the skin or damage any surrounding tissue. • A compound or open fracture is when the soft tissue or skin has been damaged. This is more serious as there is a higher risk of infection.
Dislocations	Dislocation happens when the ends of bones are forced out of position. It occurs at joints and is very painful.
Strains	Often called a 'pulled' or 'torn' muscle, a strain occurs when muscle fibres are stretched too far or tear.
Sprains	Sprains occur to ligaments (strong bands of tissue around joints that connect bone to bone) when they are stretched too far or tear.

> **Revision activity**
>
> Give some sporting examples of when each of the acute injuries in the table could occur.

> **Exam tip**
>
> Strains occur in muscles, and sprains occur in ligaments.

Chronic injuries

For your exam you need knowledge of Achilles tendonitis, stress fractures and 'tennis elbow'.

Achilles tendonitis	Tendonitis causes pain and inflammation of the tendon. The Achilles tendon is located at the back of the ankle and is the largest tendon in the body. It connects the gastrocnemius to the heel bone and is used for walking, running and jumping, so when we do a lot of regular activity it can be prone to tendonitis.
Stress fractures	Stress fractures are most common in the weight-bearing bones of the legs, often when there is an increase in the amount of exercise or the intensity of an activity rises too quickly. They happen when muscles become fatigued and so are no longer able to absorb the added shock of exercise. The fatigued muscle eventually transfers the stress overload to the bone and the result is a tiny crack called a stress fracture. The area becomes tender and swollen.

Answers and quick quizzes at **www.hoddereducation.co.uk/myrevisionnotes**

'Tennis elbow'	Tennis elbow occurs in the muscles attached to the elbow that are used to straighten the wrist.
	The muscles and tendons become inflamed and tiny tears occur on the outside of the elbow. The area becomes very sore and tender.
	Any activity that places repeated stress on the elbow through overuse of the muscles and tendons of the forearm can cause tennis elbow. As the name suggests, this injury often occurs in tennis.

Injury prevention methods

REVISED

For your exam you need to know how screening, protective equipment, warm-up, flexibility training, taping and bracing are used in injury prevention.

Screening

In sport, screening can be used to help identify those at risk of complications from exercise, prepare performers for their sport, enhance performance and reduce injury. It can be used to detect a problem early before any symptoms occur. Screening can also save lives, for example many young elite performers have CRY (cardio risk in the young) heart screening. The musculoskeletal condition of an athlete can be assessed by screening to highlight any past or current injuries. This will enable the performer to select a relevant conditioning training programme that will prevent further injury. However, screening can have disadvantages. Some screening tests are not 100 per cent accurate and may miss a problem (false negative) or can either identify a problem that doesn't exist (false positive). It can also increase anxiety when an athlete finds out they have a health problem or are more susceptible to injury.

Now test yourself

TESTED

1 Evaluate the importance of screening.

Answer online

Protective equipment

Wearing the correct protective equipment can help reduce injuries in sport. This equipment needs to fit correctly and follow NGB regulations. In football, for example, ankle and shin pads are worn to prevent injury.

Warm-up

See Chapter 4.2 on preparation and training methods.

Flexibility training

Flexibility training should involve the joints and muscles that will be most active during the activity.
- Active stretching occurs when a stretched position is held by contraction of an agonist muscle. An example is lifting your leg up and holding it in position. The tension in the hip flexors caused by holding the leg up in the air (see Figure 4.3a) helps to relax the antagonist muscles being stretched (gluteals).

Revision activity

Many games players wear protective clothing to prevent injury. Choose five games and identify what protective clothing can be worn.

Figure 4.3a Active stretching

- Passive stretching is when a stretch occurs with the help of an external force, such as another part of your body, a partner or a wall.
- Static stretching is when the muscle is held in a stationary position for 30 seconds or more.
- Ballistic stretching involves performing a stretch with swinging or bouncing movements to push a body part even further and should be performed by an individual who is extremely flexible, such as a gymnast or dancer.

Now test yourself

TESTED

2 Describe the different types of flexibility that can be used to prevent injury.

Answer online

Taping and bracing

Taping a weak joint can help with support and stability to reduce the risk of injury.

Taping can also be used on muscle. Kinesiology tape is used on muscles because it is more elastic than the tape used on joints. It is applied directly to the skin to provide controlled support, as it expands as the muscle contracts.

Bracing is much more substantial than taping and often involves hinged supports. It is used to give extra stability to muscles and joints that are weak or have been previously injured.

Injury rehabilitation methods

REVISED

Proprioceptive training

Proprioceptive training uses hopping, jumping and balancing exercises to restore lost proprioception and teach the body to control the position of an injured joint subconsciously. Sprained ankles are a common sporting injury, and proprioceptive exercises are performed on a balance board for rehabilitation.

> **Exam tip**
>
> Proprioceptive training and strength training are easily accessible rehabilitation methods.

Strength training

Strength training uses a resistance of some kind, for example weight machines or free weights, body weight or the use of thera-bands. Whatever the type of strength training carried out, it prepares the body for exercise, reducing the chance of injury.

Hyperbaric chambers

The aim of hyperbaric chambers is to reduce the recovery time for an injury. The chamber is pressurised rather like an aeroplane (in some chambers a mask is worn) and there is 100 per cent pure oxygen. The pressure increases the amount of oxygen that can be breathed in and this means more oxygen can be diffused to the injured area. The excess oxygen dissolves into the blood plasma where it can reduce swelling and pressure at the injured area as well as both stimulate white blood cell activity and increase the blood supply at the injury site. Many of the top rugby union, cricket and football teams use hyperbaric chambers.

Cryotherapy

Cryotherapy is the use of cold temperatures to treat injuries. For common sporting injuries such as muscle strains, treatment is simply **RICE**, which involves the use of ice. This has an analgesic effect and can limit pain and swelling by decreasing blood flow to the injured area.

> **Cryotherapy:** the use of cold temperatures to treat an injury.
>
> **RICE:** stands for rest, ice, compression, elevation.

Hydrotherapy

Hydrotherapy takes place in warm water and is used to improve blood circulation, relieve pain and relax muscles. Typically, hydrotherapy pools are heated to approximately 35–37 degrees Celsius, which increases blood circulation. The buoyancy of the water helps to support the body weight so that there is less load on joints, allowing for more exercise than is permitted on land.

> **Hydrotherapy:** the use of water to treat injuries.

Now test yourself TESTED

3 How can hydrotherapy help sports rehabilitation?

Answer online

> **Exam tip**
>
> Hyperbaric chambers, cryotherapy and hydrotherapy are rehabilitation methods that have limited access. It is mostly elite performers who have the opportunity to use them.

Methods of recovery from exercise REVISED

Compression garments

Compression garments have been used in medicine for a long time to try to improve blood circulation and prevent medical problems such as deep vein thrombosis (DVT).

Massage

Sports massage is a popular form of treatment which can prevent or relieve **soft tissue** injuries. The benefits of sport massage include:

- increased blood flow to soft tissue, so more oxygen and nutrients can pass through to help repair any damage
- removal of lactic acid
- stretching of soft tissue to relieve tension and pressure
- breakdown of scar tissue which, if not removed, can lead to mobility problems in muscles, tendons and ligaments.

> **Soft tissue:** includes tendons, ligaments, muscles, nerves and blood vessels.

Foam rollers

Using foam rollers is a bit like self-massage. They can release tension and tightness in a muscle, as well as between the muscles and the **fascia**. They can be used to prevent injury and improve mobility.

Cold therapy

As a method of recovery, cold therapy is useful after intense exercise where it can target any minor aches and pains. Cooling the surface of the skin using ice gives pain relief and causes vasoconstriction of the blood vessels, which decreases blood flow and reduces any bleeding or swelling. A decrease in swelling enables the muscle to have more movement. Ice can also reduce muscle spasms by decreasing motor activity, as the speed of the nerve impulse slows down in cold conditions.

Ice baths

Ice baths are a very popular recovery method. After a gruelling training session or match, sports performers get into an ice bath for 5 to 10 minutes. The cold water causes the blood vessels to tighten (vasoconstriction) and therefore reduces blood flow to the area. On leaving the bath, the legs fill up with new blood (vasodilation) that invigorates the muscles with oxygen to help the cells function better. The blood that leaves the legs takes away with it the lactic acid that has built up during the activity.

Cryotherapy

Cryotherapy can also help with recovery from exercise. Many sportspeople now use whole body cryotherapy (WBC) to aid their recovery – it targets the whole body and not just a particular muscle. This is still a relatively new practice, but WBC is a much quicker alternative to ice baths and, according to participants, more pleasant!

> **Fascia:** a layer of fibrous connective tissue which surrounds a muscle or group of muscles.

Now test yourself

TESTED ☐

4 Explain the use of an ice bath as a method of recovery from exercise.

Answer online

Sleep and nutrition

Deep sleep is important for muscle recovery. The deepest part of sleep is the third stage of **non-REM sleep**. Here brain waves are at their slowest and blood flow is directed away from the brain towards the muscles to restore energy and to repair the damage done to muscle cells. If sleep is too short, the time for repair is cut short. Most elite athletes have a minimum of 8–9 hours' sleep each night, but your body will tell you if you need more.

Nutrition is also crucial for recovery after exercise. During exercise, muscle glycogen stores decrease, so they need to be replenished when exercise is finished. Research shows that replenishing glycogen stores during the first 20-minute window after exercise can enhance performance the next day. In the 20 minutes immediately after exercise, the body is most able to restore lost glycogen.

> **Non-REM sleep (NREM):** sleep when there is no rapid eye movement. It consists of three stages of sleep, which get progressively deeper.

Now test yourself

5 Why is sleep important for improved recovery after exercise?

Answer online

Exam practice

1 The use of ice baths and cryotherapy can aid recovery. Analyse which of these methods you think is the most effective and give reasons why. [4]
2 Explain why an elite performer may suffer from Achilles tendonitis. [3]
3 Explain how hyperbaric chambers can aid injury rehabilitation. [4]

Answers and quick quizzes online

Summary

You should now be able to:
- identify acute and chronic injuries
- understand how screening, protective equipment, warm-up, flexibility training, taping and bracing are used in injury prevention
- describe how proprioceptive training, strength training and hydrotherapy can help rehabilitation

- give the physiological reasons why hyperbaric chambers and cryotherapy are used in injury rehabilitation
- explain how compression garments, massage/ foam rollers, cold therapy, ice baths and cryotherapy can aid recovery
- explain the importance of sleep and nutrition for improved recovery.

5.1 Biomechanical principles

Biomechanical principles involve an understanding of how motion (movement) and forces can be applied to performance in physical activity and sport.

Newton's laws of linear motion

REVISED

Linear motion is motion in a straight or curved line, with all body parts moving the same distance at the same speed in the same direction. A 100-metre athlete will travel with linear motion in a straight line during their race, and a 200-metre athlete will travel with linear motion in a curved line when running the bend.

Newton's first law of motion (the law of inertia)

Newton's first law of inertia states:

> 'Every body continues in its state of rest or motion in a straight line, unless compelled to change that state by external forces exerted upon it.'

In simple terms, a force is required to change the state of motion. If a body changes its state of motion, it starts, stops, accelerates, decelerates or changes direction. In the high jump, for example, the athlete runs horizontally towards the bar and then changes their state of motion at take-off when they travel vertically to try to clear the bar.

Newton's second law of motion (the law of acceleration)

Newton's second law of acceleration states:

> 'The rate of momentum of a body (or the acceleration for a body of constant mass) is proportional to the force causing it and the change that takes place in the direction in which the force acts.'

In simple terms, this law means that the magnitude (size) and direction of the force applied to a body determines the magnitude and direction of the acceleration given to a body. The rate of acceleration is directly proportional to the force causing the change. The following equation is often used to calculate the size of a force:

Force = Mass x Acceleration (F = ma)

This suggests that if the masses involved remain constant, acceleration is equal to the size of the force causing it. To provide the acceleration at the start of a sprint race, an athlete will have to apply a large force internally with their gluteals, quadriceps and gastrocnemius as they drive forward from the blocks. Similarly, a tennis player will impart a large force on the ball so that it accelerates over the net in the direction in which the force has been applied.

Linear motion: motion in a straight or curved line, with all body parts moving the same distance at the same speed in the same direction.

Newton's first law of inertia: a force is required to change the state of motion.

Newton's second law of acceleration: the magnitude (size) and direction of the force determines the magnitude and direction of the acceleration.

Exam tip

Make sure you know which law is which, as exam questions may ask for a specific law or laws, for example 'Using Newton's first and second laws...'.

Newton's third law of motion (the law of action/reaction)

Newton's third law of action/reaction states:

> 'To every action [force] there is an equal and opposite reaction [force].'

This law describes what happens when two bodies (or objects) exert forces on one another. Action and reaction are equal and opposite and always occur in pairs. Action acts on one of the bodies, and the reaction to this action acts on the other body. At a sprint start, the athlete *pushes back* on the blocks as hard as possible (the action), and the blocks *push forward* on the athlete (the reaction) – providing forward acceleration on the athlete.

Now test yourself

TESTED

1 During a race, a swimmer has to dive off the starting blocks as quickly as possible. Using Newton's first and second laws of motion, explain how the swimmer dives off the starting blocks.

Answer online

Definitions, equations and units for scalar quantities

REVISED

There are lots of different measurements used in linear motion, but for your exam you only need to study two scalar quantities: speed and distance. A scalar quantity is when measurements are described in terms of just their size or magnitude. Direction is not taken into account.

Speed

Speed can be defined as the rate of change of position and can be calculated as follows:

$$\text{Speed in metres per second (m/s)} = \frac{\text{Distance covered in metres (m)}}{\text{Time taken in seconds (s)}}$$

Distance

Distance is the length of the path a body follows when moving from one position to another. For example, a 200-metre runner who has just completed a race has run a distance of 200 metres. Distance is also a scalar quantity because it just measures size:

$$\text{Distance (m)} = \text{Speed (m/s)} \times \text{Time (s)}$$

Newton's third law of action/reaction: for every action force there is an equal and opposite reaction force.

Exam tip

Most questions on Newton's third law involve a ground reaction force: the equal and opposite force exerted on a performer who applies a muscular force on the ground.

Exam tip

Make sure you include the words 'equal' and 'opposite' when you are defining Newton's third law.

Revision activity

Give examples of how each of the laws can be applied to a sport of your choice.

Exam tip

For your exam, you have to be familiar with two scalar quantities: speed and distance.

Exam tip

An easy way to calculate speed and distance is to use the following triangle:

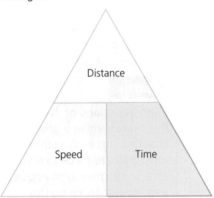

Figure 5.1a Triangle to calculate speed and distance

From this triangle you can see that: speed = distance ÷ time, distance = speed x time, time = distance ÷ speed.

When calculating speed and distance, it is important that the units used correspond with each other. If a question gives the distance in kilometres and the time in hours, then the measurement of speed should be calculated as km/h.

Now test yourself

TESTED

2 Consider an A-level PE student who runs for 40 minutes and covers 8 km. Calculate the speed the student ran in km/h.

Answer online

Speed and distance can also be used in graphs along with time:

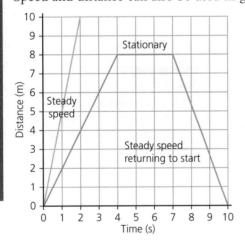

Figure 5.1b A distance–time graph

This graph shows that when a performer is stationary, the line on the graph is horizontal. Running at a steady speed in a straight line means the line on the graph remains straight but is angled. The steeper the line, the faster the speed of the performer. The runner represented by the blue line is running faster than the runner represented by the red line.

Centre of mass

The **centre of mass** is the point of concentration of mass or, more simply, the point of balance, of a body. The human body is an irregular shape, so the centre of mass cannot be identified easily. In addition, the body is constantly moving, so the centre of mass will change as a result, for example raising your arms in the air raises your centre of mass in order to keep the body balanced.

In general, the centre of mass for someone adopting a standing position is around the hip region, but it differs according to gender. Males have more weight concentrated in their shoulders and upper body, so their centre of mass is slightly higher than in females, who have more body weight concentrated at their hips.

Factors affecting stability

All sports require good balance. To increase your stability, the following mechanical principles need to be considered:

- The height of the centre of mass – lowering the centre of mass will increase stability.
- The position of the line of gravity – this should be central over the base of support to increase stability.
- Area of the base of support – the more contact points, the larger the base of support becomes and the more stable they become. For example, a headstand has more contact points than a handstand and so is a more balanced position.
- Mass of the performer – often the greater the mass, the more stability there is because of increased inertia.

> **Centre of mass:** the point of balance of a body.

Figure 5.1c The centre of mass

Now test yourself

3 How can you increase your stability in a game of football?

Answer online

Exam practice

1 Using Newton's three laws of motion, explain how a high jumper takes off from the ground. [8]
2 Calculate the distance covered if a football player runs at a speed of 9 metres per second for 15 seconds towards the ball. [2]

Answers and quick quizzes online

Summary

You should now be able to:

- identify Newton's three laws of linear motion as applied to sporting movements
- define the scalars speed and distance, giving equations and units of measurement
- define centre of mass and identify the factors affecting stability.

5.2 Levers

A lever consists of three main components, namely: a pivot (fulcrum), weight to be moved (resistance) and a source of energy (effort or force). In the body, the skeleton forms a system of levers that allows us to move. The bones act as the levers, the joints are the fulcrums, the effort is provided by the muscles and the resistance is the weight of the body part that is being moved (often against the force of gravity).

Classification of levers

There are three classes of lever, and the classification of each depends on the position of the fulcrum, resistance and effort in relation to each other.

First-class lever

Here, the fulcrum is located between the effort and the resistance. There are two examples of this type of lever in the body: the movement of the head and neck during flexion and extension, and extension of the elbow.

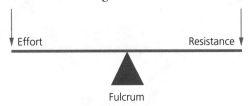

Figure 5.2a First-class lever

Second-class lever

In second-class levers, the resistance lies between the fulcrum and the effort. There is only one example of this lever in the body: plantarflexion of the ankle.

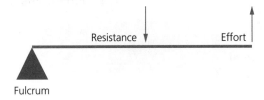

Figure 5.2b Second-class lever

Third-class lever

Third-class levers can be found in all the other joints of the body and the effort lies between the fulcrum and the resistance. Some examples are hip, knee and elbow flexion.

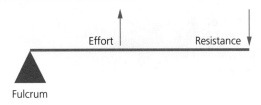

Figure 5.2c Third-class lever

> **Exam tip**
>
> Remember the rhyme FRE 123, where 123 is the type of lever and FRE refers to the component that is in the middle. So, for example, F for fulcrum is the first letter, so when the fulcrum is in the middle it is a first-class lever.

> **Exam tip**
>
> If you are asked to classify and label a lever, make sure you do not abbreviate. For example, use the label 'effort' and not the letter 'E'.

Answers and quick quizzes at **www.hoddereducation.co.uk/myrevisionnotes**

Now test yourself

TESTED ☐

1 Name and sketch the lever system that operates during flexion of the neck.

Answer online

Mechanical advantage and disadvantage

REVISED ☐

A lever can have a mechanical advantage or disadvantage. This depends on the length of the effort arm and the resistance arm. The effort arm is the name given to the shortest perpendicular distance between the fulcrum and the application of effort. The resistance arm is the shortest perpendicular distance between the fulcrum and the resistance.

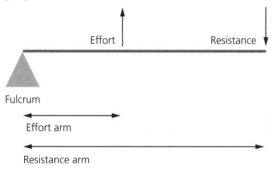

Figure 5.2d The effort arm and the resistance arm

Mechanical advantage is when the effort arm is longer than the resistance arm. This means that the lever system can move a large load over a short distance and requires little effort. However, it has a small range of movement and it is difficult to generate speed and distance.

Mechanical disadvantage is when the resistance arm is longer than the effort arm. This means that the lever system cannot move as heavy a load but can do it faster. It also has a large range of movement.

> **Mechanical advantage:** where the effort arm is longer than the resistance arm.
>
> **Mechanical disadvantage:** where the resistance arm is longer than the effort arm.

Type of lever	Mechanical advantage	Mechanical disadvantage
Second class: Plantarflexion of the ankle	Can generate much larger forces Has to lift the whole body weight	Slow, with a limited range of movement
First class: Triceps in extension of the elbow **Third class:** Biceps in flexion of the elbow	Large range of movement and any resistance can be moved quickly	Cannot apply much force to move an object

Exam practice

1 Name and sketch the lever system that operates during flexion of the elbow joint. [3]
2 What do you understand by the terms 'mechanical advantage' and 'mechanical disadvantage'? [3]

Answers and quick quizzes online

ONLINE ☐

Summary

You should now be able to:
● identify the three classes of lever and give examples of their use in the body during physical activity and sport

● give the mechanical advantage and disadvantage of each class of lever.

5.3 Linear motion

Definitions, equations and units of scalars and vectors

REVISED

There are several measurements used in linear motion. These can be divided into scalar and vector quantities:

- **scalar quantity**: when measurements are described only in terms of size or magnitude – mass, distance and speed
- **vector quantity**: when measurements are described in terms of magnitude (size) and direction – weight, acceleration, displacement, velocity and momentum.

> **Scalar quantities:** measurements described only in terms of size.
>
> **Vector quantities:** measurements described in terms of size and direction.

For your exam you need to be able to define, give units of measurement and, where relevant, equations for the following scalars and vectors.

Measurement	Definition	Unit	Calculation
Mass	Quality of matter a body possesses	Kilograms (kg)	
Distance	Path a body takes as it moves from the starting position to the finishing position	Metres (m)	
Speed	Measurement of a body's movement per unit of time with no reference to direction	Metres/second (m/s)	$\text{Speed (m/s)} = \dfrac{\text{Distance covered (m)}}{\text{Time taken (s)}}$
Weight	Gravitational force exerted on an object	Newtons (N)	$\text{Weight (N)} = \text{Mass (kg)} \times \text{Gravitational field strength (N/kg)}$
Displacement	Shortest route in a straight line between the starting position and the finishing position	Metres (m)	
Velocity	Rate of change of displacement	Metres/second (m/s)	$\dfrac{\text{Displacement (m)}}{\text{Time taken (s)}}$
Acceleration	Rate of change of velocity	Metres/second squared (m/s²)	$\dfrac{\text{Change in velocity (m/s)}}{\text{Time (s)}}$
Momentum	Product of the mass and velocity of an object	Kilogram metres/second (kgm/s)	$\text{Momentum (kgm/s)} = \text{Mass (kg)} \times \text{Velocity (m/s)}$

Now test yourself

TESTED

1 Calculate the momentum of a forward in rugby who has a mass of 110 kg and a velocity of 10 m/s.

Answer online

Graphs of motion

In your exam you need to be able to plot, label and interpret biomechanical graphs and diagrams.

Distance – time graphs

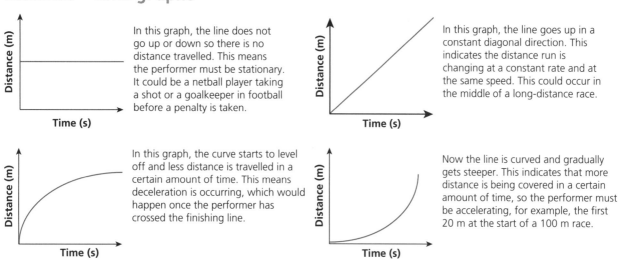

In this graph, the line does not go up or down so there is no distance travelled. This means the performer must be stationary. It could be a netball player taking a shot or a goalkeeper in football before a penalty is taken.

In this graph, the line goes up in a constant diagonal direction. This indicates the distance run is changing at a constant rate and at the same speed. This could occur in the middle of a long-distance race.

In this graph, the curve starts to level off and less distance is travelled in a certain amount of time. This means deceleration is occurring, which would happen once the performer has crossed the finishing line.

Now the line is curved and gradually gets steeper. This indicates that more distance is being covered in a certain amount of time, so the performer must be accelerating, for example, the first 20 m at the start of a 100 m race.

Figure 5.3a Distance–time graphs showing the distance travelled over a period of time

Gradient of a graph

When looking at the gradient of a graph, you just need to look at the slope. This is determined by:

$$\frac{\text{Changes in the y axis}}{\text{Changes in the x axis}}$$

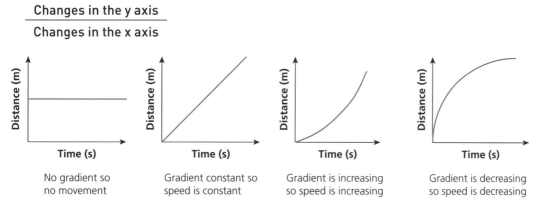

No gradient so no movement

Gradient constant so speed is constant

Gradient is increasing so speed is increasing

Gradient is decreasing so speed is decreasing

Figure 5.3b Gradients of distance–time graph showing the speed of the movement measured

Velocity–time graphs and speed–time graphs

These are essentially the same type of graph. The shape of the velocity–time graph will represent the same pattern of motion as the shape of a speed–time graph.

These graphs indicate the velocity or speed of a performer or object per unit of time. The gradient of the graph will help you to decide whether the performer is travelling at a constant velocity, accelerating or decelerating.

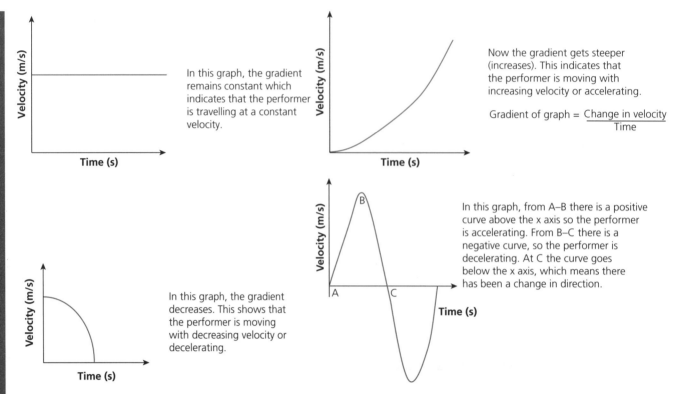

Figure 5.3c Velocity–time graphs showing constant velocity, increasing velocity, decreasing velocity and a more complex pattern of motion

In this graph, the gradient remains constant which indicates that the performer is travelling at a constant velocity.

Now the gradient gets steeper (increases). This indicates that the performer is moving with increasing velocity or accelerating.

Gradient of graph = $\dfrac{\text{Change in velocity}}{\text{Time}}$

In this graph, the gradient decreases. This shows that the performer is moving with decreasing velocity or decelerating.

In this graph, from A–B there is a positive curve above the x axis so the performer is accelerating. From B–C there is a negative curve, so the performer is decelerating. At C the curve goes below the x axis, which means there has been a change in direction.

Now test yourself

TESTED ☐

2 Which of the following distance–time graphs shows acceleration? Explain your answer.

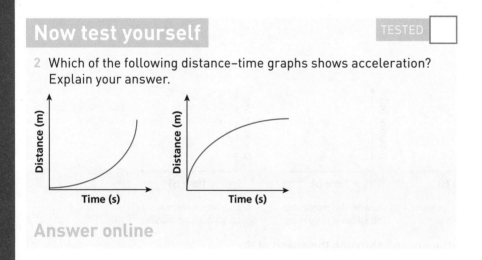

Answer online

Forces acting upon a performer during linear motion

REVISED ☐

A force changes a body's state of motion. There are two types of force:

● An internal force is applied when our skeletal muscles contract, for example the force generated as the quadriceps contract concentrically to extend the knee in a jump.
● An external force comes from outside the body, for example friction, air resistance and weight. Gravity is also an external force and is often described in terms of weight, as weight is the gravitational force that the Earth exerts on a body to pull it downwards.

For your exam you need to identify and apply the following external forces which act upon a sports performer.

Answers and quick quizzes at **www.hoddereducation.co.uk/myrevisionnotes**

Weight and gravity

Weight is a gravitational force that the Earth exerts on a body, pulling it towards the centre of the Earth (or effectively downwards). The greater the mass of the body, the greater the weight force pulling it downwards.

Weight is equal to the mass of the body multiplied by the acceleration of the body due to gravity.

Friction

There are two types of frictional force: static and sliding. Static friction occurs before an object starts to slide. When friction acts between two surfaces that are moving relative to one another, sliding friction occurs.

Friction acts in opposition to motion. This is often confusing, but try to remember that friction resists the slipping and/or sliding motion of two surfaces and an arrow is therefore drawn in the opposite direction to this slipping, usually in the same direction as the motion. However, in skiing the friction arrow opposes motion, as the slipping occurs in a forward direction.

Friction can be affected by the following factors:
- The surface characteristics of the two bodies in contact: think of a 100-metre sprinter who wears running spikes. These help to increase friction, as the spikes make contact with the track and therefore maximise acceleration.
- The temperature of the two surfaces in contact: in curling, for example, the ice is swept in front of the curling stone. The sweeping action slightly raises the surface temperature of the ice, which reduces the friction between the stone and the ice, allowing the stone to travel further.
- The mass of the objects that are sliding: a larger mass results in greater friction.

Air resistance

Air resistance opposes the motion of a body travelling through the air and depends on the following:
- The velocity of the moving body: the faster the performer moves, the greater the air resistance.
- The cross-sectional area of the moving body: the larger the cross-sectional area, the greater the air resistance. For example, think of the Tour de France and how the competitors crouch low over the handlebars, rather than siting upright.
- The shape and the surface characteristics of a moving body: a streamlined shape results in less air resistance, as does a smooth surface. For example, most elite swimmers shave off all body hair or wear half/full body swimsuits so they create a smooth surface. Those who do not shave their head wear a swimming cap instead.

Air resistance is sometimes referred to as 'drag' – although this term is most commonly used when describing resistance in water. Compare running in water to running on land. There is a much greater drag force in water due to its greater density.

How forces act upon the performer during linear motion

REVISED

Forces are vectors. How they act upon a performer can be shown using an arrow on a free body diagram. The position, direction and length of the arrow are important and need to be drawn accurately.

> **Exam tip**
>
> Weight is a vertical force.

> **Exam tip**
>
> Friction occurs when two or more bodies are in contact with one another.

> **Exam tip**
>
> The two horizontal forces are air resistance and friction.

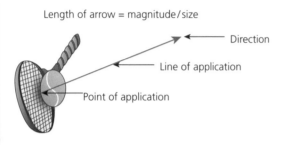

Figure 5.3d **Vectors**

Weight/gravity (W), friction (F) and air resistance (AR) can all be drawn as follows:

a   b   c

Figure 5.3e **Free body diagrams**

The length of the arrow drawn reflects the magnitude or size of the force – the longer the arrow, the bigger the force.

Figure 5.3f **From left to right: F = AR so the net force is zero and there is a constant velocity, F → AR shows acceleration, F ← AR shows deceleration**

The effects of internal and external forces can be represented as a vector diagram. In the high jump, for example, the performer uses a large internal muscular force from the leg muscles to create a big action force, in order to achieve as much vertical displacement (height) as possible. The relationship between the amount of vertical force and horizontal force provided by the muscles will lean towards the vertical component (V). As a result of the application of these forces, the resultant forces for the high jumper can be drawn as a vector diagram. The small horizontal force and the large vertical force provided by the muscles have a resultant force with a high trajectory (close to the vertical).

Figure 5.3g **A vector diagram showing the resultant forces for the high jump**

A long jumper, however, is trying to achieve as much horizontal distance as possible. This means there will be a greater contribution to the overall force from the horizontal component (H) as outlined below in Figure 5.3h:

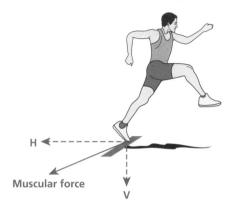

H ← - - - - - -

Muscular force

V

Figure 5.3h Forces exerted by the performer's leg muscles on the ground when performing a long jump

As a result of the application of these forces, the resultant forces for the long jumper can be drawn as a vector diagram:

Figure 5.3i A vector diagram showing the resultant forces for the long jump

Relationship between impulse and increasing and decreasing momentum in sprinting

Impulse

Impulse is the time it takes a force to be applied to an object or body. It can be calculated as:

> **Impulse:** Force x Time.

Force x Time

An increase in impulse will result in an increase in the rate of change of momentum, which causes a large change in velocity. Therefore, impulse is equivalent to a change in the momentum of a body as a result of a force acting upon it. Using impulse to increase momentum can be achieved through increasing the amount of:

● muscular force that is applied
● time in which a force is applied, for example following through with the arm in a throw.

Using impulse to decrease the momentum of an object or body occurs by increasing the time forces act upon it. In any activity that involves a landing action, such as a gymnast dismounting from the parallel bars, flexion of the hip, knee and plantar flexion of the ankle occurs, which extends the time of the force on the ground (how long the feet are in contact with the mat) and therefore allows the gymnast to control the landing and also reduces the chance of injury.

The interpretation of force–time graphs

Impulse is represented by an area under a force–time graph. The graphs below show various stages of a 100-metre sprint. In the 100-metre sprint, impulse is only concerned with horizontal forces. As the sprinter's foot lands on the ground, his muscles contract and a force is applied to the ground (action force). The ground reaction force then acts on the foot, which allows the athlete to accelerate forwards. The action of the foot in contact with the ground is referred to as a single footfall. It is important to note that in running/sprinting, negative impulse occurs first when the foot lands to provide a braking action and then positive impulse occurs as the foot takes off for acceleration.

> **Exam tip**
>
> For your exam you need to be able to interpret the relationship between impulse and increasing and decreasing momentum in a force–time graph.

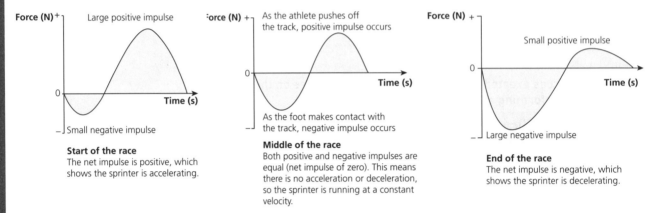

Start of the race
The net impulse is positive, which shows the sprinter is accelerating.

Middle of the race
Both positive and negative impulses are equal (net impulse of zero). This means there is no acceleration or deceleration, so the sprinter is running at a constant velocity.

End of the race
The net impulse is negative, which shows the sprinter is decelerating.

Figure 5.3j Force–time graphs to show various stages of a 100-m sprint

Now test yourself
TESTED ☐

3 How does an athlete use impulse during their sprint or take-off?

Answer online

Exam practice

1 When accelerating along the track at the beginning of a 100-metre race, a sprinter generates a large impulse. Sketch and label a graph to show the typical impulse generated by the sprinter at this stage of the race. [4]
2 Explain, in terms of the player moving towards the ball, the difference between velocity and acceleration. [3]
3 Give two horizontal forces acting on a 200-metre sprinter. [2]
4 Sketch a vector diagram to represent the differing resultant forces for a long jumper and explain your answer. [3]

Answers and quick quizzes online
ONLINE ☐

Summary

You should now be able to:
- define the scalars mass, speed and distance, giving equations and units of measurement
- define the vectors weight, velocity, displacement, acceleration and momentum, giving equations and units of measurement
- demonstrate the ability to plot, label and interpret biomechanical graphs and diagrams
- understand the forces acting on a performer during linear motion
- explain the relationship between impulse and increasing and decreasing momentum in sprinting through the interpretation of force–time graphs.

5.4 Angular motion

Angular motion is movement around a fixed point or axis, such as performing a somersault, throwing a discus or moving around the high bar in gymnastics. It occurs when a force is applied outside the centre of mass. An off-centre force is referred to as an eccentric force.

Application of Newton's laws to angular motion

REVISED

Just by changing the terminology of Newton's laws, we can relate them to angular motion:

- Newton's first law: a rotating body will continue in its state of angular motion unless an external force (**torque**) is exerted upon it. In practice, think of an ice skater spinning in the air. They will continue to spin until they land. Here the ground exerts an external force (torque), which changes their state of angular momentum.
- Newton's second law: the rate of change of angular momentum of a body is proportional to the force (torque) causing it and the change that takes place in the direction in which the force (torque) acts. In practice, leaning forwards from a diving board will create more angular momentum than standing straight.
- Newton's third law: when a force (torque) is applied by one body to another, the second body will exert an equal and opposite force (torque) on the other body. In practice, performing the hang technique in the long jump exerts an equal and opposite force. As the long jumper brings their legs forwards and upwards (action), the arms come forwards and downwards (reaction).

> **Torque:** a rotational force.

> **Revision activity**
>
> Choose a somersault, cartwheel or other rotational movement and try to apply all of Newton's laws to it.

Now test yourself

TESTED

1 Explain Newton's second law of motion in relation to a dancer spinning.

Answer online

Definitions and units for angular motion

REVISED

You need to be able to define and give a unit of measurement for each of the following:

Measurement of angular motion	Definition	Units
Angular displacement	The smallest change in angle between the starting and finishing points	Measured in radians (1 radian = 57.3 degrees)
Angular velocity	The rotational speed of an object and the axis about which the object is rotating	Measured in radians per second $(\text{rads/s}) = \dfrac{\text{Angular displacement (rad)}}{\text{Time taken (s)}}$
Angular acceleration	The rate of change of angular velocity over time	Measured in radians per second squared $(\text{rads/s}^2) = \dfrac{\text{Change in velocity (rads/s)}}{\text{Time taken (s)}}$

Conservation of angular momentum, moment of inertia and angular velocity

Angular momentum (L) depends upon moment of inertia (I) and angular velocity (ω). These two are inversely proportional: if moment of inertia increases, angular velocity decreases (and vice versa).

Inertia is a resistance to change in motion, so moment of inertia is the resistance of a body to angular motion (rotation). This depends upon the mass of the body and the distribution of mass around the axis.

The greater the mass, the greater the resistance to change, and therefore the greater the moment of inertia. For example, a medicine ball is more difficult to roll along the ground than a tennis ball.

The closer the mass is to the axis of rotation, the easier it is to turn, so the moment of inertia is low. Increasing the distance of the distribution of mass from the axis of rotation will increase the moment of inertia, for example a somersault in a straight position has a higher moment of inertia than the tucked somersault, because in the straight position the distribution of the diver's mass is further away from the axis of rotation.

> **Exam tip**
>
> Angular momentum (L) = I ω.

Figure 5.4a Tucked and open somersaults

Angular momentum is a conserved quantity – it stays constant unless an external torque (force) acts upon it (Newton's first law). When an ice skater executes a spin, for example, there is no change in their angular momentum until they use their blades to slow down the spin. A figure skater can also manipulate their moment of inertia to increase or decrease the speed of the spin (angular velocity). At the start of the spin, the arms and leg are stretched out. This increases their distance from the axis of rotation, resulting in a large moment of inertia and a large angular momentum in order to start the spin (decrease in angular velocity).

Figure 5.4b The start of a spin

When the figure skater brings their arms and leg back in line with the rest of their body, the distance of these body parts from the axis of rotation decreases significantly. This reduces the moment of inertia, meaning that angular momentum has to increase. The result is a very fast spin (increase in angular velocity).

Figure 5.4c Increasing angular velocity during a spin

Exam tip

Questions often ask you to explain how the speed of rotation can be altered or controlled. To answer this, you need to know the relationship between angular momentum, moment of inertia and angular velocity.

Exam practice

1 Explain how a gymnast can alter the speed of rotation during flight. [8]
2 Explain Newton's first law of motion in relation to a dancer spinning. [2]

Answers and quick quizzes online

ONLINE

Summary

You should now be able to:
- understand and apply Newton's laws to angular motion
- define and give units for angular displacement, angular velocity and angular acceleration

- explain how angular momentum can be conserved during flight, using moment of inertia and its effect on angular velocity.

5.5 Projectile motion

Projectile motion refers to the movement of either an object or the human body as it travels through the air. In sport, as soon as a ball is released in a kick, hit or throw, it becomes a projectile. The human body acts as a projectile in a variety of sporting situations, such as the long jump and gymnastic vault.

Factors affecting horizontal displacement of a projectile

REVISED

Three factors determine the **horizontal displacement** of a projectile:
- angle of release
- speed of release
- height of release.

> **Horizontal displacement:** the shortest distance from the starting point to the finishing point in a line parallel to the ground.

Angle of release

To ensure an object or person travels as far as possible, the angle of release is important, whether this is the angle at which the object leaves a performer's hand or the angle at which a performer takes off. The optimum angle of release is dependent upon release height and landing height.

When both the release height and landing height are equal, the optimum angle of release is 45 degrees (ignoring wind resistance and gravity). This would be the case for a long jumper who takes off from the ground and lands on the ground.

If the release height is below the landing height, the optimum angle of release needs to be greater than 45 degrees. Shooting in basketball highlights this if we assume the ring is the landing height, as the ring is above the release height.

If the release height is above the landing height, the optimum angle of release needs to be less than 45 degrees. This can be seen in the flight path of the shot put where the hand is the point of release, which is much higher than the landing point (ground).

Speed of release

The greater the release velocity of a projectile, the greater the horizontal displacement. In the shot put, the speed across the circle ensures that the shot leaves the hand at maximum velocity so a greater horizontal displacement can be achieved.

Height of release

A greater release height also results in an increase in horizontal displacement. The force of gravity is constantly acting on the mass of a shot put. This therefore means that technically the shot putter should try to release the shot at the highest point possible above the ground to gain maximum horizontal displacement.

Now test yourself

TESTED

1 Identify the three factors that affect the distance a shot put travels.

Answer online

Factors affecting flight paths of different projectiles

Weight (gravity) and air resistance are two forces that affect projectiles while they are in the air. These two factors are crucial in deciding whether a projectile has a flight path that is a true parabola or a distorted parabola. A parabola is a uniform curve that is symmetrical at its highest point (i.e. with matching left and right sides).

Projectiles with a large weight force have a small air resistance force and follow a true parabolic flight path. A good example is the shot put.

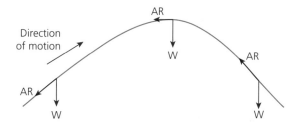

Figure 5.5a A parabolic flight path of a shot put

This diagram shows the forces acting on the flight path of a shot put at the start, middle and end of flight. As the shot put has a large mass, there is a longer weight arrow. The longer the flight path, the longer air resistance can affect a projectile and have a greater influence.

In projectiles with a lighter mass, the effects of air resistance result in a flight path that deviates from a true parabola to a distorted parabola. The badminton shuttlecock is a good example of this:

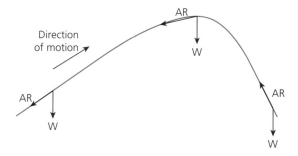

Figure 5.5b A non-parabolic flight path of a shuttlecock

This diagram shows the forces acting on the flight path of a shuttlecock. Compared to the shot put, the shuttlecock has a lighter mass and an unusual shape that increases its air resistance. In a serve, the shuttlecock starts off with a high velocity – provided by the force of the racket. As the shuttlecock continues its flight path, it slows down and the effect of air resistance reduces.

> **Revision activity**
>
> Choose projectiles from five different sports and see if you can identify and explain their flight paths.

Vector components of parabolic flight

A shot put follows a parabolic flight path. As it is released at an angle to the horizontal, its initial velocity has a **horizontal component** and a **vertical component**. These two components can be represented by vectors. A vector is drawn as an arrow and it has magnitude (size) and direction. Drawing a bigger arrow means there is more magnitude and a smaller arrow less magnitude.

> **Horizontal component:** the horizontal motion of an object.
>
> **Vertical component:** the upward motion of an object.

Now test yourself

2 Draw two vectors – one to represent the horizontal component and one for the vertical component.

Answer online

The diagram below shows both the horizontal and vertical vectors on the flight of a shot put as it follows a parabolic flight path:

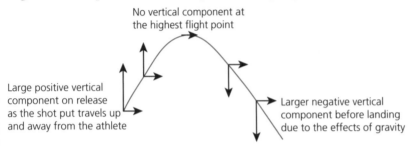

Figure 5.5c Forces acting on the flight path of a shot put

Here the vertical component can only be affected by gravity, which is why the vertical component decreases during flight. Air resistance is negligible, so both the horizontal and vertical components are unaffected by air resistance. This means the horizontal component remains constant throughout the flight.

It is also possible to add the horizontal and vertical vectors together to get a resultant vector. This shows the true flight path of the shot put:

> **Exam tip**
>
> The release point of the shot put is drawn higher than the landing point and the horizontal component arrow stays the same at each stage of the flight.

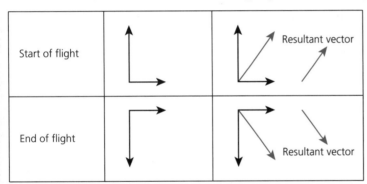

Figure 5.5d True flight path of the shot put

Exam practice

1 Elite football players use their feet to overcome the forces acting on the football so that it can travel long distances. Describe how the impact of the foot, weight and air resistance affect the velocity and acceleration of a football. [6]
2 In a game of badminton, the performer hits the shuttlecock into the air and it then becomes a projectile. Explain how the various forces act to affect the badminton shuttlecock *during* its flight. [3]
3 Draw a diagram to show the flight path of a shot put and on your diagram label and explain the changing vertical and horizontal vectors at the following points:
   ● the point of release
   ● the highest point of flight
   ● the point immediately before landing. [6]

Answers and quick quizzes online

ONLINE ☐

Summary

You should now be able to:
● identify angle of release, speed of release and height of release as the factors that affect the horizontal displacement of projectiles

● identify the factors affecting flight paths of the shot put and badminton shuttlecock
● identify the vector components of parabolic flight.

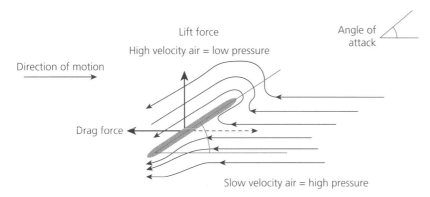

Lift force
High velocity air = low pressure
Direction of motion
Angle of attack
Drag force
Slow velocity air = high pressure

Figure 5.6b Bernoulli's principle producing a lift force on the discus

A lift force does not always have to work in an upward direction. Bernoulli's principle can also be used to describe a downward lift force, such as that required by racing cars, cyclists and speed skiers. The car, bike and skis need to be pushed down into the ground, so a greater frictional force is created.

In a Formula 1 sports car, for example, the spoiler is angled so the lift force can act in a downward direction to push the car into the track. This happens because the air that travels over the top of the car travels a shorter distance than the air underneath due to the angle of the spoiler. As a result, the air above the car travels at a slower velocity and a higher pressure. This creates a downward lift force and therefore a greater frictional force, so the tyres maintain a firm grip on the track as the car travels at high speed and around corners.

Similarly with the cyclist, the low streamlined body position over the handlebars means that the air that travels over the top of the cyclist has to travel a shorter distance than the air underneath. This results in the air above the cyclist travelling at a slower velocity, which therefore creates a higher pressure. This higher pressure above the cyclist creates a downward lift force and allows the tyres of the bike to maintain a firm grip on the track. Speed skiers need to stay in contact with the ice for faster speed because more downward-acting lift means more force, which melts the ice for a better friction-free surface.

Exam tip

The shape and angle of the rear spoiler of a racing car result in the lift force created by Bernoulli's principle acting in a downward direction.

Figure 5.6c A downward lift force is caused by the shape and angle of the rear spoiler of a racing car

Exam practice

1 Explain what would happen if the angle of attack for the discus was too high. [2]
2 Identify and explain three factors that can increase or decrease drag. [3]
3 Describe how a racing car makes use of a downward lift force. [4]

Answers and quick quizzes online

ONLINE

Summary

You should now be able to:
- understand what is meant by dynamic fluid force and relate this to drag and lift
- explain the factors that increase and reduce drag in sport

- explain Bernoulli's principle in relation to an upward lift force for the discus throw and a downward lift force for racing cars, cyclists and speed skiers.

6.1 Aspects of personality

Personality comprises the unique, psychological, temperamental features of an individual.

Some psychologists argue that personality characteristics are innate; others argue that they are learned. This 'nature versus nurture' debate is best discussed using the three perspectives outlined in this chapter.

Trait perspective

REVISED

The trait perspective of personality suggests that a performer is born with their personality – it is determined genetically from their ancestry. In other words, extroverts will show their outgoing personalities both on and off the field of play, and likewise introverts will always be reserved.

Trait theorists include Eysenck, Cattell and Girdano, and they suggest that characteristics will most likely be shown in all situations, so personality and behaviour can be predicted. They suggest personality is stable and enduring i.e. it does not change and is permanent. For example, a netballer who is very calm and controlled would always show these characteristics, even when playing against an opponent who is continually contacting her. Her coach would be confident that the player would not lash out in retaliation despite the contact. This approach does not consider any effects that environmental learning may have on the performer, that personality cannot in fact always be predicted, or that individuals may consciously decide to structure their own personality.

Social learning perspective

REVISED

This approach, associated with psychologists such as Bandura (see learning theories, page 57), suggests that personality is not innate but is learned from our experiences. It changes according to the situation, so personality and behaviour cannot be predicted. We observe and copy the behaviour and personality of significant others, e.g. parents, peers, coaches and role models in the media. Socialisation also plays an important part (see attitudes, page 155). If behaviour is successful or is praised by a coach, it is highly likely that we will imitate it. For example, your tennis coach constantly praises your team mate for showing determination and controlled emotions during matches. You decide to copy your teammate's behaviour in order to gain the same reinforcement. A performer is more likely to copy the behaviour/personality of those who share similar characteristics such as gender, age and ability levels, as well as those who are significant.

The opposing views of trait and social learning approaches give rise to the nature vs nurture debate – i.e. are we born with our personality traits or do we in fact learn them as we go (social learning)?

Now test yourself

TESTED

1 What are the differences between the trait and social learning approaches?

Answer online

The interactionist perspective of personality suggests that personality is made up of traits and the influence of what you have learned from your environmental experiences. It accepts that parts of both the trait and social learning approaches are relevant, and so combines them.

Lewin suggested that an individual's personality is produced when both their natural predispositions and the experiences they have combine in a specific situation. His equation to describe this is $B = f (P \times E)$, meaning behaviour is a function of an individual's personality traits and the environment. A performer will adapt to the situation they find themselves in, even behaving differently to how they would normally. For example, a generally introverted rhythmic gymnast is reserved ordinarily, but she has learned to adapt when performing and displays more assertive, extroverted characteristics during a competition to appeal to the judges. The interactionist approach suggests that we can predict personality and behaviour in a specific situation.

Hollander suggested that there are three aspects to an individual's personality: the core, typical responses and role-related behaviour.

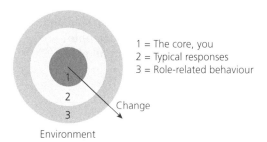

Figure 6.1a **Hollander model**

Hollander believed that personality could be represented by three concentric rings, with the innermost ring being the most difficult to penetrate:
1 The core is the real you and what your true beliefs and values are. It does not change and represents the stable aspects of your personality. Often this is kept hidden.
2 Typical responses describe how individuals usually respond.
3 Role-related behaviour is how an individual responds in a specific environment. This may be uncharacteristic behaviour. It is the most unstable aspect of your personality and does not necessarily reflect the psychological core.

What are the three parts of Hollander's model?

How knowledge of the interactionist perspective can improve performance

If a coach understands their players' innate personalities and how they would 'normally' respond in specific situations, they can use this to their advantage, for example understanding that a centre forward with an aggressive personality is likely to retaliate when fouled. The coach might therefore substitute her if they observe that her level of aggression is increasing due to the centre back continually sliding in late. The coach can try to *adapt* the responses of this player by offering cognitive and somatic strategies (see pages 191–2) to reduce her stress and therefore levels of aggression. This may form part of training sessions, where demanding situations are created in order to generate a negative response from the player. She is then given the opportunity to use the strategies. In future when she is fouled, she will respond differently to her instinctive response. She has learned to act in a more controlled way.

Exam practice

1 According to the interactionist approach, how is personality developed? Use a practical example to illustrate your answer. [4]

Answer and quick quizzes online

ONLINE

Summary

You should now be able to:
- understand each of the approaches to personality and describe them using the correct terminology
- write a balanced argument on the nature vs nurture debate – are we born with our personality or do we learn it?

- ensure your example relates specifically to personality – trait, social learning and interactionist is also seen in leadership and aggression and therefore your example must be clear to reflect the section of the specification clearly.

6.2 Attitudes

An attitude is what an individual believes, how they feel and how they act towards an attitude object. Attitude objects can include other people, places, situations and items. Attitudes, while usually deep rooted, are not permanent and can be changed although this can prove difficult.

Attitude formation

REVISED

Attitudes can be positive or negative and are developed through experiences rather than being innate. They often begin to form at an early age. They can be formed by the following:

- Past experiences: winning matches or titles, for example, is an enjoyable experience and can lead to the individual developing a positive attitude. As a result, the individual may develop a high perception of their own ability, which increases their confidence. A bad experience, e.g. losing or being injured, may lead to a negative attitude. The individual may have low self-confidence and a poor perception of their ability. This may manifest itself as the individual developing a negative attitude towards physical activity as a whole. They may develop learned helplessness.
- Socialisation: this describes how an individual wishes to fit in with the cultural norms surrounding them. If it is the norm for your friendship group or family to participate regularly in and have positive attitudes towards physical activity, then you will conform in order to fit in. For example, they might all play for a team or attend the gym on a regular basis and therefore you do the same because you do not want to feel 'left out'. However, if it is the norm for your peers/family not to participate and to hold negative attitudes, you will adopt these to be consistent with the people around you.
- Social learning: imitating the attitudes of significant others, for example parents, teachers and peers. If your parents/friends have a positive attitude towards a particular sporting activity, it is likely that you will copy them, especially if you are reinforced or praised for doing so. Conversely, if they hold a negative attitude and abstain from participating, it is likely that you will copy the same attitude and behaviour.
- Media: high-profile role models in the media/on TV often display positive attitudes and, as we regard them highly, we are likely to adopt their positive attitudes towards being active.

Triadic model

REVISED

The triadic model suggests that an attitude is made up of three components. An individual shows a positive attitude towards squash, for example, thus:

1 Cognitive – beliefs/thoughts, for example 'I *believe/think* that I can be a successful squash player'.
2 Affective – emotions/feelings, for example 'I *enjoy* playing squash and *feel energised* after each training session'.
3 Behavioural – actions/responses, for example 'I *have 1–2–1 training twice a week and compete on the club's squash ladder*'.

Attitudes, however, are very inconsistent. An individual may believe that attending the gym is good for them and really enjoy it when they go but may not actually attend due to lack of time or motivation. Beliefs do not always correspond with behaviour, and sometimes all three aspects of a person's attitude may be negative.

Now test yourself

TESTED

1 How would a performer demonstrate a positive attitude towards pre-season training?

Answer online

Changing attitudes

REVISED

It is important to be able to change the negative attitude of an individual. Some general strategies include:
- ensuring positive, successful experiences
- praising positive attitudes/behaviour
- punishing negative attitudes/behaviour, for example substitution/bans
- using positive role models to highlight positive attitudes.

Coaches might also try persuasive communication, particularly by significant others who encourage you to change your mind and take on board their more positive point of view. If you have a deep-seated, negative attitude, realistically you are only likely to want to change if a significant other or an expert is asking you to. They have to give a very clear message about why you should change your attitude, and you have to understand what they are saying! They might enlist the help of your peers to support their view/message. This strategy is very difficult to get right. Ultimately, the individual must *want* to change.

An alternative strategy is cognitive dissonance. When an individual's attitude components all match, whether positively or negatively, they are in a state of cognitive consonance. Their beliefs, feelings and actions are in harmony and the individual's attitude will remain. To change the attitude, you can create cognitive dissonance. Dissonance is caused by generating unease inside the individual. This unease is created by changing one or more of the negative attitude components into a positive, causing the individual to question their attitude and thus change it into a positive one.

The table below shows the negative attitude of one individual towards attending their local gym. Using any of the strategies in the right-hand column can cause dissonance/unease and therefore instigate an attitude change.

> **Revision activity**
>
> Find a picture of a sportsperson who, in your view, has demonstrated a negative attitude. Make a poster with their face in the middle and write the cognitive, affective and behavioural ways this negative attitude was shown. In a different colour pen, write how you would change their negative attitude, with reference to cognitive dissonance theory.

> **Exam tip**
>
> Questions about changing negative attitudes are common.

Component	Negative attitude	Change by:
Cognitive	I think that going to the gym is a waste of time.	Educating – preferably by a significant other. Highlight to them that attending the gym can make you healthy. It creates muscle tone, improves appearance and reduces the risk of disease.
Affective	I hate going to the gym.	Ensuring a positive, varied experience. Make it fun/enjoyable. Ensure that they are successful.
Behavioural	I don't go to the gym.	Persuasive communication – preferably by an expert. Praise them to reinforce their behaviour so they continue to go to the gym.

Exam practice

1 Explain how a coach can use cognitive dissonance to change a performer's negative attitude into a positive attitude. [4]

Answer and quick quizzes online

ONLINE

Summary

You should now be able to:
- fully understand the three components of an attitude and how they are formed, giving clear examples

- describe effectively how to use cognitive dissonance and persuasive communication.

6.3 Arousal

Arousal is the level of **somatic** or **cognitive** stimulation that gets us ready to perform. Being aroused to the correct level and being motivated is important in sport.

> **Somatic:** of the body.
>
> **Cognitive:** of the mind.

Drive theory

REVISED

- As arousal increases, so does performance in a linear fashion .
- Performance is a function of drive multiplied by habit: $P = f(D \times H)$.

However, it is unrealistic to suggest that performance always keeps improving:

- At high arousal, the performer reverts to their dominant response. This is a well-learned skill that the performer will use when under competitive pressure.
- If the performer is in the autonomous phase of learning, their dominant response is likely to be correct. Performance levels are therefore high.
- If the performer is in the cognitive phase of learning, their dominant response is likely to be incorrect. Performance levels are therefore low.
- This theory does not account for elite performers deteriorating under pressure.

> **Typical mistake**
>
> There are *three* graphs related to arousal. Students often confuse them! Revise each one thoroughly.

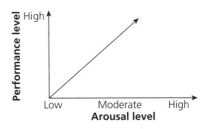

Figure 6.3a **Drive theory**

Inverted-U theory

REVISED

This is a more practical theory, as it accounts for how experience, personality and skills can impact on success. However, it does not account for the dramatic decrease in performance seen by some elite performers once they have exceeded their optimum level of arousal.

Inverted-U theory suggests that as arousal increases, so does performance quality, up to an optimum point at moderate arousal. After this, performance quality decreases as a result of over-arousal. Under- and over-arousal can both be detrimental to performance.

Inverted-U theory in relation to experience, personality and skills

A moderate level of arousal is not always the best for peak performance. The optimum level of arousal can very depending on the performer's experience and personality and the type of skill being performed. This is shown in Figure 6.3c.

Optimum performance occurs at *lower* levels of arousal (shown by the green curve) in situations involving:

- novice/cognitive performers
- introverts who have a high resting level of adrenaline
- fine skills that require a high level of precision and control
- complex skills where several decisions are made.

Figure 6.3b **Inverted-U theory showing how increased arousal affects performance**

Optimum performance occurs at *higher* levels of arousal (shown by the blue line) in situations involving:

● advanced/autonomous performers
● extroverts who have a low resting level of adrenaline and who strive for 'exciting' situations
● gross skills where precision and control is not needed
● simple skills with few decisions to make.

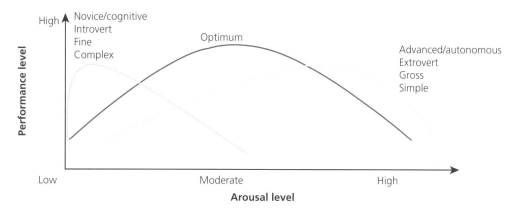

Figure 6.3c **Adaptations to the inverted-U theory showing how the performer and the skill can affect the optimal level of arousal for best performance**

What is the optimal level of arousal when performing a pistol shot?
What is the optimal level of arousal for a complex skill?

Catastrophe theory

This theory accounts for the sudden drop in performance once the optimum has been exceeded. It illustrates why there is a total 'catastrophe' for some performers, including the elite.

This theory is multi-dimensional. It considers the effects of both somatic and cognitive anxiety. As arousal increases, so does performance quality up to an optimum point at moderate arousal, as shown by the inverted-U theory. However, there is then a dramatic decrease in performance as a result of high somatic anxiety combined with high cognitive anxiety. The body and the mind have become over-aroused, causing an immediate and catastrophic decline in performance.

The effects can be reversed by performing relaxation techniques, for example deep breathing exercises or progressive muscle relaxation. The performer can then continue to play, providing they have reached a level of relaxation below the point of catastrophe.

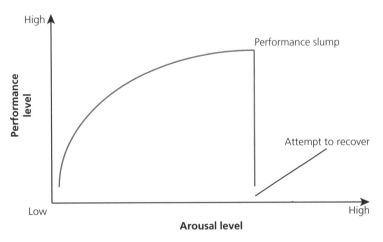

Figure 6.3d Catastrophe theory

TESTED

2 What causes a 'catastrophe' and what happens as a result?

Answer online

Hanin's zone of optimum functioning

REVISED

A more recent theory by Hanin suggests optimum performance is reached during a band or zone, not at a single point as described by the inverted-U theory.

The 'zone' is a mental state that autonomous performers normally only experience once or twice in their entire sporting career, when everything is 'perfect'. Characteristics of the zone include:
- performing at optimum arousal levels
- feeling completely calm
- complete attentional control – fully concentrated on the task
- performing on 'autopilot' – some performers have no memory of it
- feeling completely confident that success is inevitable
- performing smoothly, efficiently and effortlessly.

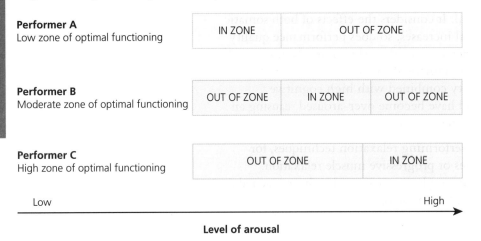

Figure 6.3e Zone of optimal functioning

Looking at Figure 6.3e, performer A enters the zone, achieving best performance at low levels of arousal. Performer B is in the zone at moderate levels of arousal. Performer C enters the zone at high levels of arousal. Individuals have a variety of somatic and cognitive strategies to get them into the zone.

Peak flow experience

Peak flow describes the ultimate positive psychological state for a performer. It is very rare and intense. The performer is fully concentrated on the task, has absolute control over their actions, which seem effortless, and may feel an 'out of body' experience that they have difficulty in remembering.

Peak flow happens to a performer when they:
- are presented with a level of challenge that matches their skill level
- have a clear goal
- have the correct attentional style
- have a positive attitude before and during the performance
- have control of their arousal levels.

It is very difficult to achieve peak flow. If a performer is presented with a challenge that is perceived as too high for them, it will result in anxiety. For example, a novice skier attempting a black piste will undoubtedly feel nervous. If the task is too easy for a performer's level of skill, they will become bored. For example, a club-level high jumper would find it very monotonous while his classmates were being taught the basics. An apathetic view would be taken by a performer who has a low skill level and is presented with a very easy task.

To achieve peak flow, performers should be given a task which is realistic yet which challenges them at an appropriate level. They then enter the most rewarding psychological and physical state.

> **Revision activity**
>
> This section is heavy on theory. Read the chapter out loud and record yourself using a voice recorder/voice recorder app. Listen to it repeatedly!

How will a performer feel if they achieve peak flow?

Exam practice

1 Explain how over-arousal can affect performance with reference to the catastrophe theory. [4]

Answer and quick quizzes online

Summary

You should now be able to:
- draw, explain and give examples for each of the three theories of arousal
- understand how the inverted-U theory addresses the different arousal requirements for various skills and performers
- understand and give characteristics of the zone of optimal functioning
- explain the characteristics of peak flow and what is required to enter a peak flow state.

6.4 Anxiety

Anxiety negatively affects performance. It is caused by a performer's perception that their ability is not good enough.

Types of anxiety

- Somatic anxiety: physiological symptoms of anxiety, for example increased heart rate, blood pressure, sweat levels and muscle tension.
- Cognitive anxiety: mental symptoms of anxiety, for example worrying, irrational thoughts, confusion and learned helplessness.
- Competitive trait anxiety: the performer has a natural tendency to become anxious in all sporting situations. They have a genetic predisposition (trait anxiety), for example a skier thinks that they will fall when attempting to ski down any piste, regardless of whether it is black, red or blue!
- Competitive state anxiety: the performer is only anxious in specific sporting situations and often in high-pressure moments. It can be caused by negative past experiences, for example a footballer experiences worry and heightened blood pressure when taking a penalty as he has missed one before.

Somatic anxiety and cognitive anxiety often occur together in sport. To achieve maximal performance, the athlete should experience *low* levels of *cognitive* anxiety. They should not be worried about performing. As described in the inverted-U theory, performers should have *moderate* levels of *somatic* anxiety, as this produces the best performance. Low levels mean the performer is not stimulated enough, high levels mean there are excessive levels of adrenaline in the body, increasing the likelihood of the somatic symptoms occurring and therefore reducing performance levels.

> **Now test yourself**
>
> 1 What is the difference between competitive trait anxiety and competitive state anxiety?
>
> **Answer online**
>
> TESTED

Causes of anxiety

Causes of anxiety include:
- task importance, e.g. playing in a final
- losing/fear of failing
- perceived inaccuracy of official's decisions
- being fouled
- injury/fear of being injured
- lack of self-confidence/efficacy
- audience effects, e.g. an abusive crowd
- evaluation apprehension.

Measuring anxiety

Anxiety can be measured using questionnaires, observation and physiological methods such as heart rate monitors, measuring sweat etc.

Questionnaires

Self-report questionnaires are often used to measure anxiety. Martens' Sport Competition Anxiety Test (SCAT) was devised specifically to measure anxiety in sporting situations. Performers answer statements rating their level of anxiousness. Coaches and psychologists can therefore evaluate which performers need help with managing anxiety.

The State–Trait Anxiety Inventory (STAI) is a 40-question test that distinguishes between specific state and trait anxiety. Performers score themselves on a scale of 1–4 in each question, which measures feelings of nervousness, worry, apprehension and tension based on the performer's current feelings (state) and their general feelings (trait).

The Competitive State Anxiety Inventory-2 (CSAI-2) was developed to measure cognitive and somatic anxiety and self-confidence in competitive situations. Performers rate themselves on a four-point scale as to how they are currently feeling in 27 statements. Usually this is given out on more than one occasion leading up to an event, i.e. in the week before, day before, then hour before, as this will indicate the level and type of anxiety experienced and when.

Questionnaires are cheap and efficient. A lot of information can be gathered in a short period of time. However, the performer may not answer truthfully, they may not understand the question being asked and the responses that are given can be affected by environmental factors, for example the time of day the questionnaire is being completed.

Observation

Observation is a real-life method whereby performers' behaviour is analysed before, during and after play. However, it is very subjective. Each observer will perceive the situation differently. It is also time-consuming. The observers will need to be aware of the performer's 'normal' anxiety levels so they can see the changes, if any, during competitive situations. Also, the performer may change their behaviour as soon as they realise they are being observed!

Physiological methods

Physiological methods generate factual data on somatic responses such as heart rate and blood pressure levels. These measures can be taken immediately during performance. However, they involve the performer wearing monitors that may restrict their movements, the equipment could be very expensive and the performer realises they are being monitored, which may cause a physiological response and therefore an inaccurate reading.

Revision activity

Try out each of the cognitive and somatic strategies.

What are the advantages and disadvantages of using observation as a way of measuring anxiety?

Exam practice

1 Using sporting examples, describe somatic and cognitive anxiety. [4]

Answer and quick quizzes online

ONLINE

Summary

You should now be able to:
- define somatic, cognitive, competitive trait and competitive state anxiety
- describe how anxiety can be measured by questionnaires, observation and physiological testing
- describe the advantages and disadvantages of each method.

6.5 Aggression

Aggression or assertion?

REVISED

Aggression is when an individual purposefully harms or injures their opponent. It is outside of the rules, hostile and reactive, for example a rugby league player angrily punching his opponent when getting up to play the ball.

Assertion is often confused with aggression. This is when an individual plays hard, but within the rules, perhaps using more effort than usual, but there is no intention to harm the opposition. A very strong, quick bowl at the batter in rounders/cricket or a crunching but fair tackle in rugby union are both examples of assertive play.

There are many causes of aggression including:
- playing badly
- feeling that team mates are not trying
- disagreement with officials' decisions
- provocation by opponent/crowd
- important game, e.g. semi-final/final/local derby
- religious/cultural reasons, e.g. Celtic 'versus' Rangers
- contact sport (therefore expected), e.g. ice hockey/Gaelic football
- naturally aggressive personality
- social learning
- over-arousal.

> **Typical mistake**
>
> Definitions of aggression and assertion are sometimes unclear – make sure you know the difference.

> **Exam tip**
>
> Make sure you give a range of answers from across the mark scheme to access all the marks available. For example, playing badly/losing might appear on the same mark scheme point and can only be credited once.

Theories of aggression

REVISED

Instinct theory

As humans, we have a natural trait or predisposition to be aggressive. It is genetically determined and we are born with a tendency to defend ourselves and, in sport, our territory. Instinct theorists believe that inevitably aggression builds up within us. If we are provoked enough, we will react aggressively. Once the aggressive act occurs, there is a cathartic effect – the aggression is released and we calm down.

This theory has the following drawbacks:
- It does not consider the effect of environmental/social learning on aggression.
- Individuals often experience increased aggression during sporting competition, rather than it having a cathartic effect.
- The instinct approach suggests that as humans we are all genetically determined to behave aggressively. This is not true. Some people never act aggressively!

Frustration–aggression hypothesis

When a performer has a drive to achieve a goal but is then stopped from achieving that goal, they experience frustration. According to this hypothesis, frustration always leads to an aggressive response. For example, a basketball player is dribbling and running towards the basket.

They are fouled and their goal has been blocked. They feel frustrated, which leads to an aggressive act such as pushing their opponent. This will have a cathartic effect, reducing frustration and aggression. However, if they are then unable to release their aggression and experience the cathartic effect, perhaps due to the presence of the officials, more frustration builds, leading to an increased aggressive drive. The performer is likely to retaliate at a later point in the match.

This theory does not account for performer who:
- experience frustration and aggression even when goals have not been blocked
- have their goals blocked and experience frustration but do not react aggressively.

Aggressive cue hypothesis (Berkowitz)

Berkowitz updated the frustration–aggression hypothesis. When a performer has their goal blocked, their arousal levels increase and they experience frustration. This leads to them being *ready* for an aggressive act, rather than inevitable aggression. An aggressive act will only happen if learned cues or triggers are present. For example, aggressive objects such as bats/clubs or aggressive contact sports such as rugby/ice hockey are more likely to produce aggressive responses. A footballer who has been praised by their coach for aggressive, dangerous tackles may learn that this is a positive behaviour and the coach acts as a cue in future matches to be aggressive.

Social learning theory

This opposes the trait approach to aggression and is based on the work of Bandura. It asserts that aggression is learned by watching and copying the behaviour of significant others. If an aggressive act is reinforced or is successful, it is more likely to be copied. For example, a young rugby player watches his idol high tackle an opponent. The crowd cheers and the opponent is prevented from scoring a try. As this aggressive act is reinforced and successful, the rugby player copies this behaviour in his next match.

Performers may also become aggressive due to socialisation. For example, a footballer observes many of his team mates shouting abuse and acting aggressively towards the referee as they disagree with a penalty call. He joins in to fit in with his team mates. Aggression is more likely to be copied if the model shares similar characteristics with the performer.

This theory does not take into account any genetic explanations as to why aggression may happen. For example, it will discount the trait approach even though studies have shown that there may be an aggressive gene in humans.

According to the aggressive cue hypothesis, when will an aggressive act occur?

Strategies to control aggression

Players can:	Coaches can:
Use cognitive techniques (see page 192): ● mental rehearsal ● imagery ● visualisation ● selective attention ● negative thought-stopping ● positive self-talk Use somatic techniques (see page 191): ● relaxation techniques ● deep breathing ● biofeedback ● count to ten ● walk away ● mantra Displace/channel aggressive feelings by playing hard, e.g. kick the ball harder	● Praise non-aggressive acts ● Highlight non-aggressive role models ● Punish aggression, e.g. substitution/fines ● Use peer pressure to remind each other that aggression is unacceptable ● Set process and performance goals rather than product goals ● Ensure their own behaviour is not aggressive ● Give the performer responsibility within the team ● Ensure the performer understands their specific role

Now test yourself

TESTED

2 Name three cognitive and three somatic strategies to combat aggression.

Answer online

Revision activity

Divide an A3 sheet of paper into four and in each quadrant make a bullet list for each of the four main theories of aggression.

Exam practice

1 What strategies can a coach use to eliminate aggressive actions? [5]

Answer and quick quizzes online

ONLINE

Summary

You should now be able to:
● give clear definitions and examples of aggression and assertion
● explain the instinct, frustration–aggression, aggressive cue and social learning approaches to aggression using the correct terminology

● support your explanations with sporting examples
● outline strategies to control aggression.

6.6 Motivation

Motivation is a person's desire to succeed. It is an individual's drive that inspires them to perform in sport.

Types of motivation

Extrinsic motivation

This is anything received from an outside source. It could be tangible, such as money, trophies or medals, or intangible, such as praise from the coach or crowd.

This type of motivation attracts performers to the sport to begin with and is therefore a useful strategy for cognitive performers. It raises their confidence and increases participation.

However, it should be used sparingly, especially with young performers. They may begin to perform only for the rewards, losing enjoyment and the satisfaction gained from performing. Ultimately for these performers, withdrawing extrinsic rewards can lead to total withdrawal from participation.

Intrinsic motivation

This comes from the performers themselves. They participate for the 'love' of the sport, for self-satisfaction and the pride of achieving their own goals. Developing their health and fitness may be the driving factor. This could be learning to somersault on a trampoline for their own gratification, or a javelin thrower attempting to throw a personal best distance.

This type of motivation will maintain participation for a longer period of time than extrinsic motivational methods.

Coaches should try to encourage performers to set personal goals and to generate intrinsic motivation whenever possible.

What is the difference between extrinsic and intrinsic motivation?

Motivational strategies

A range of strategies should be used to maintain drive in all performers:
- Tangible, extrinsic rewards will initially attract performers and should be given periodically, for example certificates, medals or player of the match awards.
- Intangible extrinsic rewards will increase the confidence of performers, for example praise and positive reinforcement.

- Make the activity fun/enjoyable.
- Set easily achievable tasks to ensure success.
- Use positive role models/significant others that performers can identify with.
- Highlight the health and fitness benefits of participation.
- Use variable practice.
- Generate intrinsic motivation through performance goals, for example beating personal best time in 100 metres.
- Continually set new, challenging goals, just within the reach of performers.
- Punish lack of motivation.
- Use peer group pressure.

Exam practice

1 Which of the following is an example of intrinsic motivation? [1]
   - Receiving a trophy for being voted 'players' player'
   - Praise from your coach for having excellent serving technique
   - Pride in achieving a personal best in the long jump
   - Receiving money for winning a golf tournament

Answer and quick quizzes online

ONLINE

Summary

You should now be able to:
- define motivation
- distinguish between intrinsic and extrinsic motivation and give practical examples.

6.7 Achievement motivation theory

Atkinson's model

Atkinson suggested that in demanding situations performers will exhibit either NACH (need to achieve) or NAF (need to avoid failure) characteristics. This is based on both their personality and the situational factors in hand. It can be defined as the drive to succeed minus the fear of failure.

	NACH performer	NAF performer
Personality characteristics	• Exhibits approach behaviour • Has high self-efficacy/confidence • Enjoys competition and challenges • Will take risks • Sticks with the task until it is complete • Regards failure as a step to success • Welcomes feedback as they use it to improve • Takes personal responsibility for the outcome • Attributes success internally (see attribution, page 181) • Likes an audience when performing	• Exhibits avoidance behaviour • Has low self-efficacy/confidence • Dislikes competition and challenges • Will take the easy option • Gives in easily, especially if failing • Does not welcome feedback • May experience learned helplessness • Attributes failure internally (see attribution, page 181) • Dislikes performing in front of an audience
Situational characteristics	Very competitive – likes tasks with: • a low probability of success, i.e. a challenging task • a high incentive, i.e. they will be extremely proud to have achieved their goal	Not competitive – likes tasks with: • a high probability of success, i.e. an easy task • a low incentive, i.e. they have little satisfaction in achieving their goal
Example	A snowboarder decides to take the risky black off-piste route rather than the easier blue run down the mountain, knowing that she is likely to fall over but seeing it as a challenge.	A mid-table squash player prefers to play opponents from the bottom of the table rather than those near to him in ranking as he is highly likely to win.

What type of competitive situations would a NACH performer prefer?

Achievement goal theory

This theory suggests that every performer will have their own perception of what achievement means to them and what being successful looks like. In specific situations or tasks, individuals can set either outcome-orientated goals or task-orientated goals.

Outcome-orientated goals are set with the specific aim to beat and show superiority over others, for example to win the 5000-metre race. If a performer continually achieves their goal, then motivation and confidence will be high. However, it is unrealistic to expect victory in every sporting encounter and therefore being defeated may reduce confidence.

Task-orientated goals do not seek to measure a person's ability against others. The aim is to master a skill or to improve on your own performance. The process is more important than the outcome, for example to master a somersault on the trampoline or achieve a personal best distance in the hammer throw. Regardless of the result in the hammer competition, the task-orientated goal can be achieved.

To generate approach behaviours:
● ensure success by setting achievable goals
● raise confidence by giving positive reinforcement, praise and rewards.
● highlight successful role models that have comparable characteristics.
● credit internal reasons, e.g. ability, for success.

Revision activity

Create two mind maps – one for NACH and one for NAF. Include personality and situational characteristics.

Exam practice

1 What are the personality characteristics of a performer with a need to avoid failure (NAF) profile? How would a coach develop a need to achieve (NACH) attitude in this performer? (6)

Answer and quick quizzes online

ONLINE

Summary

You should now be able to:
● give the personality and situational characteristics of NACH and NAF performers
● explain the different types of goal in relation to achievement goal theory
● suggest ways to increase approach behaviour in performers.

6.8 Social facilitation and inhibition

Performers react differently to being observed while participating. Some enjoy performing with an audience and as a result their performance improves. This is known as social facilitation and it may well motivate performers.

However, some dislike performing with an audience and their performance worsens when being observed. This is known as social inhibition. These performers might find it stressful to perform with an audience and many lose motivation as they cannot deal with the pressure of being watched.

Zajonc's model

REVISED

Zajonc suggested that four types of 'others' may be present during performance, and these can be categorised as passive or interactive.

Passive others

Passive others do not interact with the performer, but have an effect by simply being present. These include:
- Audience: people present who do not speak but just watch, for example a TV audience, silent observers during a tee-off in golf or a scout turning up unannounced to observe you performing. Their mere presence may make you feel anxious and can affect your performance.
- Co-actors: those who perform the same task at the same time but are not competing against you, for example seeing another cyclist in front of you makes you speed up in order to overtake them. Although you win nothing by doing so, their presence has made you cycle faster.

Interactive others

Interactive others communicate directly with the performer and include:
- Competitive co-actors: the opposition, for example other swimmers in a race who are in direct rivalry with the performer
- social reinforcers: the coach/crowd, for example the spectators at a rugby match cheer and applaud but may also shout abuse at performers. They give you the motivation to improve.

Audience effects

Even when passive others such as an audience are present, the main effect on the performer is that they will experience increased arousal levels. The presence of an audience has varied effects on performance, depending on the skill classification and the performer's level of experience.

Performance will be facilitated if the performer is:
- an expert, as they are used to performing in front of an audience
- performing a simple skill, which requires limited decision making/ information processing
- performing a gross skill of large muscle group movements that does not require precision/accuracy.

In the above circumstances, the performer will be able to cope with the additional arousal caused by the presence of the audience and their performance will improve.

However, performance will be inhibited if the proformer is:
- a novice, as they find performing in front of an audience intimidating
- performing a complex skill, as this requires several decisions to be made and lots of information processing, which may not be carried out successfully at high arousal
- performing a fine skill, as it requires precision and accuracy, which is difficult to maintain at high arousal.

In the above circumstances, the performer cannot cope with the extra arousal, which means their performance will deteriorate.

Now test yourself

TESTED ☐

1 According to Zajonc, what effect would an audience have on a cognitive performer?

Answer online

Dominant response

Drive theory (see page 158) explains the linear relationship between drive and performance. There is a strong link between drive theory and Zajonc's model. At heightened levels of arousal, performers revert back to their dominant response. This is a well-learned skill that the performer will use when under competitive pressure.

If the performer is an expert, they will have overlearned motor programmes stored in their long-term memory and their dominant response is likely to be performed correctly. Therefore, performance will be facilitated. As described earlier, if the response is gross or simple, it will be enhanced.

However, if the performer is a novice, they have not yet grooved their responses. By being under competitive pressure and in the presence of an audience, their performance will be inhibited. Fine or complex skills will deteriorate.

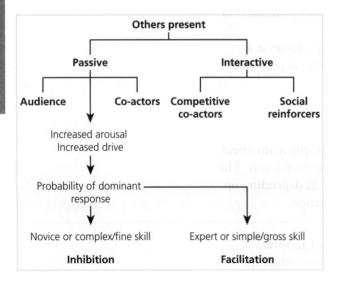

Figure 6.8a Zajonc's model

Evaluation apprehension

Evaluation apprehension is the fear of being judged. The performer may not be actually being judged, but if they *perceive* that they are then this will have an effect on their performance. Other factors causing evaluation apprehension include:

- if the audience is knowledgeable if you will be increasingly nervous, for example if a scout is watching
- if significant others such as parents/peers are present, positive and negative effects are seen based on task/performers, as described above
- if the audience is supportive/abusive, performance will be facilitated/ inhibited
- if the performer naturally has high trait anxiety (see page 162), they will be inhibited by an audience
- if the performer has low self-efficacy, they do not believe in their ability and will be inhibited.

Strategies to combat social inhibition

Key strategies to combat social inhibition include:

- familiarisation training – allow an audience to watch you training/play crowd noise during training
- increase self-efficacy
- practise skills until they are grooved
- use selective attention to improve focus/concentration – block out the crowd and concentrate on the relevant stimuli such as the ball or opposition.

Use other cognitive strategies such as:

- mental rehearsal – going over the performance in your mind will maintain focus and lower arousal levels
- imagery
- positive self-talk
- negative thought-stopping.

In addition, the coach could:

- decrease the importance of the task
- offer encouragement, positive reinforcement and praise to the performer to support them
- slowly introduce evaluation in training.

Exam practice

1 What strategies can a performer use to combat the effects of social inhibition? [5]

Answer and quick quizzes online

Summary

You should now be able to:
- explain each part of Zajonc's model
- define evaluation apprehension and suggest causes for it
- give a range of strategies to combat social inhibition.

6.9 Group dynamics

Group formation

A group is two or more people who:
- interact with each other, i.e. communicate
- share a common goal, i.e. they have the same aim
- have mutual awareness, i.e. they influence and depend on each other
- have a collective identity, e.g. a specific kit that makes them feel they belong.

Tuckman's model

Tuckman suggested that there are four stages that a group goes through in order to begin working together effectively. The time it takes per team will vary, depending on the experience of the players and the size of group.

1 Forming	• Group members initially get together • Roles and responsibilities are unclear • Members start to work together • Members decide if they fit in with the team
2 Storming	• Many teams fail at this stage as there is conflict • Relationships can be strained • Competition for positions/roles • Boundaries are pushed – positions of authority are challenged • Goal is unclear or questioned
3 Norming	• Conflicts are resolved • Goal is clarified • Greater commitment to achieving goals • Authority figures are respected • Appreciation of team mates' strengths • Group cohesion develops – both task and social
4 Performing	• Players interact effectively • Full commitment to achieving team goals • Individual roles and responsibilities are completely understood

Now test yourself

1 According to Tuckman's model, what are the four stages of group development?

Answer online

Group cohesion

A cohesive team has unity and a structure, and all members pull together in order to reach their shared aim. The more cohesive a team is, the more successful it will be; the more successful the team is, the more cohesive it becomes. The one causes the other!

There are two types of cohesion, and the most effective groups show both:

- Task cohesion is when group members work in unity to meet a common aim. They may not socialise away from the team and may not share views. However, in order to achieve their potential in the sporting arena they come together and can get good results. This is important in interactive sports, for example football and volleyball, where the team members must work together and rely on each other's timing and co-ordination to achieve.
- Social cohesion is when group members get along and feel attached to others. They communicate and support each other both inside and outside the sporting arena. This is important in more co-active sports, where you perform individually but your effort contributes to a whole team performance, e.g. the Davis Cup in tennis or in a swimming team.

Task and social cohesion are reasons for being attracted to the group. Perhaps the other members share your goal of wanting to win, but also your friends may be part of the team which makes you want to join. Also you integrate within the group to work effectively with others, in order to achieve your goal and to attempt to get along socially with the other members.

Carron's antecedents

Carron suggested that there are four factors or antecedent that affect task and social cohesion. These factors can bring a team together, making the team more effective, stable and satisfied.

They include:

- personal: level of motivation shown, how satisfied you feel within the group and if you share individual characteristics such as age, gender, ability etc.
- environmental: whether a player has a contract or scholarship, their location, age, and the size of the group
- leadership: leadership style, and relationships between the leader and group members
- team: the stability of the group, common experiences in victory and defeat, common will to win.

Revision activity

Use the mnemonic 'PELT' to help you remember Carron's antecedents.

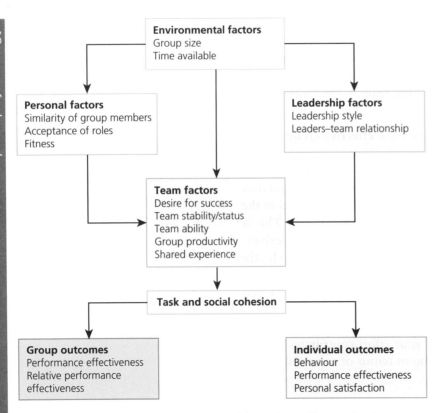

Figure 6.9a **Carron's antecedents and how they affect cohesion**

Steiner's model of group performance

REVISED

Steiner proposed that the results of group effort could be based on an equation that sums up the influences on cohesion:

Actual productivity = Potential productivity − Losses due to faulty processes

- Actual productivity is the team's level of achievement in a specific task, for example a netball team reaching the semi-final of a cup competition.
- Potential productivity is the team's best possible level of achievement when it is cohesive, for example the netball team could have won the cup competition.
- Losses due to faulty processes are the things that go wrong, including the co-ordination and motivation problems the team faces. These losses reduce the level of cohesion and therefore lower the actual productivity. For example, the arousal and motivation levels of some team members were lower than expected and therefore the team did not reach/win the cup final.

Steiner suggested that teams face many problems which affect their productivity, including:
- co-ordination problems, such as team members failing to communicate properly with each other, resulting in poor timing and set plays breaking down
- team members failing to understand their role in the team
- lack of understanding of tactics or strategies set by the coach
- the Ringlemann effect (see next page)
- motivation losses, such as team members withdrawing effort when training and/or playing
- social loafing (see next page).

The Ringelmann effect

The Ringelmann effect and social loafing are both faulty processes which have a detrimental effect on the cohesion and attainment of a team.

The Ringelmann effect was suggested after a tug-of-war experiment showed that eight participants failed to pull eight times as hard as a single participant. Ringelmann's study therefore found that as the number of people in the group increases, the level of performance of individuals in the group decreases. For example, a rugby union player performs much better when playing in a seven-a-side tournament than when playing in a full fifteen-a-side game.

It was suggested that the reduction in performance in the tug-of-war was due to the lack of co-ordination, i.e. the participants were not all pulling on the rope in unison. However, follow-up studies showed that it may be due to a reduction in motivation rather than a loss of co-ordination.

Social loafing

Social loafing is when a performer lowers the level of effort they contribute to the team because they believe that they are not a valued member of the group and their input is not noticed, so they stop trying. If the coach does not praise you when you feel you have played well, you will, eventually give up. Other factors that may cause performers to loaf include:

- no clear role within the group, e.g. being unsure of their position within the team
- low self-efficacy/confidence, e.g. believing that they are not good enough; they may be experiencing learned helplessness
- team mates not trying so you also stop putting in effort, e.g. your winger fails to chase a ball which goes into touch, so you think 'why should I bother?'
- the coach and/or captain are poor leaders; they do not provide encouragement and/or use weak strategies
- experiencing high levels of trait/state anxiety
- carrying an injury, e.g. you twisted an ankle in training, therefore you decide not to bother reaching to return wide serves in tennis
- experiencing social inhibition as a result of an offensive crowd.

Strategies to improve team performance

By improving cohesion, making individuals feel valued and reducing faulty processes – for example social loafing – within a team the coach can improve individual and whole-team performance.

Methods include:

- highlighting individual performances, e.g. giving statistics such as shots on target/tackles assists.

- giving specific roles/responsibilities within the team
- developing social cohesion, e.g. team-building exercises, tours and encouraging friendship.
- praising/rewarding cohesive behaviour, e.g. encouragement when performers work as a team
- raising individuals' confidence
- encouraging group identity, e.g. have a set kit.
- ensuring effective leadership that matches the preferred style of the group
- selecting players who work well together rather than individual 'stars'
- setting achievable process/performance goals rather than outcome team goals
- continually emphasising the team goal
- selecting players who are less likely to social loaf
- punishing social loafing
- grooving set plays/completing vast amounts of co-ordination practice
- training with an audience present.

Now test yourself

TESTED

3 What is Steiner's model of group performance?

Answer online

Revision activity

Complete a copy of the table below.

Reason for social loafing	Strategy to overcome
	Coach ensures everyone understands their position and responsibilities
Injured	
	Remind them of past successes and praise them
Experiencing social inhibition	
	Performer tries mental rehearsals and breathing control

Exam practice

1 What is social loafing? Suggest reasons why some performers might experience this. [5]

Answer and quick quizzes online

ONLINE

Summary

You should now be able to:
- describe what a group/team is and how it is formed
- describe the various aspects of the Steiner model
- discuss task and social cohesion and give clear examples
- describe the causes of the Ringelmann effect and social loafing and explain what a coach can do to try to eliminate these.
- give strategies to improve team performance.

6.10 Importance of goal setting

Benefits of goal setting

Psychological research has shown that setting goals has a positive effect on performance. Generally, performers who set goals are more committed, maintain participation and are more task persistent.
The benefits of setting goals include:
- giving the performer an aim or focus
- increasing motivation when the goal is accomplished
- increasing confidence levels
- controlling arousal/anxiety levels
- focusing efforts in training and game situations.

Types of goal

- Task-orientated goals do not seek to measure a person's ability against others. The aim is to master a skill or to improve on your own performance. The process is more important than the outcome, for example to achieve a personal best time in a 10 km race. Regardless of the place the performer came in the race, their goal can be achieved.
- Process goals are relatively short-term goals set to improve technique, for example a speed skater aims to improve their cross-over technique.
- Performance goals are intermediate goals often set against yourself to improve performance from last time, for example to get a faster time than in the last competition.
- Outcome (product) goals are long-term goals reached after extensive work. They are often set against others and are based on the outcome, for example to win the short track junior championships.

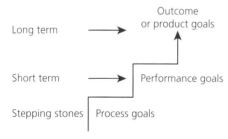

Figure 6.10a **Goal-setting summary**

Define process, performance and outcome goals.

Principles of effective goal setting

When setting goals, the SMARTER principle should be followed:

	Explanation	Example
Specific	The goal must be clear and exact. It should reflect a performer's individual playing position or event.	A full back in rugby aims to improve the number of high ball catches he successfully completes when in his own 22-metre area by 5%.
Measurable	The goal must be quantifiable so progress can be assessed.	A GA in netball aims to achieve an 80% shot success rate.
Achievable	The performer must be able to achieve their goal within the time frame set.	You and your coach both decide to reduce your 400-metre time by 2 seconds.
Realistic	The goal must be within the performer's reach from where they are now, in order to ensure sustained effort and motivation. If the target set is insurmountable, it may cause distress/anxiety.	Aim to run 10 kilometres in under 55 minutes in the road race in 12 months' time.
Time – phased	A set period must be stated clearly in order for progress to be tracked and to sustain motivation.	Perform a personal best time in the 100-metre freestyle by the end of next month.
Evaluate	The coach and performer should gauge whether or not the goal was achieved and the reasons for any progress made – positive or negative. The effective strategies can then be used when setting future goals.	The coach and performer check times and realise that she did not manage to reduce her personal best 100-metre time by 0.5 seconds within the given time frame. The coach realises that more time should have been allocated to improving the sprint start.
Re-do	The performer should repeat their efforts for any goals that have not been met. Following the evaluation, the coach and/or performer might decide to adjust the goal to ensure success.	The coach and performer decide to adjust the goal to reduce personal best time by 0.3 seconds and will spend more training time focused on the sprint start.

Exam practice

1 What are the benefits of goal setting? [4]

Answer and quick quizzes online

ONLINE

Revision activity

Using each component of the SMARTER principle, set goals in your sport.

Summary

You should now be able to:
- understand that goal setting is a key part of mental preparation and important to develop confidence, concentration and emotional control
- describe the types of goals
- understand that goals do not always have to measure performance against others as this may cause stress on the performer
- know that process/performance goals are equally, if not more, important and be able to give examples
- be able to refer to goal setting in terms of achievement motivation
- describe the SMARTER principle used for setting effective goals.

6.11 Attribution theory

Weiner's model

Attribution theory tells us how individuals explain their behaviour. In a sporting context, performers use attributions to offer reasons for winning or playing well, or reasons for losing or playing badly.

Weiner suggested that four key attributions lie on two dimensions:

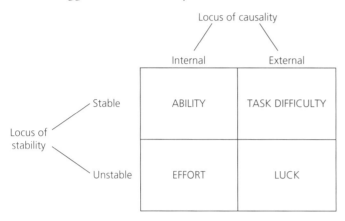

Figure 6.11a **Weiner's model of attribution**

The locus of causality describes where the performer places the reason for the win/loss:

- Internal – winning or losing was within the performer's control, e.g. it was due to the amount of natural ability they possess or the amount of effort they put into training.
- External – winning or losing was out of the performer's control and under the control of the environment, e.g. the task difficulty in terms of the level of opposition they faced, or luck, which relates to the decisions made by the officials or environmental factors such as an unlucky ball bounce.

The stability dimension describes how fixed the attributions are:

- Stable – the reason is relatively permanent, e.g. the ability (internal, stable) of the performer remains the same over a long period of time, as does the task difficulty (external, stable), which is the ability of the opposition.
- Unstable or very changeable – this change could be from week to week or even within minutes in a fixture, e.g. the effort (internal, unstable) shown to chase down a ball may be higher when winning at the beginning of the match than the effort shown towards the end of the same match when losing. Luck (external, unstable) is also very changeable, e.g. the tennis ball hitting the top of the net and bouncing either on your side or the opposition's side is down to luck.

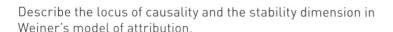

Describe the locus of causality and the stability dimension in Weiner's model of attribution.

Link between attribution, task persistence and motivation

REVISED

Attributions can be used to ensure that even when individuals or teams lose, they keep trying to improve and do not just give up. The locus of causality tells us that we have control of effort, for example, and therefore if we put more effort into training sessions we may well be victorious in the future. Similarly, if we attribute success to high ability or to the amount of effort we put into a match, then we may well see success in a similar task in the future. In addition, the stability dimension tells us that things can change, for example a 50/50 decision went against us today, but in future fixtures with a different official the decision could go the other way. Attributing in this way can help performers to understand the need to practise, persevere and stay motivated – to be task persistent.

Both performers and coaches should attribute the reasons for winning internally to ability and effort (rather than externally to luck), and failure should be attributed externally rather than internally to ability. This is known as self-serving bias. This will raise self-efficacy and esteem and increase the likelihood of an individual continuing to participate.

Learned helplessness

REVISED

Learned helplessness develops when performers attribute failure internally to stable reasons, for example I lost the swimming race as I simply do not have the stamina (ability). They believe that no matter what they do or how hard they try, they are destined to fail and therefore are not persistent. This can be either general, relating to all sports (*for example*, I cannot play any sport) or specific, relating to one skill in sport (for example, I cannot take penalty flicks in hockey as I will miss) or to a single sport (for example, I cannot play badminton). This usually occurs when performers have low self-confidence due to past failings and so they completely withdraw their effort and stop participating. It may be due to having unrealistic goals set by the coach. Learned helpless performers share similar characteristics with NAF performers; if their attributions remain unchanged, it is likely that they will not participate in sporting activity, as they have such low self-esteem relating to sport.

Now test yourself

TESTED

2 What are the causes of learned helplessness?

Answer online

Strategies to avoid learned helplessness, leading to improvements in performance

In order to reduce the effects of learned helplessness, the performer should change their negative attributions into positive ones. This process is known has attribution retraining. The performer's perception of why they have failed is altered – they attribute success to external factors such as luck, or to controllable factors such as effort, which they know they can improve on. Success is attributed internally to ability; the performer knows that they have what is necessary to repeat the victory in the future.

In addition to this, the coach can:
- set realistic/achievable process and/or performance goals
- raise self-efficacy by using Bandura's model
- highlight previous successful performances
- give positive reinforcement and encouragement.

Revision activity

Make a list of the reasons why you have won/lost fixtures before. Use Weiner's model and categorise them as ability, effort, task difficulty or luck.

Exam practice

1 What is learned helplessness and what can a coach do to combat the effects of it? [5]

Answer and quick quizzes online

ONLINE

Summary

You should now be able to:
- understand all aspects of Weiner's model
- draw and label Weiner's model
- explain the locus of causality and the stability dimension
- understand the link between the attributions given by a performer, how task persistent they are and their level of motivation
- explain and give examples of:
  - self-serving bias
  - general and specific learned helplessness
  - attributional retraining
- describe the strategies coaches can employ to avoid learned helplessness in their performers.

6.12 Self-efficacy and confidence

As a performer, you may be generally confident in all sports. This is known as trait sports confidence, which is a performer's natural confidence levels, for example they are a generally confident performer and will show this in all sporting situations. However, some performers are only confident in specific tasks, sports or situations. This is known as state sports confidence or **self-efficacy** and is directly linked to positive past experiences, for example they are confident that they will score as they have kicked many conversions successfully before.

> **Self-efficacy:** the amount of confidence you have in a specific task, sport or situation.

Bandura's self-efficacy theory

REVISED

Self-efficacy is specific rather than general and varies in different circumstances. Bandura suggested that four factors can influence the level of self-efficacy shown by a performer. By addressing these factors, coaches/teachers can raise the performer's self-esteem, resulting in a more positive, successful performance and increased task persistence.

A young gymnast is experiencing fear when asked to perform on a full-height beam. To increase her self-efficacy, the coach should use the four factors described in the table below.

> **Typical mistake**
>
> Read the question very carefully. Students often write about Bandura's social learning theory when asked about self-efficacy. Bandura has a range of theories – check which one the question is asking about!

Factor	Description	Example
Performance accomplishments	Self-efficacy is affected by past experiences. The coach should therefore remind the performer of past success in similar situations.	Remind the gymnast that she was brilliant on the lower beam and that she did not fall off. The width of the full-height beam is the same, so she is equally unlikely to fall.
Vicarious experiences	The coach should ask a performer who shares characteristics with the gymnast (e.g. ability, gender or age) to show that the task is possible for them to achieve also, thereby increasing self-efficacy.	Ask a gymnast of a similar age and standard to perform on the full-height beam. The young gymnast will feel 'if they can do it, so can I'.
Verbal persuasion	Giving praise and positive reinforcement increases self-efficacy. Significant others should be used to enhance this.	The coach and friends of the gymnast persuade her that they believe she can perform well on the full-height beam.
Emotional arousal	The coach should show the performer how to cope with and control their arousal levels. This may include both cognitive and somatic strategies. Often a performer perceives they are unable to meet the demands of the task.	The coach tells the performer to use mental rehearsal to go over the moves on the full-height beam in her mind before mounting. This will allow her to focus and lower her arousal levels.

Vealey's model of sports confidence

Athletes who have high sports confidence in one sporting situation will feel more confident in their ability to succeed in others.

Vealey suggested that the performer will undertake the task (objective sporting situation), such as taking a conversion in rugby, with a certain amount of:

- trait sports confidence (SC–trait) – their natural, innate confidence levels, e.g. they are a generally confident performer in a range of sports
- state sports confidence (SC–state) – their level of confidence in this situation (self-efficacy) based on past experience, e.g. they are confident that they will score as they have kicked many conversions before
- competitiveness orientation – how driven the performer is and the types of goal they may have set themselves, for example the kicker is very motivated to succeed and has set himself the performance goal of kicking 90 per cent of his attempts.

The performer produces the response (for example attempts the conversion) and considers the subjective outcomes. If they perceive the outcome as being a positive result (for example they successfully kick the conversion), then the level of general SC–trait and specific SC–state will increase. This will further the chances of approach behaviour being shown in other situations. A successful attempt will also increase the level of competitiveness orientation shown by the performer. For example, the kicker becomes even more motivated and sets himself a new goal of a 95 per cent success rate. A negative outcome will lower trait and state confidence along with competitiveness and may lead to future avoidance behaviour and an inactive lifestyle.

> **Exam tip**
>
> If you find it difficult to explain Vealey's model, try using the example of a penalty and work your way through the boxes, describing each as you go.

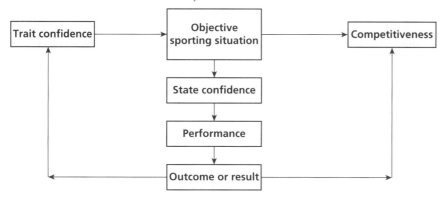

Figure 6.12a **Vealey's model of sports confidence**

Define SC–trait, SC–state and competiveness orientation.

Home-field advantage

REVISED

Home-field advantage suggests that performers usually perform better when playing at home, as they have a large number of supporters present and are familiar with the venue. This keeps the level of uncertainty, and therefore arousal, low. The influence of the home crowd and familiar venue can increase confidence – often more home games are won than away fixtures. The larger and more supportive the crowd is, the greater the effect on the performer's confidence. If the audience is very close to the playing area, home-field advantage is even more important. In basketball, for example, seating is very close to the court.

However, there can be some negative effects, which can reduce confidence. This might happen during the later stages of a competition when the home crowds expect a win. If the team is losing, the home crowd can become hostile. The pressure may be extremely high and can cause social inhibition.

Strategies to develop high levels of self-efficacy

REVISED

A coach can use all aspects of Bandura's model:
- Point out when the performer succeeded previously.
- Ask one of the performer's peers to demonstrate the skill to show them that they can do it too.
- Give praise and positive reinforcement.
- Use cognitive and somatic strategies to control the performer's arousal and anxiety levels.
- Allow success in training, then gradually increase the difficulty of the task.
- Set achievable process and performance goals.
- Attribute success internally.

> **Revision activity**
>
> Use the abbreviations PA, VE, VP, EA (see table on page 184) to help you to remember Bandura's model of self-efficacy. Think of a skill in your sport and describe how you would use each part of the model to raise the self-efficacy of a young performer trying to groove the skill.

Exam practice

1 Using Bandura's model, explain how a coach could increase self-efficacy by using performance accomplishments and vicarious experiences. Give practical examples to illustrate your answer. [4]

Answer and quick quizzes online

ONLINE

Summary

You should now be able to:
- understand the four key components of Bandura's model and give clear examples
- understand Vealey's model
- explain ways that a coach could raise self-efficacy in their team.

6.13 Leadership

Characteristics of effective leaders

REVISED

Effective leaders are often ambitious, have a clear vision or goal and have the ability to motivate others to achieve that goal.

Leaders often show other characteristics, including being:
- an effective communicator
- charismatic
- knowledgeable about the sport/skilful
- empathetic
- confident
- flexible.

> **Exam tip**
>
> Qualities of a good leader is an easy starter question, so make sure you can give a range of answers to access several points on the mark scheme.

Prescribed and emergent leaders

REVISED

Prescribed leaders are chosen from outside the group. For example, national governing bodies appoint national team managers. They often bring new ideas to the group but can cause disagreements if the group members are opposed to the appointment.

Emergent leaders are selected from within the existing group, often as they are nominated by the other group members. For example, a Sunday-league football team votes the previous season's 'players' player' as the new captain. There is already a high level of respect for this person, but as they have had the same experiences as the other team members, they may not be able to bring any new strategies to enable the team to progress.

What is the difference between a prescribed leader and an emergent leader?

Styles of leadership

REVISED

Leadership style	Features	When to use	Example
Autocratic/task-orientated	• Dictatorial • Only interested in ensuring the task is fulfilled • Sole decision maker	• In dangerous situations • With large groups • If time is limited • With hostile groups • With cognitive performers • Preferred by male performers	A basketball coach calls a time out towards the end of a match and instructs the players to run a specific set play in the remaining seconds as he has decided it is the most effective strategy.

| Democratic/ social-orientated | • Interested in ensuring relationships are developed within the group
• Group members are involved in making decisions | • With small groups
• If lots of time available
• With friendly groups
• With advanced performers
• Preferred by female performers | A doubles tennis coach spends time with the players discussing which strategies are best to use in their upcoming fixture. He takes on board their suggestions before making a final decision. |
| Laissez-faire | • Leader is more of a figurehead than an active leader; they take a hands-off approach
• Group members make all of the decisions | • If a problem-solving approach is required
• Only effective with advanced performers | A football manager allows the team to decide which skills/drills to work on during their training sessions. |

Revision activity

Create a revision card for each leadership style. On one side write the type and on the other side write the features of the style and when you would use it. Ask a friend to test you!

Now test yourself

TESTED

2 What leadership style would be most appropriate when teaching a novice group of rock climbers?

Answer online

Typical mistake

Questions on the style of leadership are often confused with theories of leadership or vice versa.

Theories of leadership

REVISED

Fiedler's contingency model

Fiedler suggested an interactionist approach, in which an effective leader will match their style with the situation facing them. One of two leadership styles should be adopted:

- A task-orientated leader is mainly concerned with achieving goals and takes a pragmatic approach to get thing done. They are very direct and authoritarian. This style should be used in both most- and least-favourable situations.
- A person-orientated leader focuses on developing harmony and good relationships within the group. They are open to suggestions and take more of a democratic approach. This style should be used in moderately favourable situations.

Exam tip

Make sure you use the correct terminology when describing Fiedler's model – 'task-orientated' not 'autocratic' and 'person-orientated' rather than 'democratic'.

The favourableness of the situation dictates which leadership style should be adopted:

- In the most-favourable situations, the leader is in a strong position of authority and has the respect of the group, the members have good relationships with each other and the task is clear. For example, a team which has played together for a number of years under the same captain and whose members have good relationships with one another may have a number of set plays rehearsed. When the captain calls the play, they are all aware of what should happen and complete the move immediately. In this situation, a task-orientated approach would work best to complete the task effectively.

- In the least-favourable situations, the leader has no power or respect from the group, there may be infighting in the group and hostility towards the leader, with the task being unclear. For example, an unpopular caretaker manager is placed in charge of a team. The team members may not show the new leader any respect. The new leader is unclear as to what is needed to motivate the team and what strategies to employ. In this situation, a task-orientated approach would also need to be used.
- In moderately favourable situations, the leader would choose a person-orientated style which allows other team members to contribute to the decision-making process. The leader would have some power/respect, there would be some good relationships and parts of the task would be clear. For example, two new players join a netball team. The whole team discusses which positions are best for them.

Task-orientated leadership is used effectively with cognitive performers, large groups, when time is limited and in dangerous situations. Males also prefer this style.

Person-orientated leadership is used effectively with advanced performers, smaller groups, when large amounts of time are available and when tasks are not dangerous. Females prefer this style.

Chelladurai's multi-dimensional model of leadership

Chelladurai suggests that in order to ensure group satisfaction and high levels of performance, leaders must be able to adapt their leadership style. He suggests the leader gets the best from their team if the leadership style 'fits' with what the situation and the team need.

Leaders should consider three factors before adopting a specific leadership style:
- Situation, e.g. the strength of the opponents or if there is any danger involved. For example, learning to trampoline is dangerous and requires an autocratic approach.
- Leader, e.g. their ability, personality and preferred leadership style. For example, the leader is highly experienced and prefers to use an autocratic style.
- Group, e.g. ability levels and relationships between members and with the leader. For example, the group members are cognitive performers and therefore need to be given direct instructions about how to perform moves on the trampoline bed.

The leadership style is also affected by the following:
- Required behaviour or what the situation demands – a dangerous task such as trampolining would require an autocratic rather than a democratic approach, in order to maintain safety levels.
- Actual behaviour or what style and approach the leader decides to take in a given situation – this is based on their own ability. For example, the leader considers all the factors and decides to adopt an autocratic style of leadership
- Preferred behaviour or what style of leadership the team members would like best, based on their own experiences and characteristics such as ability. For example, the group likes the autocratic approach as they find it straight forward to develop their basic skills and can therefore move onto more difficult skills quickly.

Once these factors have been considered, the leader must try to balance their style of leadership with each of them in order to gain the highest level of performance and satisfaction from the group. The more the leader's actual behaviour matches (known as congruence) what the group wants and what the situation needs, the better the performance will be. In the example given above (trampolining), the leader decides to use the autocratic style. As this matches what the group likes and what the situation needs, there is a greater chance that the group will be satisfied and performance levels will be high.

Revision activity

Many students find the Chelladurai model difficult. Try working backwards through the model in order to explain it, describing each component and what it means. Use the same example at each stage.

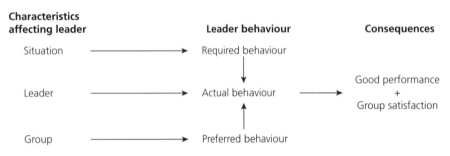

Figure 6.13a Chelladurai's model of leadership

Now test yourself

TESTED

3 In terms of the situation, group and leader, what should be taken into consideration before beginning to lead a group?

Answer online

Exam practice

1 Fiedler states that the favourableness of the situation dictates which leadership style should be used. What are the characteristics of an unfavourable situation and what style of leadership does Fiedler suggest should be used? [5]

Answer and quick quizzes online

ONLINE

Summary

You should now be able to:
- describe the qualities of a good leader
- give clear descriptions and examples of the various leadership styles
- explain Fiedler's model
- explain Chelladurai's model, giving a clear example throughout.

6.14 Stress management

Stress can be defined as an individual's physical response to prepare the body for action when a threat is perceived. Unlike anxiety, stress is not always negative. Individuals react differently; one person's **stressor** might be another person's motivator:

- Eustress is used to describe positive responses to stressful situations. The performer rises to the challenge they are facing, feels confident and is motivated to complete the task. Performance can be facilitated.
- Distress is used to describe negative responses to stressful situations. The performer finds the stressor threatening and difficult to cope with. Performance can be inhibited.

There may be cognitive or somatic responses to stressors:

- Somatic responses to stressful situations are physiological, for example increases in heart rate, blood pressure, sweating, adrenaline production and muscle tension.
- Cognitive responses to stressful situations are psychological, for example anxiety, irrational/negative thoughts, reduced concentration/ attentional narrowing and poor decision making.

> **Stressor:** the cause of a stressful response, for example playing in an important competitive situation (final or semi-final), sustaining an injury, being fouled/injured, perception that you are playing badly/letting the team down, fatigue or climate.

What is the difference between eustress and distress?

Stress management techniques

REVISED

Somatic strategies

- Biofeedback – using equipment, e.g. heart rate monitors reading bpm, to generate physiological data. The data can show which sporting situations cause the most stress and which strategies are the most effective for them, as heart rate etc. will reduce. These strategies are very effective but time-consuming. Using equipment during performance can distract athletes and increase anxiety levels as they are aware they are being monitored.
- Progressive muscular relaxation – concentrating on each muscle group in turn. By tensing, holding and then relaxing each group, the performer begins to relax.
- Breathing control – by controlling and concentrating on the rate and depth of breathing, the performer becomes less distracted and is able to focus on the task.
- Centring – used alongside controlled breathing, this is useful during breaks in performance, e.g. during time-outs or at the end of a tennis set. Concentrate fully on your body (often the centre, i.e. your belly-button region) and breathe in. As you breathe out, chant a word or phrase describing how you wish to perform – strong, focused, calm etc. By doing this, you maintain focus on yourself and any negative thoughts are disregarded.

- Warm-up – traditionally the warm-up focused on preparing the body through a session including cardiovascular work, stretching and sport-specific skills and drills. However, the psychological importance of the warm-up should not be underestimated. It controls arousal and allows the performer to achieve a state of readiness, fully concentrate using selective attention, and adopt the correct attentional style. A warm-up reduces the chance of attending to incorrect environmental cues and therefore reduces stress and anxiety. Cognitive strategies, e.g. imagery, should form part of the warm-up in order to mentally review skills and tactics.

Cognitive strategies

- Psychological skills training describes an individualised programme that regularly and methodically utilises a range of mental training strategies. This will be tailor-made for the performer and will take into consideration their specific sport, and position within the sport, as well as their current psychological condition. As a result, athletes are more successful and demonstrate increased confidence and motivation, improved focus and lower stress.
- Mental rehearsal involves going over the performance in your mind before the action begins, e.g. seeing all the subroutines of the triple jump without moving.
- Visualisation – when you perform a skill successfully in training, you lock in the mental image of it. This is then re-lived in the competitive situation. It can be internal (e.g. visualising a successful smash shot and how it 'feels' kinaesthetically) or external (e.g. visualising your successful slam dunk as if seen by a spectator on TV).
- Imagery involves recalling a successful previous performance, using all the senses including kinaesthesis to recreate the feeling of success, e.g. remembering how the serve felt when you hit an ace. This can also be internal or external.
- Positive self-talk is verbally reminding yourself of the key points of the movement and telling yourself that you can achieve. For example, a Rugby League player taking a conversion will talk himself through the run-up, contact and follow-through. He will tell himself that he can take the points. He might also have a mantra or saying that he continually repeats.
- Negative thought-stopping is often used with the above. A tennis player whose first serve is letting them down and who begins to think, 'I cannot hit one in' should replace that thought with 'I can and I will hit the next one in'.
- Attentional control and cue utilisation – Easterbrook's cue utilisation hypothesis links a performer's ability to sustain focus on the correct cues in the environment with their level of arousal. At low levels of arousal the performer is not stimulated enough and takes in a large number of environmental cues. They are unable to distinguish what the relevant cues are and can become confused, reducing performance levels. At high levels of arousal, the performer takes in a very small number of cues as they are excessively stimulated and may begin to panic. The correct cues are missed, again reducing performance levels. At moderate levels of arousal, the performer filters out the irrelevant cues and focuses only on the relevant cues. This lowers the level of stress that the performer is experiencing and allows them to complete the task to the highest level.

Revision activity

Guess the strategy! Write each strategy on a sticky note. Place them face down and shuffle. With a partner, take it in turns to select one and stick it to your forehead without looking at it. Your partner has to describe the strategy to you without naming it.

Nideffer's model of attentional focus

Nideffer suggested that different activities require different types of attentional focus. For example, invasion games often require a broad focus, whereas net/wall games usually often require a more narrow style. Performers are required to apply a variety of attentional styles, with the best athletes being able to switch from one style to another. Having attentional focus and the correct attentional style will reduce the level of stress experienced by the performer and therefore performance is improved.

There are two dimensions of attentional focus:
- Broad–Narrow is concerned with how many cues are being focused on. Broad is many cues, while narrow is one/two.
- Internal–External is concerned with where the focus is being placed. Internal is the thoughts and feelings of the performer; external is focus on the environmental cues.

Four attentional styles arise from this:
- Broad–Internal: many cues concerning the performer, for example a footballer planning their team strategies/next set piece
- Narrow–Internal: one/two cues concerning the performer, often used to calm nerves, for example a swimmer mentally rehearsing the sound of the starter signal and subsequent dive into the pool
- Broad–External: many cues in the environment, for example a centre player in netball focusing on many team mates whom she might pass to
- Narrow–External: one/two cues in the environment, for example a basketballer focusing on the net during a free throw.

Describe the two dimensions of attentional focus according to Nideffer.

Exam practice

1 Explain how performers can utilise somatic and cognitive techniques to manage their stress. [6]

Answer and quick quizzes online

Summary

You should now be able to:
- explain the various somatic and cognitive strategies used for stress management
- fully describe and apply clear examples to explain Nideffer's model of attentional focus.

7.1 Concepts of physical activity and sport

When observing or watching people taking part in physical activity, you might notice a number of different features (i.e. **characteristics**). For example, at one end of the 'continuum' there might be a relaxed/fun atmosphere evident, as opposed to a more serious attitude when watching top sports performers.

Sporting development continuum

Different forms of physical activity can be viewed on a **sporting development continuum**, with the 'foundation level' being the first introduction to physical activity/sport (for example at grass roots level in primary school PE programmes). This is followed by the 'participation level', with its emphasis on fun, socialising and developing friendships; it involves participating in a recreational, relaxed manner. More dedicated, focused individuals can reach the 'performance level', where there is a commitment to regular involvement in sport and an emphasis on winning.

Characteristics of physical recreation

Physical recreation can be defined as the active aspect of leisure. Leisure is free time, which can be spent actively or passively.

The following is a list summarising a number of characteristics commonly associated with physical recreation:

- It is fun, enjoyable, non-serious and informal in nature, so winning is not important.
- It is physically energetic, i.e. it involves effort being applied to physical activity.
- Participating is a matter of choice; it is voluntary and up to you whether you take part or not in the free time you have available.
- It tends to involve adults at the **participation level** of the sporting development continuum.
- It is flexible in nature, so how long you take part for and the rules being followed can be adjusted by participants as they wish.
- It is self-officiated/self-regulated (i.e. any decisions during activities are made by the participants themselves).

> **Characteristics:** key features used to identify a particular concept (e.g. fun/enjoyment in physical recreation or a serious attitude in sport).
>
> **Sporting development continuum:** participation in different forms of physical activity at various stages of development. For example, grass roots 'foundation level' in primary school PE or 'participation level' involvement as an adult in physical recreation.
>
> **Participation level:** taking part in physical activity recreationally, with enjoyment as a key motivator.

Now test yourself

1 Identify the characteristics of physical recreation.

Answer online

Functions of physical recreation

The functions of physical recreation can be looked at in terms of positive outcomes for individuals, as well as how society can benefit if more people increase their physical activity levels and recreation.

Regular participation in physical recreation increases an individual's health and fitness and helps in the development of physical skills (e.g. improvement of a golf swing). It provides individuals with a challenge which, if they overcome it, will lead to a sense of achievement and increased levels of self-esteem and self-confidence. Recreation can provide a chance to refresh oneself and it can act as a stress relief from work, helping individuals to relax. Involvement in physical recreation can help people to socialise and meet up with friends (for example as members of a regular circuit training class at a leisure centre). As recreation takes place in a relaxed atmosphere, it provides people with a sense of fun and enjoyment. For many, it helps ensure participation in physical activity for as many years as possible, well into later life, as the emphasis is on taking part at your own level and pace, rather than trying to beat others.

Participation in physical recreation provides a number of benefits to society, including:
- decreasing strain on the NHS as a result of improved health and fitness
- decreasing crime levels as a result of more positive use of free time
- improving community morale and cohesion as a result of different groups participating together
- economic benefits via increased leisure spend and more job opportunities in the active leisure industry.

Explain the benefits to society of increasing participation in physical recreation.

Characteristics of sport

REVISED

Sport can be viewed as a serious and/or competitive experience and can be identified by a number of key features (characteristics), including the following:
- It is highly structured and has set/strict rules (e.g. set time limits and boundaries).
- It involves the use of specialist equipment/set kit.
- Officials are present who are trained or appointed by national governing bodies to enforce the rules.
- Strategies and tactics are involved to try to outwit opponents and win.
- Rewards are received as a result of success, which can be extrinsic rewards such as medals/trophies or intrinsic rewards such as gaining personal satisfaction from your performance.
- High skill levels/high prowess are visible in sporting performance.
- High levels of commitment and/or strict training are involved to maintain and improve fitness and skill levels.
- It is serious and competitive (i.e. winning is important).

Serious/competitive — 'win at all costs' attitude or sportsmanship (*how?*)

Prowess — high skill levels, particularly by professionals (*who?*)

Organised — sport has rules/regulations (*how?*)

Rewards — available for winning (extrinsic) and intrinsic satisfaction (*why?*)

Time and space restrictions apply (*when?/where?*)

Figure 7.1a Key characteristics of SPORT

Functions of sport

REVISED

Taking part in sport has a number of important functions for individuals, as well as society in general. These are similar in many ways to the functions of physical recreation.

For individuals:
● Sport can help improve health and fitness and physical skill levels. Self-confidence often increases as a result of skill improvement and success, which can lead to a feel-good factor for participants.
● Sport often provides increased social opportunities, for example the chance to communicate, socialise and work as part of a team and make friends at sports clubs.
● Participation in sport can help develop positive sporting morals and attitudes, such as fair play and sportsmanship, which can influence a person's general behaviour and keep them out of trouble through positive use of their free time.

The benefits of sports participation for society can be remembered via three 'S' factors and three 'E' factors:
● **S**train on the NHS is reduced as levels of obesity decline etc.
● **S**ocial control is increased as individuals make more positive use of free time.
● **S**ocial integration is increased, along with community cohesion/morale, via increased joint participation in sport by different socio-economic and ethnic groups.
● **E**mployment opportunities increase (e.g. via employment as sports coaches, fitness trainers etc.).
● **E**conomic benefits result as people pay to participate and spend money on new equipment and the latest fashionable kit.
● **E**quality of opportunity is achieved via 'sports participation for all'.

Now test yourself

3 Sport has an emphasis on winning, with high rewards at stake for elite-level performers. Identify other characteristics of sport.

Answer online

TESTED

Revision activity

Draw a spider diagram of the 'S' and 'E' factors, identifying the benefits of sports participation for society.

Now test yourself

TESTED

4 Lots of people take part in sport to increase their health and fitness. Identify the functions of taking part in sport for an individual.

Answer online

Characteristics of physical education (PE)

The National Curriculum for Physical Education was introduced following the 1988 Education Reform Act. It has been reviewed and modified slightly since, but essentially its key characteristics and aims have remained broadly similar.

The key characteristics of PE can be summarised as follows:
- It is compulsory.
- It involves formally taught lessons.
- It has four key stages as part of the National Curriculum from ages 5 to 16.
- It begins at primary school 'foundation level'.
- Teachers are in charge and deliver lessons.
- Lessons are pre-planned; it is highly structured.
- It takes place during school time.

Functions of physical education (PE)

PE has a variety of different functions, including the following:
- The development of health and fitness, as well as positive attitudes, will hopefully lead to healthy lifestyles being continued when PE is no longer compulsory. Ultimately, PE is about encouraging life-long participation and trying to create a sporting habit for life after pupils finish compulsory PE at the age of 16.
- PE provides opportunities for increased participation in a variety of activities, developing and improving a range of physical skills and competencies.
- The development of personal and social skills is an important aim of PE (for example teamwork, communication, leadership and co-operation). PE also aims to develop positive sporting ethics, such as morality, fair play and sportsmanship.
- Cognitively, PE can help improve problem solving, decision making and creativity (for example developing a new sequence in dance or gymnastics). It also aims to develop pupils' skills of self-analysis, as well as learning to recognise strengths and weaknesses in performance and where improvements have occurred.

Figure 7.1b **Objectives of National Curriculum PE**

Characteristics of outdoor education REVISED

National Curriculum PE includes the opportunity to participate in outdoor and adventurous activities (OAA) as **outdoor education**. Such activities provide the opportunity for pupils to overcome fears, face personal challenges and experience an adrenaline rush. Outdoor education is therefore an element of NC PE so the characteristics as stated on page 197 apply to it. In addition, outdoor education takes place in the natural environment and provides opportunities for personal challenges to try to overcome any fears.

Functions of outdoor education   REVISED

> **Outdoor education:** activities which take place in the natural environment and utilise nature/geographical resources, such as mountains, rivers, lakes etc.

There are a number of functions of outdoor education for young people, as identified below:

- It helps children learn to appreciate and engage with the natural environment, as well as increase its conservation. While in the natural environment, they are learning to develop new physical and survival skills (e.g. abseiling and climbing), which can result in increased self-esteem. Outdoor education activities such as climbing are physically challenging, so they result in increased levels of health and fitness.
- Working with others is a key feature of outdoor education activities, so increased co-operation and an improvement in social skills and leadership skills often result.
- Mentally, there are a number of different functions of outdoor education, including learning how to deal with a challenging situation, allowing the pupil to learn how to **perceive risk**, as well as learning to get excited as a result of participation in activities such as abseiling and climbing. Increased cognitive skills and improved decision making can also be gained by children as a result of participating in outdoor education.

> **Perceived risk:** a challenge that stimulates a sense of danger and adventure for beginners or inexperienced performers in a safe environment, with danger minimised via stringent safety measures (e.g. wearing a safety harness when climbing).

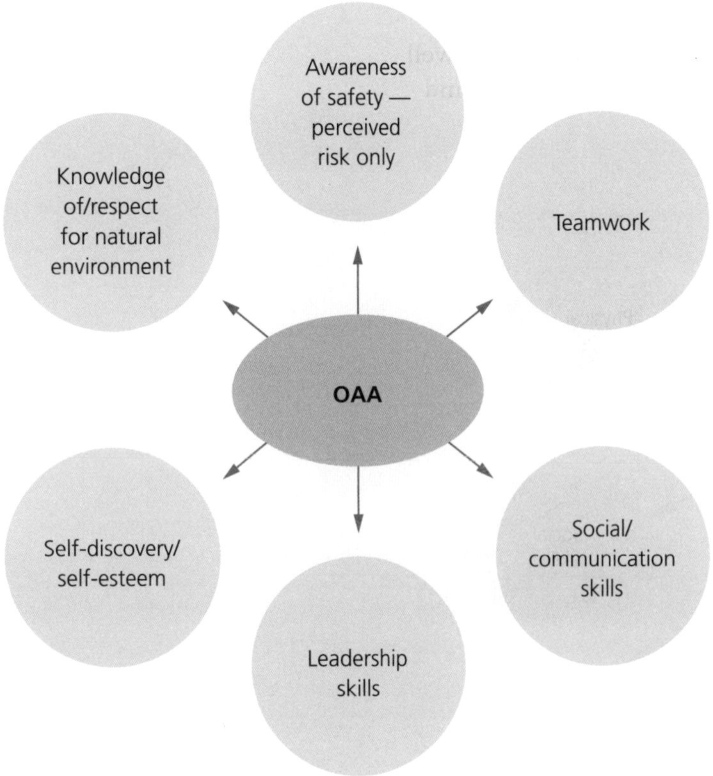

Figure 7.1c **Benefits of OAA as outdoor education**

Now test yourself

5 OAA form part of a school's overall PE programme. Identify the benefits of participating in OAA such as climbing.

Answer online

TESTED

Characteristics of school sport

School sport is different to PE as it mostly occurs in extra-curricular time as a choice for young children attending school. School sport is competitive and has been promoted as important by governments, with initiatives introduced such as **School Sport Partnerships** and **School Games**. Schools sometimes use sports coaches to help increase the range of extra-curricular sporting opportunities available to pupils, as well as using their specialisms to develop pupils' talents to the full.

> **School Sport Partnerships:** the creation of increased opportunities for school sport via junior/primary schools working together with secondary schools and further education providers.
>
> **School Games:** an initiative to increase participation in school sport from intra-/inter-school level through to county and national levels.

Functions of school sport

There are a number of benefits to participating in school sport. Physically, increased activity levels result in increased health and fitness and skill levels, which can improve a child's self-esteem. Socially, new groups can be formed and new friendships developed via extra-curricular involvement in school sport. Improved cognitive skills can result in improved decision-making capabilities, as well as an improvement in academic performance if pupils become more motivated to attend and achieve at school.

Having considered the concepts of physical activity and sport mainly in isolation, it is also important to consider how they compare and contrast in a variety of different ways (i.e. their similarities and differences).

Similarities and differences between physical recreation and sport

Physical recreation and sport are similar in that they both involve physical activity, which helps increase health and fitness. They can be performed in a person's free time as voluntary activities, with individuals gaining intrinsic benefits as a result of participating, for example achieving a sense of personal satisfaction as a result of accomplishing goals/aims.

Physical recreation and sport have a number of differences, including those identified in the table below.

Physical recreation	Sport
Available to all/voluntary/choice	More selective/obligation/for some an occupation
Emphasis on taking part/participation focus	Emphasis on winning/serious/competitive
Limited/varied effort or commitment required	Involves a high level of effort or commitment, e.g. to train for a specific event/competition
Rules can be modified, e.g. timings or numbers involved	Set rules apply
Self-officiated/self-regulated	External officials enforce rules
Mainly intrinsic rewards	Extrinsic rewards available for success, e.g. winning trophies/medals
Varied skill/fitness levels	Higher skill/fitness levels
Basic equipment and clothing used or worn	High-tech equipment and clothing used or worn

Similarities and differences between physical recreation and PE

Physical recreation and PE are similar in that they both develop physical skills and are energetic, therefore providing health and fitness benefits. They can both be enjoyable and fun to participate in, offering intrinsic benefits.

The differences between physical recreation and PE are summarised in the table below.

Physical recreation	PE
Voluntary/choice	Compulsory
In a person's free time	In school time
Informal/relaxed	Formal teaching and learning
Participants control activity; self-regulated	Teacher in charge
Participation level	Foundation level at primary school
Simple/limited organisational structure	Highly structured

Now test yourself

TESTED

6 Identify the similarities and differences between physical recreation and PE.

Answer online

Comparison between PE and school sport

As mentioned above, the overall concept of PE can be experienced in a number of different ways. A direct comparison can be made between PE as a compulsory National Curriculum subject and school sport as a choice for young people, as illustrated in the table below.

National Curriculum PE	School sport
In lesson time; curriculum time	In free time; extra-curricular
Compulsory	Element of choice; voluntary involvement
For all	For the chosen few; elitist
Emphasis on taking part	Emphasis on winning; competitive
Teacher-led	Coaches involved
Wide variety of activities experienced	Specialisms developed

Now test yourself

TESTED

7 Identify the differences between National Curriculum PE and school sport.

Answer online

School sport remains an extra-curricular activity for pupils. This has a number of advantages:
- It allows the ethos of PE to dominate and an educational focus is maintained within school sport provision.
- It allows individual choice for both teachers and pupils, who are under no pressure to involve themselves/participate if they do not want to.
- Schools can cater for those who are interested in competitive sport via provision of a range of sporting opportunities to develop and improve their talents.
- School sport is relatively easy to access and cheaper than joining a sports club.

School sport remaining as an extra-curricular activity also has a number of disadvantages:
- If optional as an extra-curricular activity, it does not necessarily reach the maximum number and some talented individuals might miss out; it might be viewed as elitist if only a minority of pupils stay behind at school/compete for the school at weekends.
- It relies heavily on teacher goodwill; teachers may sometimes opt out due to other pressures on their time (e.g. attendance at staff meetings).
- School sporting facilities may not be used to their full capacity.

Exam practice

1 Which of the following statements best describes a characteristic of physical recreation? [1]
  (a) Voluntary with an emphasis on participation
  (b) Compulsory with an emphasis on winning
  (c) Strict rules apply, which are externally enforced
  (d) Serious and competitive in nature
2 What are the functions of physical recreation for the individual? [3]
3 Explain the potential benefits to society of increasing participation in sport and physical recreation. [8]
4 Outline the functions of National Curriculum PE in schools today. [4]
5 Identify the problems schools face in offering OAA within their school PE programmes. [3]
6 Modern-day sport performers face high levels of pressure to succeed, which sometimes has a negative effect on their behaviour. Explain why there are fewer acts of negative behaviour during physical recreation compared to sport. [8]

Answers and quick quizzes online

ONLINE

Summary

You should now be able to:
- identify the key characteristics and functions of a range of key concepts at the base of the sporting development continuum (i.e. physical recreation, sport, physical education and school sport)
- identify the similarities and differences between these key concepts.

7.2 Development of elite performers in sport

Factors required to support progression from talent identification to elite performance

REVISED

Personal factors

It is important that all young, talented athletes in the UK are able to fulfil their sporting potential and have in place all they need to support and develop their talents. When considering the factors necessary to progress to **elite** performance level, a useful starting point is to identify some key **personal qualities** (for example physical/psychological) which are viewed as important in talented athletes.

Below is a summary of key personal factors and qualities necessary to develop as an elite performer:

- commitment/dedication and self-discipline
- determination to succeed, as well as being single-minded and mentally tough/focused
- highly motivated/self-motivated with the desire to achieve/clearly set goals to achieve
- willing to self-sacrifice in order to succeed
- high pain tolerance/resilience/perseverance/patience
- high levels of self-confidence and self-efficacy
- highly skilled physically and/or naturally talented
- high level of physical fitness (as required by the sport, e.g. endurance for distance runners)
- good communication skills.

> **Elite:** the best, highest level sports performers.
>
> **Personal qualities:** attributes and personality characteristics of an individual person.

Now test yourself

TESTED

1 Identify the psychological qualities you feel are necessary for an individual to develop as an elite performer.

Answer online

Social and cultural factors

A wide range of social and cultural factors can influence the progression of a young talented individual to elite performance level. Of key importance is the support of friends and family when starting out in sport and trying to progress. Having friends and family present in the crowd at sports events to support and encourage is viewed as very important, both socially and emotionally. The financial resources of a family can also influence an individual's development, as money is required for specialist equipment, travelling expenses, specialist coaching and medical support. (This is sometimes referred to as the 'bank of mum and dad'!) An important social and cultural influence on performer progression is therefore an individual's **socio-economic status**.

> **Socio-economic status:** an individual's position in the social structure, which depends on their job, level of income and the area they live in.

Below is a summary of the social and cultural factors necessary to develop as an elite performer:
- highly supportive family/high socio-economic status
- evidence of equal opportunities and anti-discriminatory practice within a sport and setting of equity targets
- high-quality, supportive educational provision/clear links to clubs
- structured levels of competition to progress through
- high levels of media coverage and role models to aspire to.

Identify the socio-cultural factors which encourage the development of elite performers and improve the chance of UK athletes winning medals at the Olympics.

Organisations providing support and progression from talent identification through to elite performance

REVISED

The syllabus focuses on three organisations as being particularly important when considering **talent identification** and elite performer progression. UK Sport, the English Institute of Sport (EIS – as an example of a national institute of sport) and the national governing bodies (NGBs) of sport are each considered below, with any inter-relationships between them explained as and when appropriate.

> **Talent identification:** the multi-disciplinary screening of athletes in order to identify those with the potential for world-class success.

UK Sport

UK Sport is singularly focused on developing high-performance sport in the UK and it works to create and implement various strategies to increase sporting excellence. Its primary role is to strategically invest and distribute National Lottery funding for elite performer development, in order to maximise the performance of UK athletes in the Olympic and Paralympic Games.

It does this via two main channels. The first is to provide funding to NGBs, which enables them to operate a World Class Programme (see page 207) covering all funded summer and winter Olympic and Paralympic sports. The second channel provides funding directly to athletes via an Athlete Performance Award, which contributes to their living and sporting costs once they have reached elite performance level.

In terms of financial support at elite performance level, UK Sport also provides funding for the national institutes of sport, such as the English Institute of Sport (EIS), and the British Olympic and Paralympic preparation plans (for example the preparation camp at Belo Horizonte at Rio 2016).

UK Sport is therefore the nation's high-performance sports agency investing in Olympic and Paralympic sport. Working with partner organisations, it runs a number of centralised strategic support services across the UK, including the development of World Class Coaches for example, via the Elite Programme. This is delivered in conjunction with Sports Coach UK and is aimed at developing programmes and innovations to support coaches involved in the World Class system.

UK Sport is a lead agency involved in running Talent ID programmes, with the EIS providing host venues, as explained in more detail below. As part of such programmes, UK Sport is keen to develop lifestyles in young performers which enable elite performer progression to occur unimpeded by personal issues or work demands. Performance Lifestyle advice has been developed by UK Sport and is delivered at national institutes of sport to help with mentor support and advice on issues such as time management, budgeting and so on.

UK Sport promotes positive sporting conduct and ethics at elite level in the UK's high-performance athletes. It also attaches importance to developing and managing the UK's international sporting relationships, via liaison with International Federations on the International Voice programme for example.

Now test yourself

TESTED

3 Describe the role of UK Sport in elite performer development.

Answer online

National institutes of sport

One example of a national institute of sport is the English Institute of Sport (EIS), which has a network of high-performance centres across England, providing a range of services to elite performers.

The EIS is a subsidiary of UK Sport and wholly owned by that organisation. It receives a grant of £40 million over four years from UK Sport and generates its own income by providing services to NGBs such as performance analysis and sports medicine. In the year of London 2012, for example, NGBs invested £6.1 million in EIS services to help and support elite performer development.

The EIS is UK Sport's science, medicine and technology arm (e.g. via 'Research and Innovation' programme), which acts as the team behind many of Team GB's most successful Olympians and Paralympians. Its job is to increase the probability of a potential elite athlete being successful by providing a range of different services to improve their health, fitness, training and preparation.

In terms of such sporting services, the EIS operates World Class Performance environments via a number of high-performance centres, as well as numerous other training bases across England. Their partner sites include the Team GB Intensive Rehabilitation Unit at Bisham Abbey, as well as the Holme Pierrepont National Watersports Centre in Nottingham. Its staff work with high-level coaches and NGB performance directors to help improve the performance of their best athletes, by delivering a range of services to enable them to optimise training programmes and maximise performance in competition (e.g. Performance Lifestyle programmes).

> **Typical mistake**
>
> It is important to link the key services of the national institutes of sport to the level of service they provide. They do not just provide facilities and coaches; they provide high-quality facilities and high-level coaching to develop performers.

Now test yourself

TESTED

4 England, Northern Ireland, Scotland and Wales all have national institutes of sport. Describe how these national institutes are aiding the development of the UK's elite athletes.

Answer online

National governing bodies (NGBs)

A **national governing body (NGB)** can help ensure the development of elite performers in a number of different ways. Initially, it can promote and increase participation in its sport, providing equality of opportunity for all. It can also use regional scouts and talent identification schemes to try to identify young sporting talent. Once talent has been identified, it needs to be supported in a number of different ways (e.g. via provision of Performance Lifestyle support, structured levels of competition and development squads to progress through).

NGBs are the organisations which make decisions on who in their sport should receive funding, for example from UK Sport's World Class Programme. They work with organisations such as the national institutes of sport and UK Sport to provide elite performers with various support services necessary to help them develop and progress. For example, high-quality coaches and top-class training facilities are important in enabling performers to develop their talents to the full. NGBs provide sport-specific coaching awards, from basic, low-level qualifications through to the high levels necessary to support and develop elite performers.

For example, the Lawn Tennis Association (LTA) has developed a Coaching Pathway from Level 1 Coaching Assistant through to Level 5 Master Performance, which develops tennis players to an elite standard.

> **National governing body (NGB):** an organisation which has responsibility for managing its own particular sport (e.g. British Cycling).

Identify ways in which a national governing body can help to ensure the development of elite performers.

Key features of national governing bodies' Whole Sport Plans

A **Whole Sport Plan** is a lottery-funded, Sport England 'approved' outline of how an NGB intends to increase participation in the sport for which it is responsible, as well as identify and develop talent in it. In 2012, NGBs submitted their Whole Sport Plans to Sport England, giving information on how investment in their sports would nurture young talent.

For the four-year period the Whole Sport Plan is in operation, for example 2013–17, a sum of £83 million was allocated to develop talented young athletes.

> **Whole Sport Plan:** a business plan/document submitted to Sport England outlining national governing body strategies to increase participation and enhance talent in the sport(s) for which they are responsible.

Talent development and support services

REVISED

Working in partnership, UK Sport, the national institutes of sport (e.g. the EIS) and national governing bodies (NGBs) of sport are committed to systematically unearthing sporting talent with the necessary potential and mind-set to win medals and world titles. This is done through talent identification programmes, which are important for the following reasons:
- All potential performers can be screened.
- Performers can be directed to the sports most suited to their talents.
- The development process can be accelerated as a result of the information gained.

- Efficient use can be made of available funding for Talent ID schemes.
- The chances of producing medallists are improved.
- They provide a co-ordinated approach between organisations such as NGBs, the EIS and UK Sport.

Possible disadvantages of talent identification programmes include:
- They may miss late developers.
- They require high levels of funding.
- They require large numbers to be tested to be of use.
- There are no guarantees of success.
- Many sports are in competition for the same talent pool; high-profile sports may attract more performers or the best performers.

The EIS is one of the national institutes of sport which provides various support services to help ensure talent development. Its **Performance Pathway Team** works with UK Sport to support the World Class Programme in identifying talented athletes and providing them with the necessary support services to ensure their progress.

> **Performance Pathway Team:** a combination of EIS and UK Sport expertise used to identify and develop world-class talent.

The team at the EIS has identified a number of areas of support as important for the identification and development of talent:

1 Pathway Frontline Technical Solutions: these are designed to meet the specific needs of each sport when identifying and developing talent (e.g. establishing talent recruitment and confirmation programmes for different sports, such as the UK Athletics Futures programme).

2 Pathway Education: this provides educational opportunities for development coaches, covering a variety of topics linked to elite performer development.

3 Pathway Analytics: this gives sports the ability to provide meaningful measurements of the effectiveness of their performance pathways by using a range of diagnostic tools; they can also take a 'Performance Pathway Health Check'.

4 Performance Pathway Health Check (PHC): the PHC is an important diagnostic tool, supporting summer and winter Olympic and Paralympic sports. It provides an evaluation of current systems and practices for supporting the development of potential medal winners in any given sport. It includes a review of the sport's long-term vision and strategy for elite development, as well as consideration of the coaching and training environments a sport has in place to develop elite performers.

5 Pathway Strategy: this is designed to assist sports to develop and put in place a clear progressive pathway from Podium Foundations level to Podium level.

The ultimate aim of support services provided by national institutes of sport such as the EIS is to identify new athletes with clear sporting potential, help them progress onto the World Class system and successfully represent the UK in major international sporting events.

> **Revision activity**
>
> Draw a spider diagram identifying and describing the key roles/purposes of NGBs, UK Sport and national institutes of sport in developing elite performers in the UK.

Key features of UK Sport's World Class Performance Programme, Gold Event Series and Talent Identification and Development programmes

World Class Performance Programme (WCPP)

It can take athletes many years to develop the high-level skills and competitive maturity required to be successful at the top level of international sport. UK Sport has therefore adopted a funding philosophy which reflects potentially long journeys to the top, investing around £100 million annually into elite sport. This funding philosophy is called 'no compromise' and bases its decisions on performances at major sporting competitions.

UK Sport has adopted this approach to raise standards/performance levels among Team GB athletes. It is designed to make the best use of the funding available to elite sport by funding athletes/sports deemed to have the best chance of success (i.e. it is directed at potential medal winners.) Such an approach has increased Team GB medal chances and helps justify the large National Lottery investment in elite sport.

The World Class Performance Programme (WCPP) covers all funded summer and winter Olympic and Paralympic sports and works on the basis of the two levels that comprise the World Class Pathway:

1 Podium: designed to support athletes with realistic medal-winning capabilities at the next Olympics/Paralympics (i.e. a maximum of four years away from the podium). UK Athletics, like other NGBs, receives funding from UK Sport and the National Lottery, which enables it to offer financial support to a selected group of performers in their sport via the WCPP. In the lead-up to Rio, UK Athletics funded 21 podium group athletes in 2015–16, including Jessica Ennis-Hill, Mo Farah, Adam Gemili and Laura Muir.
2 Podium Potential (previously known as Development): designed to support athletes whose performances suggest they have realistic medal-winning capabilities at subsequent Olympic/Paralympic Games (i.e. a maximum of eight years away from the podium).

Beneath Podium Potential is the 'Talent' level, which provides funding and support to identify and confirm athletes who have the potential to progress to the World Class Pathway. The Futures Programme in place for British Athletics underpins the WCPP and was designed to provide financial and medical support to young, talented athletes (typically aged 17–20) and their coaches.

Gold Event Series

UK Sport is the lead agency attempting to ensure the UK successfully bids to host and stage major sporting events. It has a flagship programme called the Gold Event Series, which is working hard to bring 100 targeted major international sporting events to the UK during the ten years it is operating (i.e. from 2013 to 2023). Successful bids were made as part of the programme to host the UCI Track Cycling World Championships in London in 2016, as well as the World Athletics Championships at the Olympic Stadium in 2017.

Exam tip

If asked to explain the World Class Performance Programme, you should use the correct terms to identify the different levels of the pathway before providing clear/correct explanations of the levels to distinguish them.

Revision activity

Review and summarise UK Sport's investment decisions following Rio 2016 through to Tokyo 2020 by looking at:

www.uksport.gov.uk/our-work/investing-in-sport/current-funding-figures

The Gold Event Series focuses mainly on attracting World Championships, European Championships and premium world circuit events to the UK. Prior to developing event bids, UK Sport works with the sport and host location, helping them to draw up a detailed business plan and giving a budget to work to. When UK Sport agrees a financial award to support an event bid, it continues to work with the NGB involved to develop and support their planning and delivery of the actual event.

Ultimately, UK Sport has a number of objectives as a result of staging major international sporting events in the UK, including:
- supporting high-performance success
- creating high-profile opportunities for people to engage in sport
- using and demonstrating the legacy of London 2012 and Glasgow 2014
- driving positive economic and social impacts for the UK.

Now test yourself

TESTED

6 Identify the key objectives UK Sport aims to achieve through its Gold Event Series.

Answer online

Talent Identification and Development (Talent ID) programmes

UK Sport is a lead agency in running Talent ID programmes, with national institutes of sport acting as host venues. The co-ordinated work of the EIS and UK Sport supporting talent identification and development is described above. Additional information provided here focuses more on UK Sport's specific roles when looking to discover sporting talent of the future.

UK Sport has a clearly defined mission to drive forward Olympic and Paralympic Performance Pathways, which help to ensure continued success at future Games events. Its Performance Pathway Team supports World Class Programmes to identify and develop talented athletes and construct the necessary support systems to help ensure success. Frontline Technical Solutions are provided via the Performance Pathway Team, looking to create a 'talent profile' which is capable of predicting future Olympic and Paralympic potential. It is also involved in possible positive transfer of sporting talent from one sport to another, following in the footsteps of dual Olympic medal winner Rebecca Romero, who successfully switched from rowing to cycling.

The Performance Pathway Team also provides specialist knowledge for Olympic and Paralympic talent development managers and coaches on the issues they face in identifying and developing future generations of elite performers. UK Sport's educational work involves creating a unique learning programme for talent development managers and coaches nominated into the WCPP by their NGB. It draws on best practice in developing excellence from many areas of life other than sport, including astronauts, junior surgeons and musicians, to try to learn from 'gold standard' examples of how to create successful opportunities to progress for elite performers.

Pathway Analytics enables sports to measure and benchmark the effectiveness of their performance pathway using a Talent Health Check, which is delivered every four years by the Performance Pathway Team. It discusses topics such as junior to senior transition, as well as retention and attrition rates of athletes on the pathway. Overall, UK Sport looks

Answers and quick quizzes at **www.hoddereducation.co.uk/myrevisionnotes**

to develop and implement a clearly defined pathway, vision and strategy, from foundation through to podium level.

UK Sport's talent recruitment and confirmation programmes involve a number of different phases. Campaigns start with a 'talent search', which can involve the general public and/or the sports community. Interested athletes are invited to submit an application form to UK Sport, with successful applicants invited to Phase 1 testing, hosted at venues around the home nations. Phase 1 involves performing a range of different fitness and skill tests linked to the sport. Results from these influence progression onto Phases 2 and 3, which further assess an athlete's suitability for a sport via medical screening, performance lifestyle workshops and psychological/behavioural assessments.

Following these assessment phases, selected athletes then embark on a 6–12-month confirmation phase, where they are totally immersed in the sport's training environment, with exposure to a carefully constructed developmental experience. Rates of progression are tracked to see if individuals are suitable for the sport and therefore eligible for potential funding on their WCPP.

UK Sport also operates a World Class Talent Transfer initiative for athletes exiting an Olympic or Paralympic World Class Programme who are interested in exploring their possible potential to achieve elite-level performance in another sport.

Exam practice

1 Which of the following best describes the Podium level of the World Class Performance Pathway? [1]
   (a) Supporting athletes 10 years away from the podium
   (b) Supporting athletes 8 years away from the podium
   (c) Supporting athletes 6 years away from the podium
   (d) Supporting athletes 4 years away from the podium
2 UK Sport plays a key role in co-ordinating Talent ID programmes to help achieve its aim of developing elite performers. Outline and explain the characteristics of an effective Talent ID programme. [6]
3 Explain how the structure of the World Class Performance Pathway supports the development of elite athletes in the UK. [3]
4 Discuss the use of Talent ID programmes in the UK to support the development of elite performers. [8]
5 Large numbers of Team GB athletes successful in Rio 2016 were supported by UK Sport National Lottery funding. Justify the decision to allocate this funding based on performances at major competitions. [6]

Answers and quick quizzes online

ONLINE

Summary

You should now be able to:
- identify and describe a range of personal, social and cultural factors which are required when developing talented sports performers to reach their potential
- describe the roles, purposes and inter-relationships between various organisations involved in elite performer development, such as national governing bodies of sport (e.g. their

Whole Sport Plans), national institutes of sport (e.g. the EIS) and UK Sport
- identify and explain a number of key features of UK Sport programmes supporting elite performer development in the UK, including the World Class Performance Programme, the Gold Event Series and Talent Identification and Development programmes.

7.3 Ethics in sport

Amateurism

REVISED

Amateurism was a nineteenth-century code or ideal of sporting ethics, which developed among the upper then middle classes during the Victorian era. In the nineteenth century, elite sport was dominated by the upper and middle classes, who had high status in sport as well as in society. Upper- and middle-class amateurs held a higher status than professionals at the time.

> **Amateurism:** participation in sport for the love of it, receiving no financial gain; it is based on the concept of athleticism (i.e. physical endeavour with moral integrity).

In modern-day British sport, amateurism is still evident in a number of ways, including through:

- fair play/sportsmanship: this is still viewed positively encouraged and promoted in a number of ways, for example the Fair Play Awards in football, shaking of hands prior to and at the end of sporting contests, and through the Olympics with the 'Olympic ideal' based on principles of amateurism
- sports such as rugby union, which maintained their amateurism until late into the twentieth century and still have codes of conduct based on such principles, such as calling the referee 'Sir'.

Olympic oath

REVISED

Written by Baron de Coubertin, the founder of the modern Olympic Games, the Olympic oath was first taken at the 1920 summer Olympics in Antwerp. It is a promise made by one athlete as a representative of the participating competitors, one judge as a representative of the Olympic officials who commit to impartiality at the opening ceremony of each Olympics and one coach.

The oath of the athlete reads as follows:

> 'In the name of all competitors, I promise that we shall take part in these Olympic Games, respecting and abiding by the rules that govern them, committing ourselves to a sport without doping and without drugs, in the true spirit of sportsmanship, for the glory of sport and the honour of our teams.'

You could argue that it is still relevant in modern-day sport because the Olympics are still viewed by large numbers of people as a festival of sport with fair play and sportsmanship very much in evidence. However, there are unfortunately lots of examples of doping and positive drugs tests at Olympic Games. Some argue that this leaves the relevance of the Olympic oath in question. Ben Johnson is thought to have sparked a significant increase in drugs testing and a tightening up of procedures and practices, following his positive test for drugs the day after winning the 100-metre gold medal at the 1988 Seoul Olympics, breaking the world record in the process. In addition, with professional athletes now allowed to compete in the Games, more examples of 'win-at-all-costs' behaviour and stretching of the rules to their absolute limit are occurring in Olympic sport, which further questions respect and adherence to the oath. (See, for example, Russian athletes during the London 2012 Olympic.)

Sportsmanship

Sportsmanship involves playing by the unwritten rules to a high code of ethics. Fairness, maintaining self-control and treating others with respect are all positive virtues associated with sportsmanship. It involves maintaining high levels of etiquette to ensure fair play is clearly evident in a sporting contest. It therefore involves playing the game in a positive spirit, with respect shown for opponents and officials alike.

Examples of sportsmanship at elite level include professional footballers returning the ball to the opposition when it has been kicked out of play to allow an injured player to have treatment, and cricketers 'walking' before being given out when they know they have made contact with bat on ball and it has been caught. Professional sports performers sometimes show 'good grace' when returning to play at former clubs by not celebrating the scoring of a goal or try, as a mark of respect to their old football or rugby club.

In modern-day sport, sportsmanship is under attack as winning becomes increasingly important. For example, when a team is winning they often stretch the rules and waste time in order to ensure a victory. Some performers have earned a negative reputation for **simulation**/diving in the penalty area to try to unfairly win a penalty. In addition, violent actions have seemingly replaced the civilised behaviour more evident in the amateur era of many sports. On occasions, performers constantly question the decisions of referees or refuse to adopt sporting etiquette with their opponents (for example refusal to shake hands at the end of a match).

Define the term 'sportsmanship'.

While the pressure is on to 'win at all costs', sportsmanship can still be encouraged in a number of ways, including:
- use of NGB campaigns promoting sportsmanship/fair play (e.g. FA Respect)
- the giving of awards for fair play to encourage it in top-level sport, thereby providing positive role models for youngsters to follow (UEFA Fair Play Awards include a place in a European competition awarded on the basis of fair play/sportsmanship)
- use of technology to help match officials reach the correct decisions and allow performers to be cited after matches for behaviour which goes against the rules
- introduction of NGB rules promoting fair play (e.g. banning high or late tackles)
- punishing foul play and unsporting behaviour on the field of play and within the sporting event (e.g. officials can 'sin bin' – book a player or send a player off)
- punishing foul play and unsporting behaviour after the event (e.g. fines or bans imposed by NGBs)
- use of positive role models to promote sportsmanship and fair play
- use of rigorous drug testing to try to ensure fairness in sporting contests and catch out drugs cheats.

Sportsmanship: conforming to the unwritten rules, spirit and etiquette of a sport.

Simulation: trying to deceive an official by over-acting, for example diving to win a free kick.

Typical mistake

When defining sportsmanship, students often link it purely to 'playing by the rules' instead of focusing on playing by the unwritten rules/positive codes of conduct.

TESTED ☐

2 Identify different ways in which elite-level sports performers fail to adopt the sportsmanship ethic, and suggest ways in which sportsmanship is encouraged and maintained in high-level/elite sport.

Answer online

Gamesmanship

REVISED ☐

Gamesmanship can be described as the art of winning games by cunning means, but without actually breaking the rules – although, on many occasions, it is a very fine line between gamesmanship and actually cheating! Gamesmanship therefore involves stretching the rules to the limit and failing to follow the etiquette of the game or sporting contest. There are many examples of gamesmanship in elite-level modern-day sport:

- delaying play at a restart to get back in defence (e.g. by keeping possession of the ball)
- time-wasting when ahead in a game to try to ensure victory
- verbally 'sledging' an opponent to distract or upset them, e.g. in cricket, a bowler or fielder might say something to upset the concentration of a batsman in an effort to get them out
- psyching out an opponent at a pre-match press conference
- taking an injury time-out, toilet break or appealing a decision to the umpire even when it is not necessarily needed, to upset the concentration or rhythm of an opponent (e.g. in tennis or cricket)
- deliberate deception of an official to try to gain an advantage, e.g. over-appealing for a wicket in cricket or a penalty in football and claiming for a decision which is not necessarily theirs
- over-reacting to a challenge in a bid to put pressure on a referee to book or send off an opponent.

> **Gamesmanship:** bending the rules and stretching them to their absolute limit without getting caught; using whatever dubious methods possible to achieve the desired result.

> **Typical mistake**
>
> Gamesmanship does not refer to breaking the rules, cheating or taking performance-enhancing drugs. Remember, it is about bending the rules to their limit in order to win.

TESTED ☐

3 Define the term 'gamesmanship'.

Answer online

Win ethic

REVISED ☐

The win ethic links to the sporting ethic of 'win at all costs', where coming second is not viewed as an option and the outcome is all that matters. The win ethic has sometimes been called the 'Lombardian ethic' after the Green Bay Packers American football coach, Vince Lombardi. Lombardi claimed that for him, 'winning is not a sometime thing, it's an all the time thing'. In modern-day rugby, where the code of amateurism was protected until late in the twentieth century, top-level coaches have even resorted to using fake blood capsules to mimic a blood injury so that a specialist kicker can enter the field at a crucial game stage, when kicking a penalty is required to win. Performers also try to ensure victory when the stakes are so high by cheating in various ways. Diego Maradona was famous for his 'hand of God', which involved illegally punching a ball into the back of the net to help Argentina to victory over England in the 1986 Football World Cup. Seemingly, winning is all that matters when the rewards for winning are so high and livelihoods are at stake.

The win ethic is evident in modern-day elite sport via the following examples:
- no drawn games, i.e. there is always a winner in basketball, American football and League Cup football in England
- managers and coaches are fired if unsuccessful
- high amounts of deviance (see below), e.g. violence, over-aggression and doping
- media praise for winners; positive newspaper headlines
- media negativity for losers.

The Lombardian ethic is a dominant sporting ethic in twenty-first century elite sport. How is such a 'win at all costs' ethic displayed in sporting contests?

Positive and negative deviance in relation to the sports performer

Positive deviance

Deviance is behaviour which goes against the norms of society and is deemed unacceptable. In terms of sports performers, **positive deviance** involves over-adherence or over-conformity to the norms and expectations of society. For example, a performer might over-train or try to compete in a sporting event despite being injured. Retired marathon runner Paula Radcliffe is one example of an elite performer doing her best to win for her country at the 2004 Athens Olympics, despite carrying an injury which ultimately led to her pulling out of the race part-way through. Another example of positive deviance is where a performer striving to win within the rules or etiquette of a sport accidentally and without intent injures another player.

Negative deviance

Negative deviance in sports performers involves under-conformity to the norms and expectations of society. The motivation to win at all costs encourages performers who lack moral restraint to act against the norms of society and sport in various ways and cheat. Examples of negative deviance include:
- taking illegal performance-enhancing drugs
- deliberately fouling or harming an opponent through aggression or violent actions
- accepting a bribe to lose; match-fixing
- diving to win a penalty or free kick.

Positive deviance: behaviour which is outside the norms of society but with no intent to harm or break the rules. It involves over-adherence to the norms or expectations of society.

Negative deviance: behaviour that goes against the norms and has a detrimental effect on individuals and society in general.

Now test yourself

TESTED ☐

5 Using examples, explain the terms 'positive deviance' and 'negative deviance' in relation to the performer.
6 Identify the similarities and differences between gamesmanship and negative forms of deviance in sport.

Answers online

Exam practice

1 Which of the following statements best describes the term 'gamesmanship'? [1]
   (a) Over-adherence to the rules
   (b) Breaking the rules
   (c) Stretching the rules to their limit
   (d) Playing to the rules
2 Using examples, explain the difference between sportsmanship and gamesmanship. [4]
3 Discuss the suggestion that increased commercialisation of sport has had a negative effect on traditional sports performer values such as sportsmanship/fair play and the Olympic oath. [8]
4 Outline strategies that sporting authorities such as national governing bodies could use to encourage higher standards of individual performer behaviour. [3]
5 Describe how deviance in sport has increased in the twenty-first century. [8]

Answers and quick quizzes online

ONLINE ☐

7.4 Violence in sport

Causes of violence in sport in relation to the performer

REVISED

A number of sporting ethics are introduced and explained in Chapter 7.3. Of these, the 'win ethic' in particular can help explain why performers resort to **aggression** and ultimately **violence** during sporting contests. On occasions, pre-match media hype and intense build-up to a key contest can 'over-psych' a performer and lead them to become over-aggressive (for example via a high tackle in rugby).

Frustration with decisions made by match officials may create a sense of injustice and increase frustration for sports performers, which ultimately leads them to become violent on the field of play (for example performing a late tackle or retaliation against an opponent). Performer violence might also occur as a result of abuse or provocation from opponents and/or the crowd. Some sports are viewed as naturally more violent than others, as aggression and high levels of physical contact are considered part of the game.

Some of the causes of player violence can be remembered via the mnemonic 'WINNER':
- **W**in ethic and high rewards for success
- **I**mportance/emotional intensity of an event (e.g. local derby/Cup Final)
- **N**ature of the sport is aggressive/intense
- **N**ational governing bodies are too lenient with their punishments
- **E**xcitement/over-arousal
- **R**efereeing decisions are questionable/poor, leading to frustration.

> **Aggression:** an emotional response (involving anger) to an individual perceived as an enemy or a frustrating rival; an intent to harm outside the laws of the game.
>
> **Violence:** physical acts committed to harm others. It often occurs in sports such as American Football, rugby, football and ice hockey.

Suggest possible reasons why a performer may become violent during a sporting contest.

Strategies for preventing violence in sport in relation to the performer

REVISED

Players can often become aggressive in fast-moving, highly competitive sporting contests. A coach can use a range of strategies to reduce aggressive behaviour in a sports performer, for example:
- remove the performer/player from the pitch/substitute them
- punish aggressive behaviour, e.g. by fining them/leaving them out of the team for a certain number of matches
- increase peer pressure (e.g. on the field of play via a team mate/Captain) to act less aggressively
- educate the performer/reinforce use of assertive behaviour
- provide positive role model behaviour to aspire to

- highlight their responsibility to the team/the negative impact on them if aggression leads to being sent off/banned from future matches
- decrease the emphasis on winning
- use stress management techniques with a sport psychologist (e.g. positive self-talk)
- work on improving fitness to decrease the likelihood of fatigue negatively affecting mood/mind-set.

The frustration caused by poor officiating can be decreased by using more officials to help reach decisions as actions occur on the field of play. For example, extra officials have been trialled and adopted in the Europa League, where two additional officials are employed to help with decisions close to goal and one additional official is situated on each goal line. Off the field of play, sporting contests can be stopped and video technology used to help reach the correct decision, for example via a fourth official. This can help decrease performer frustration with officials and any perceived injustice in them, as the decision is taken out of the referee's hands and given to an individual in the stands, using technology to help them reach the 'correct' decision. For example, in rugby league the **television match official (TMO)** reviews plays by looking at TV footage as and when asked to by the on-field referee.

If a lack of punishment or effective deterrents are a cause of violence, then the sporting authorities/NGBs and even the law need to apply tougher sanctions. These sanctions could include longer bans, higher fines on players, or the deduction of points from clubs. In extreme cases, where there are particularly violent actions by performers on the field of play, court action might be taken and a possible prison sentence imposed (as was the case with Rangers player Duncan Ferguson, who received a three-month prison sentence for his head butt on Raith Rovers player Jock McStay in 1994).

In most sporting situations where particularly aggressive actions have occurred, it is normally the NGB of the sport which is responsible for discouraging performer violence and promoting higher standards of behaviour. Controlling violent behaviour in their sport is therefore an important responsibility of the NGBs, who are keen to present a positive image to fans and future performers, as well as potential sponsors. They can take a number of actions to try to prevent player violence, including:

- supporting the decisions of match officials when dealing with violence by performers by using a TMO/video replays to check decisions being made, changing/clarifying rules on violent acts (e.g. 'high tackles') and training officials to develop the skills necessary to diffuse or calm down match situations which could potentially develop into aggressive behaviour
- punishing violence by performers missed by officials after the match by using video evidence and taking retrospective action as appropriate to the offence committed; this might be against the performer and/or the club itself if it is deemed not to be in control of its players; fines and/ or point deductions might be imposed on clubs for repeat offences of violence among its players
- post-match video evidence where individuals have been cited by referees as performing violent actions worthy of further investigation; for example, the rugby league 'on-report' system allows a referee who sees what they believe to be an act of foul play to highlight the incident immediately to independent reviewers

> **Television match official (TMO):** a referee who can review plays by looking at TV footage as and when asked to by the on-field referee.

> **Exam tip**
>
> When questions ask for solutions/strategies to decrease aggression among sports performers, relate your answers as appropriate to the question set. For example, if it asks for solutions a coach could employ, focus on these as opposed to those of NGBs.

- promoting performers with good disciplinary records as positive role models in their sport
- imposing punishments for violent actions on the field of play (e.g. sin bin/booking/sending off).
- introducing education campaigns and/or awards/rewards linked to fair play, for example the FA and its Respect campaign (West Ham qualified for the Europa League after topping the Premier League Fair Play table in 2014–15).

Implications of violence in sport in relation to the performer

REVISED

If such strategies/actions do not work, there may be a potential negative impact for a sport as a result of the negative publicity associated with a performer's over-aggressive behaviour. This may take the form of:
- lower attendances/gate receipts at a sporting event
- declining participation numbers in a sport
- negative/decreased media coverage
- lower sponsorship/media revenue
- negative role models encouraging an increase in poor behaviour in the sport among the young/amateur performers
- increased pressure on NGBs to introduce strategies to eliminate/decrease negative aggressive behaviour in their sport.

Causes of violence in sport in relation to spectators

REVISED

Spectator violence has been particularly evident over the years in the sport of football. This section therefore reviews a number of different causes of **football hooliganism** before considering the negative implications of such violence.

Causes of football hooliganism include:
- emotional intensity and the ritual importance of the event, e.g. a local derby, team loyalty taken to extremes
- too much alcohol and/or the 'highs' caused by drug-taking
- pre-match media hype stirring up tensions between rival fans
- poor policing, stewarding and crowd control (one of the key reasons identified for the Hillsborough Stadium disaster in 1989)
- lack of effective deterrents and punishments to discourage individuals from involving themselves in violence at football matches
- diminished responsibility by individuals in a large group (i.e. a football crowd); organised violence as part of a gang and peer pressure to get involved in violence
- reaction of the working classes who perceive the middle classes to be taking over 'their game'
- poor officiating or frustration with match officials, which heightens tensions between rival fans
- violence by players on the pitch being reflected in the crowd
- religious discord, e.g. at a Celtic vs Rangers match tensions are particularly high between rival fans of the Protestant and Catholic religions

> **Football hooliganism:** unruly, violent and destructive behaviour by over-zealous supporters of association football clubs.

- a negative violent reaction occurring as a result of chants and taunts by rival fans; frustration at one's own team losing causing some in the crowd to become violent (e.g. when fans from opposition teams keep chanting reminders of the score!)
- violence sometimes being used by young males as a display of their masculinity caused by an adrenaline rush when attending a match.

Now test yourself

TESTED

2 Hooliganism is sometimes associated with young males, who are often drunk, as a sign of their masculinity. Identify other causes of spectator violence at football matches.

Answer online

Exam tip

When questions are set which have 'solutions' already in them, avoid making points which are already stated. In the case of 'Now test yourself' question 2, this would be things such as too much alcohol and the points linked to a display of masculinity.

Strategies for preventing violence in sport in relation to spectators

REVISED

The strategies employed to combat crowd violence at football matches include:

- bans on or control of alcohol sales, for example ban pubs where known trouble-makers gather from opening prior to kick-off
- increased use of police intelligence and improved liaison between forces across the country to gather information on known or potential hooligans
- imposing tougher deterrents such as bans from matches, higher fines and prosecution/imprisonment for violent offenders, banning individuals from travelling abroad
- using CCTV in and around stadiums to identify and then eject or arrest individuals for crowd disorder
- removal of terraces, building of 'all-seater' stadiums, segregation of fans, and introduction of family zones to create a better, 'more civilised' atmosphere at football matches, promoting football as family entertainment
- encouraging responsible media reporting prior to matches, decreasing the hype and potential tensions between rival fans
- playing games at kick-off times imposed by the police (e.g. early kick-offs to try to avoid high levels of alcohol consumption)
- passing specific laws preventing 'trespass' onto the pitch to try to stop pitch invasions and potential clashes between rival fans in the ground.

Typical mistake

If a synoptic question is set linking solutions to hooliganism with sport and the law, you need to make sure the answers you give have a clear link to law enforcement. For example, encouraging responsible media reporting is not a legal solution, but passing a trespass law to discourage pitch encroachment is.

Implications of violence in sport in relation to spectators

REVISED

When football hooliganism was at its height towards the end of the twentieth century (i.e. in the 1970s and 1980s), there were a number of negative consequences for the sport of football.

- The image of football declined, causing participation numbers to fall.
- Spectator attendance at matches fell, causing a decrease in gate receipts.
- More stringent security measures were imposed on all fans, which negatively impacted on law-abiding fans (e.g. their treatment en route to grounds).

Identify the negative effects of hooliganism for law-abiding football fans.

Hooliganism also had negative implications for clubs as a result of the ever-increasing costs of security and policing before, during and after matches. This was particularly the case for clubs in the lower leagues, where money was tighter.

The negative images of football hooliganism involving English 'fans' at home and abroad were often viewed globally and portrayed England as a nation of violent thugs who were out of control. This then had a negative influence on relations with other countries and on bids to host international sporting events. It also has repercussions for commercial deals/sponsorship of leagues/cup competitions as these come up for renewal.

Explain the negative implications of hooliganism for the sport of football.

Exam practice

1 Identify the possible solutions to violent behaviour among spectators in high-level sports such as football. [4]
2 Elite sport performers are expected to act as positive role models for others to follow. Outline possible reasons why an elite performer might act in an over-aggressive way which is deemed unacceptable by society. [4]
3 Using psychological theories, suggest reasons why sports performers may display acts of violence and outline possible strategies national governing bodies could use to eliminate such behaviour. [15]

Answers and quick quizzes online

ONLINE

Summary

You should now be able to:
- identify and explain different causes and implications of performer violence in sport, linked to a variety of examples
- identify and explain the strategies used to try to combat violence among sports performers
- identify and explain the causes and implications of violence in sport in relation to the spectator and sport in general, as well as strategies for preventing hooliganism at football matches.

7.5 Drugs in sport

Reasons for using illegal drugs and doping methods to aid performance

REVISED

The use of illegal drugs and **doping** methods to enhance performance at elite level continues to be a major issue in sport in the twenty-first century.

> **Doping:** in competitive sports, the use of banned performance-enhancing drugs by athletic competitors.

Social reasons

The social reasons for using illegal drugs and doping methods to enhance performance include:

- a 'win-at-all-costs' attitude, which dominates modern-day elite sport
- the fame and fortune attached to success at elite level (i.e. the very high level of extrinsic rewards/money received for sporting success via prize money, sponsorship deals and so on)
- the high levels of pressure to win from a variety of different sources such as coaches, family and the media (coaches might persuade athletes to take drugs illegally because their main competitors do so and they will not be able to compete with them on a level playing field if they do not)
- the lack of effective deterrents and firm belief that a performer will get away with it and not get caught
- poor role models setting a bad example that drug taking in certain sports is viewed in some way as being acceptable (e.g. athletics/cycling).

Psychological reasons

In addition to the various social reasons, elite performers also use illegal performance-enhancing drugs and doping to aid their psychological performance in a variety of different ways. Some may use beta blockers to steady their nerves where fine motor control is required (e.g. snooker players), while others may use anabolic steroids to increase their aggression in high-contact sports (e.g. rugby players). When athletes are suffering from a lack of confidence, **stimulants** can be used to raise a performer's belief that they can achieve, even when the competition is of the highest standard like at the Olympic Games.

> **Stimulants:** drugs that induce a temporary improvement in mental and physical function (e.g. increase alertness and awareness).

Now test yourself

TESTED

1 Identify the social and psychological reasons why elite performers continue to take illegal performance-enhancing drugs despite obvious dangers to their health.

Answer online

Physiological effects of drugs on the performer and their performance

All athletes want to improve their performance, and there are both legal and illegal methods, in addition to training, of achieving this. The table below lists the illegal drugs that some athletes feel the need to use.

Type of drug	Physiological benefits	Used by	Side effects
Anabolic steroids Artificially produced hormones, e.g. tetrahydrogestrinone (THG) which was tweaked by chemists to make it undetectable by 'normal' tests	Aid storage of protein and promote muscle growth and development of muscle tissue in the body, leading to increased strength and power Lead to less fat in the muscle and a lean body weight Improve the body's capacity to train for longer at a higher intensity and decrease fatigue associated with training	Power athletes, such as sprinters	Liver damage Heart problems Immune system problems Acne Behavioural changes, such as aggression, paranoia and mood swings
Beta blockers Medication used for heart conditions that works by widening the arteries, allowing increased blood flow and reducing involuntary muscle spasms	Improve accuracy in precision sports by steadying the nerves Calm performance anxiety and aid performance by keeping heart rate low and decreasing tremble in the hands Calm performance anxiety by counteracting the adrenaline that interferes with performance by preventing it from binding to nerve receptors	High-precision sports, such as archery, snooker and golf	Tiredness due to low blood pressure Slower heart rate, which will affect aerobic capacity
Erythropoietin (EPO) A natural hormone produced by the kidneys to increase red blood cells; it can now be artificially manufactured to cause an increase in haemoglobin levels	Stimulates red blood cell production leading to an increase in the oxygen-carrying capacity of the body, which can: ● increase the amount of work performed ● increase endurance ● delay the onset of fatigue	Endurance performers (e.g. long-distance runners and cyclists) who need effective oxygen transport to succeed in their sport	Blood clotting Stroke Death (in rare cases)

Some performers break the rules and use banned substances to enhance their performance. Identify the physiological reasons why a performer may use (a) beta blockers and (b) EPO.

Revision activity

Create a 'drugs in sport' mind map to include the social and psychological reasons why performers take performance-enhancing drugs (PEDs), as well as identifying the physiological effects of anabolic steroids, beta blockers and EPO on performance.

Positive and negative implications for the sport and the performer of drug taking

REVISED

In terms of the sport, drug taking and doping threaten the spirit and integrity of sport. It is cheating and negatively damages the reputation of a sport and decreases interest in it. Certain sports are strongly associated with drugs cheats, such as Ben Johnson in athletics and Lance Armstrong in cycling.

In terms of the performer, drug taking can positively impact on performance and bring fame and fortune for those who manage to evade detection. But there are a number of negative implications of drug taking. It provides negative role models, which set a bad example to young people. It can also be very damaging to a performer's health (steroids can lead to high blood pressure; EPO can increase the risk of heart disease and strokes). There are also a number of negative social consequences, as athletes involved in doping may lose their good reputation following a positive test. Future career prospects may be negatively impacted, with a loss of income and sponsorship deals resulting from doping infringements being widely reported in the media. In certain cases it can result in legal action against an individual, who can be fined, banned from competing, stripped of medals and earnings and even end up in jail, like Marion Jones as part of the **BALCO** scandal.

Doping can lead to social isolation from peers, as well as having a negative effect on an individual's emotional and psychological well-being.

BALCO: the Bay Area Laboratory Cooperative, which was behind one of the biggest scandals in drugs history as the source of THG, with several athletes implicated and subsequently banned from sport, including sprinters Dwain Chambers and Marion Jones.

Strategies for the elimination of performance-enhancing drugs in sport

REVISED

UK Anti-Doping (UKAD) is the organisation responsible for protecting UK sport from the threat of drug taking and doping. It administers the testing programmes for over 40 sports and has a number of anti-doping strategies designed to try to eliminate the use of illegal performance enhancers in sport.

Educationally, UKAD works with athletes and their support staff (e.g. coaches) to increase their knowledge and understanding of the dangers of drugs and the moral issues associated with doping. It promotes ethically fair, drug-free sport via its '100% Me' programme. This programme is delivered to athletes at all stages of the performance pathway and includes rising stars at the 'School Games' as well as elite athletes preparing for the Olympics and Paralympics.

Investment in drug-detection technology, science and medicine is also used by UKAD to try to ensure that it can prevent and detect doping. It works in a co-ordinated manner with other organisations involved in drug detection and prevention, such as the **World Anti-Doping Agency (WADA)** and the national governing bodies of sport. Such a co-operative approach is important when trying to develop and enforce stricter testing procedures to try to catch out drug takers. These procedures include random testing, out-of-competition testing and the **whereabouts system**).

Once detected and caught, it is important that organisations punish drugs cheats as harshly as possible to act as a deterrent to those considering following a similar route to success. Harsher punishments might include longer or lifetime bans and the return of career earnings and money gained from sponsorship. It is important to try to adopt a standardised, consistent approach between different countries and different sports

World Anti-Doping Agency (WADA): a foundation created in 1999 through a collective initiative led by the International Olympic Committee to promote, co-ordinate and monitor the fight against drugs in sport.

Whereabouts system: a system designed to support out-of-competition testing, which requires athletes to supply the details of their whereabouts so that they can be located at any time and anywhere for testing, without advance notice.

when punishing drugs cheats, so elite performers who are 'clean' gain confidence from a unified system which deals strongly with convicted drugs cheats.

Where positive role models exist, they should be used to promote ethically fair, drug-free sport (e.g. Sir Chris Hoy and the 100% Me campaign, which promotes the fact that winning clean is possible). In addition, drugs cheats should be 'named and shamed' to try to dissuade others from following their negative example.

You can remember a number of strategies being used to decrease drug usage via the mnemonic 'DOPING':
- **D**rug-free culture created via education programmes (e.g. 100% Me)
- **O**rganisations involved in drug detection/enforcement need to work together (i.e. co-operate)
- **P**unishments need to be harsher
- **I**nvestment is required into new testing programmes/technology
- **N**ame and shame negative role models
- **G**uilty lose funding/sponsorship deals.

Explain the advantages of all sports in all countries testing for performance-enhancing drugs.

Arguments for and against drug taking and testing

REVISED

Various arguments can be used in favour of the legalisation of drugs in sport, allowing them to be just another training aid. These are outlined below:
- The battle against drugs is expensive and time-consuming.
- Drugs are quite easy to access and some would argue that they are very difficult to eliminate and the money spent on testing could be better spent on things like participation initiatives and/or investment in elite sport.
- Detection is not always effective; drug testers are always one step behind as new drugs become available and masking agents are developed.
- Sometimes it is difficult to define what a 'drug' is, compared to a legal supplement; other technological aids, such as oxygen tents and nutritional supplements, are not regulated.
- Drugs are sometimes taken 'accidentally' (e.g. stimulants in cold cures, as with skier Alain Baxter).
- Sacrifices made by a performer are personal choice.
- If everyone takes drugs, it levels the playing field and increases performance standards physiologically and psychologically.
- If drug taking is properly monitored, health risks may be lessened.
- Athletes do not ask to be role models and individuals have a right to choose as it is their body.
- Drugs can be particularly helpful in allowing athletes in allowing recover more quickly from gruelling training.

The majority of people, however, would argue against the points above and point out that drugs should continue to be banned in sport for a variety of reasons. These are outlined below:

- There can be health risks and dangerous side effects (e.g. addiction/heart disorders).
- Drug taking creates negative role models who set a poor example to the young, who might then be tempted to use drugs.
- Drug use gives a negative image to certain sports (e.g. weight lifting, cycling and athletics).
- Pressure to take drugs increases from coaches and peers who take drugs.
- Success in sport should be about hard work and natural talent, and drug use is outside this concept.
- Drugs give an unfair advantage and are immoral, unethical and against the fair-play ethic.
- Taking drugs is cheating.
- Only richer countries can afford drugs.
- There are a variety of negative consequences if caught doping, such as the loss of sponsorship, medals and lottery funding.
- Drug taking is illegal.

> **Typical mistake**
>
> It is too vague to justify legalising drugs by saying that it would make a sport more exciting or that it would lead to money being saved.

> **Exam tip**
>
> When discussing the issues surrounding drugs and sport, make sure you clearly identify and outline both sides of the argument, for and against the legalisation of drugs in sport.

Exam practice

1. Which of the following is a key physiological reason why an elite performer takes EPO in order to improve their chances of success? [1]
   (a) Increased power
   (b) Increased confidence
   (c) Increased endurance
   (d) Increased anxiety
2. Elite athletes continue to take performance-enhancing drugs, despite obvious risks to their health and the negative implications of being caught. Give reasons why drug taking continues at elite sporting events such as the Olympics. [4]
3. Describe the physiological reasons why an elite performer might use anabolic steroids just like any other training aid. [3]
4. Outline the strategies being used by sports organisations to try to decrease the use of drugs by elite performers. [4]
5. Explain the problems which are being faced by drug enforcement agencies in the world of sport (e.g. WADA/UK Anti-Doping) in their fight to eliminate performance-enhancing drugs at elite performer level. [8]

Answers and quick quizzes online

ONLINE

Summary

You should now be able to:

- understand the different social and psychological reasons why elite performers use illegal performance-enhancing drugs/doping methods to aid performance
- understand the physiological impact of drugs on sport performance such as anabolic steroids, beta blockers and EPO
- understand the positive and negative implications to the sport and the performer of drug taking
- identify and explain a variety of different strategies being implemented in the continuing battle to eliminate performance-enhancing drugs in sport
- discuss the arguments for and against drug taking and testing.

7.6 Sport and the law

Sports legislation and the performer

Sports law includes the laws, regulations and judicial decisions that govern sports and athletes who perform in them. Lots of injuries occur to performers while playing sport, and more often than not they are seen as an expected side-effect of participating in sport. However, sometimes injuries occur that are not considered part and parcel of the sporting contest and involve a deliberate act by a participant to injure another. In certain instances, these are illegal. For example, criminal cases have been brought for dangerous tackles and violent actions such as punches in football matches, which have resulted in serious career-ending injuries.

In such cases, civil claims for **damages** (e.g. for injuries suffered and/or loss of earnings) can also be made against the person who has committed the illegal act. In order to be successful, claims made by sports performers for injury or loss of earnings (e.g. ex-Reading footballer Chris Casper) need to prove that the act was outside the playing culture of the sport; the incident must be shown to be an unacceptable means of playing the sport.

Loss of earnings may also result from an inequality issue (e.g. members of the USA women's soccer team took action against their federation and filed a wage discrimination complaint based on the fact that their male counterparts were paid four times more, despite generating less money) or a legal 'injustice'.

Performers may also interact with the law in a number of other ways, including contractual disputes. Performers are employees and as such should have the same employment rights as other workers. Their rights were greatly improved in 1995 by the **Bosman ruling**, which gave professional footballers within the EU the right to move freely to another employer (i.e. football club) at the end of their contract, and their existing club could not demand a transfer fee or retain the individual's playing licence. Players within the EU therefore have the right to work anywhere within the EU without restriction.

In terms of contracts with sponsors, a rare example of a brand suing an endorser was when Oakley brought an action against golfer Rory McIlroy when he left the sportswear company without allowing it the 'right of first refusal' before he signed a deal with Nike. Eventually, the case was resolved amicably without the need to go to court. Wayne Rooney's legal dispute with Proactive Sports Management, however, did go to court. The sports management company claimed it was owed commission by Rooney, but the Court of Appeal ruled that the deal he signed as a 17-year-old was unenforceable and was a '**restraint of trade**'.

> **Damages:** monetary compensation awarded by a court in a civil action to an individual when it has been proved that they have been injured through the wrongful conduct of another party.
>
> **Bosman ruling:** a ruling by the European Court of Justice, which gave a professional football player the right to a free transfer at the end of their contract.
>
> **Restraint of trade:** action that interferes with free competition in a market. In sport, this might involve a clause in a contract which restricts a person's right to carry out their profession.

Identify the reasons why sports performers may need protection from the law during their careers.

Sports legislation and officials

Negligence is when someone (e.g. an official) fails to take reasonable care for another person to avoid any dangers that could cause them harm. Officials have a **duty of care** towards participants to make sure that all dangers around them are eliminated so they can take part in a contest in a safe environment. If they fail to do 'everything possible' to keep participants safe, they may be seen as being 'negligent', for example allowing a match to be played on a dangerous surface that has not been checked prior to the match starting.

Negligence cases are brought against officials at both professional and amateur levels of sport. For example, in rugby some court cases have highlighted the position whereby a referee can be found liable for injuries sustained by a player during the game. In the case of *Smoldon* v *Whitworth and Nolan*, a referee was found liable for serious injuries sustained by the claimant following a scrum collapsing. It was found that the official was at fault because he allowed a number of scrums to collapse during the course of the fractious match he was refereeing. The referee was found to have failed in following Rugby Football Board guidelines in relation to collapsed scrums; he had allowed two packs to come into the scrum too hard, leading to a scrum collapse on more than twenty occasions.

In the case of *Allport* v *Wilbraham*, a claim against a rugby referee failed. Allport, the claimant, was left paralysed from the neck down following a scrum collapse. He argued that the referee had failed to ensure that the scrum had been adequately controlled. In this case, the court preferred the evidence of the defendant (Wilbraham) and dismissed the claimant's claim for compensation.

Such cases illustrate that it is likely there will continue to be litigation against referees and officials in rugby, as well as in other sports. They need to do everything in their power to ensure they are not negligent in the performance of their duties.

> **Negligence:** conduct that falls below a 'reasonable person standard' and leads to a breach of the duty of care, which results in foreseeable harm to another.
>
> **Duty of care:** a legal obligation to ensure the safety or well-being of others.

Now test yourself

TESTED

2 Define the term 'negligence' and give an example of how a sporting official might be deemed negligent in the execution of their duties.

Answer online

Sports legislation and coaches

In terms of sports coaches, the duty of care means they have a legal obligation to take 'reasonable' measures to eliminate all the potential dangers and risks so that players can participate in a safe environment.

Coaches therefore need to be aware of their legal responsibilities, especially with respect to the advice they give sports performers and the way they manage and supervise participation in sport. Coaches have a legal responsibility to their athletes in a variety of ways, including the following:

● Health and safety: coaches are responsible for the health and safety of the performers and athletes in their care. They should have access to first aid facilities and the means to contact the emergency services should this be required. A coach could be deemed liable if evidence shows that normal standards and practices were not followed.

- Protection from abuse: coaches have a responsibility to protect children from all forms of abuse, including emotional (threats or taunting) and physical (being hit by someone). All organisations (local sports clubs, local authorities etc.) should have a policy statement and guidelines regarding child abuse, which a coach should adhere to. The issue of sexual abuse rose to prominence at the end of December 2016 in football, with a number of historical cases reported and investigated.
- Supplements: coaches have a legal and ethical responsibility to educate their athletes about drug use and abuse and to provide general and appropriate advice on legal nutrition and supplements which can be used to enhance performance.
- Duty of care: it is widely accepted that, in relation to children and young people, sports organisations and the individuals who work for them have a duty of care. When coaching young children, ensuring the participants' safety and welfare can be due to a legal duty of care or a moral duty of care.

Legally, liability issues would only arise if an incident occurs and it can be demonstrated that the risk was foreseeable, but no action was taken to remedy it. In the sporting environment, when working with children and young people (e.g. at a sports club), coaches should ensure they follow a number of steps to demonstrate a reasonable standard of care. These include:

○ keeping up-to-date contact details, medical details and registers of attendance
○ maintaining appropriate supervision ratios
○ ensuring first aid provision is available
○ ensuring individuals regularly involved in coaching children have current DBS clearance
○ ensuring they have undertaken an appropriate risk assessment for the activities being coached.

Morally, coaches have a responsibility for the safety and welfare for those under their control. Where children are involved, those in charge have to act **'in loco parentis'**, which requires the coach to act as a reasonable parent would.

> Identify the steps a sports coach should follow in order to demonstrate a reasonable standard in terms of a legal duty of care to children and young people.

'In loco parentis': a Latin phrase which means 'in the place of a parent'. It is the authority parents assign to another responsible adult who will be taking care of their child (e.g. a sports coach at a sports club).

Sports legislation and spectators

REVISED

Spectators at sports events must act within the law. It is now illegal to trespass onto the field of play and chant in a racist manner towards players and opposition fans. Some of these new laws are particularly applicable to the sport of football, where clubs have a responsibility to ensure the health and safety of all spectators.

A variety of measures have been introduced to try to ensure safety and overcome hooliganism at sports events, including football matches. These include:

- removal of perimeter fences and terraces; all-seater stadia to replace the terraces
- control of alcohol sales on the way to grounds as well as in the grounds
- specified kick-off times imposed by police (e.g. in the case of a local derby, an early kick-off time can be imposed to decrease the likelihood of alcohol consumption)
- increased security and police presence, intelligence gathering, improved police liaison between forces across the country and indeed the world
- tougher deterrents, e.g. banning orders, fine and imprisonment for offenders.

Typical mistake

Make sure you can be specific when describing legal measures taken to control crowd behaviour at football matches. It is not just a case of fining clubs, deducting points, segregating fans or banning alcohol.

The various pieces of legislation that have emerged over the years to try to control fan behaviour at sporting events and improve safety can be considered as a 'timeline of crowd safety legislation':

1 The Occupiers' Liability Act (1957) is considered to be the fundamental law governing spectator safety at sporting events. It states that an 'occupier' of a premises owes a common duty of care to its 'visitors'. An occupier is in charge of the premises, while the visitor is someone that is invited or permitted to be at the premises.

2 The Safety of Sports Grounds Act (1975) protects all spectators and covers all grounds in all sports.

3 The Sporting Events (Control of Alcohol etc.) Act (1985) was introduced to ban possession of alcohol at a football match or on a journey to a match. It also empowered magistrates to impose conditions on licensed premises within sports grounds to ensure no alcohol can be sold by them during a match.

4 The Fire Safety and Safety of Places of Sport Act (1987) requires that a fire security certificate/licence is gained from the local authority for an event to happen. The Act also sets the maximum number of spectators who will be safely allowed into a stand, as well as stating that stands have to be made from fire-proof materials.

5 The Football Spectators Act (1989) allows banning orders to be put on individuals who have committed offences. The Act prevents them from attending sports events for a certain period of time at home and abroad (e.g. as at West Ham at the start of the 2016 Premier League season, following the move to its new home of the London Stadium where a number of security issues were experienced).

6 The Football (Offences) Act (1991) created three offences at football grounds to prevent the throwing of missiles, the chanting of racist remarks and trespassing onto the field of play. Supporters face legal consequences for their unacceptable behaviour, such as running onto the pitch (i.e. trespass) and attacking players. In February 2013, Wycombe goalkeeper Jordan Archer was attacked by a fan in the closing stages of his side's 1–0 win at Gillingham. A 17-year-old was arrested and charged with assault. Prior to this, in October 2012, Leeds fan Aaron Cawley was jailed for 16 weeks for attacking Sheffield Wednesday goalkeeper Chris Kirkland.

Describe how the use of sports legislation has helped improve spectator safety.

Answer online

Exam practice

1 Which of the following is a legal solution put in place to control football hooliganism? [1]
   (a) Fine the football club/deduct points
   (b) Improve segregation of rival fans to keep them apart
   (c) Pre-match appeals for good behaviour to fans by players/managers
   (d) Pre-match banning orders on fans who are known trouble makers
2 Identify the potential benefits of the law becoming more closely linked to the world of sport. [3]
3 Explain how the law aims to protect spectators from hooliganism at football matches. [8]

Answers and quick quizzes online

ONLINE

Summary

You should now be able to:
● understand the uses of sports legislation in relation to performers (contracts, injury, loss of earnings), officials (negligence), coaches (duty of care) and spectators (safety, hooliganism).

7.7 Impact of commercialisation on physical activity and sport and the relationship between sport and the media

Impact of the media, commercialisation and sponsorship on sport and sports performers

Golden Triangle

Sport, commercialisation/sponsorship and the **media** are closely interconnected and form what is known as the 'golden triangle' (see page 92).

> **Media:** an organised means of communication by which large numbers of people can be reached quickly.

There are a number of advantages to elite sport as a result of the golden triangle, including the following:

- Increased income to the sport allows events to be televised. This money can be spent at all levels of the sport – funding participation initiatives at grassroots level as well as providing finance to support elite athletes at the top of their profession.
- Increased promotion of the sport can attract more fans and increase its popularity.
- Increased sponsorship and income from business sources pay for advertising at grounds and sporting events.
- Sports are organised and funded, which in turn improves the way they are run (i.e. in a more professional manner).
- Improved facilities benefit performer and spectator alike.

However, there are also a number of possible disadvantages to elite sport resulting from its links to the media and sponsorship. These include the following:

- Sensationalist media reporting may sometimes focus too much on negative aspects of a sport.
- The media and sponsors can dictate kick-off times and scheduling of sports events, to the detriment of performers and spectators.
- The media and sponsors can change the nature of a sporting activity (e.g. introducing more or longer breaks in play to allow for advertising).
- The media only televise already popular, high-profile sports.
- The media and sponsors can be too demanding on elite performers and coaches (e.g. in relation to personal appearances and giving interviews).
- Sponsorship deals can increase the pressure to win in order to maintain lucrative contracts with companies willing to pay for an association with successful sports and sports performers.

Media

The media use sport to gain viewers, or readers, and to increase their income/advertising revenue. For the majority of people, the information and knowledge gained about sport is as a result of what they have seen or heard in the media (ranging from television, newspapers, magazines, radio, the internet and social media). The presence of the media as an influence on modern-day sport has turned it into a highly marketable commodity worth billions of pounds.

The **Ofcom** Code on Sports and Other Listed and Designated Events provides a series of regulations designed to protect the availability of major listed events in sport. The list of **ring-fenced** sporting events, however, has declined in recent years, as satellite channels offer riches which the sporting authorities cannot refuse.

There are a number of reasons for the continued ring-fencing of certain major sporting events, including to:

- access the widest number and range of viewers
- avoid restricting coverage to subscription channels available only to those who can afford them
- increase geographical access for all viewers in all parts of the country to major sporting events
- enable viewing of certain events which are seen as part of the UK's sporting heritage and culture
- enable access to sporting events which should be freely available to all to view (e.g. the Olympic Games, Football World Cup etc.).

> **Ofcom:** the communications regulator in the UK (e.g. it regulates the television sector).
>
> **Ring-fenced:** a number of sporting events at national and international level must be available for viewing on terrestrial or free-to-access TV, rather than on satellite and subscription channels.

Discuss the relationship between sport, sponsorship and the media. State the reasons why certain sporting events should continue to be 'ring-fenced'.

Sports which have the following characteristics are particularly attractive to the media:

- They have high levels of skill for viewers to watch and admire, which comes through a competitive, relatively well-matched competition.
- They are visually appealing and demonstrate physical challenge, lots of action-packed excitement and aggression (e.g. rugby).
- They are easily understood, with relatively simple rule structures.
- The sport or sporting event is easy to televise and has a relatively short timescale which fits into viewers' busy schedules.
- They are seen as nationally relevant with easily identifiable personalities and role models. TV companies focus their coverage on sports like these (e.g. association football and golf).

The advantages and disadvantages of media coverage for a sport are outlined in the table below.

Advantages of media coverage	Disadvantages of media coverage
It increases the profile of the sport and individual performers within the sport.	National governing bodies/sports performers lose control to TV/sponsors. The traditional nature of a sport is lost, e.g. rule structures/timings of a sport are adapted to suit the demands of TV or sponsors.
It increases participation levels within a sport as a result of TV coverage encouraging others to take it up (e.g. cycling as a result of Tour de France coverage or football as a result of World Cup coverage).	The media control the location of events, as well as kick-off times and, in some cases, playing seasons (e.g. Super League Rugby switched to a 'summer' game). There is sometimes too much sport on TV, which can lead to possible boredom of spectators and/or lower attendance at events which are on TV.

More variations of a sport are developed to make it more 'media friendly', leading to more matches/fixtures for fans to watch (e.g. Twenty20 cricket).	There are inequalities of coverage – more popular sports such as football gain at the expense of minority sports such as squash. Certain prestigious events are now available only on satellite TV, which requires a subscription payment (e.g. test cricket and golf's Ryder Cup). This means there are fewer viewers for some sports due to the increasing control of Sky and BT Sport.
It generates higher levels of income and makes a sport more appealing to sponsors. It increases commercial opportunities, which further increases the financial gain of a sport or sports performers (e.g. golf, tennis and football).	The demands of the media and sponsors negatively impact on high-level performers (e.g. demands for interviews and personal appearances).
Increased standards in performance as well as behaviour result from an increased media focus.	The media can sometimes over-sensationalise or over-dramatise certain negative events in sport. A win-at-all-costs attitude develops due to high rewards on offer, which leads to negative, deviant acts and players becoming poor role models (e.g. in football arguing with officials or diving to try to win a penalty).
Rule changes lead to a speeding up of action/more excitement/entertainment in a sport (e.g. penalty shoot-outs).	More breaks in play (e.g. for adverts) can disrupt the spectator experience.

Now test yourself

TESTED

3 Describe the possible disadvantages of media coverage for a sport.

Answer online

Commercialisation and sponsorship

There are a number of reasons why sport is attractive to businesses. Businesses use television companies to promote and advertise their products.

Businesses give their support to elite teams and performers in a variety of ways, including sponsorship, advertising contracts and product endorsements. Due to the following characteristics, sport becomes very attractive as a commercial enterprise:

- It has extensive media coverage.
- It gains large audiences, viewing figures and high levels of ticket sales.
- It links to professional/high-profile sport.
- Players are contracted to perform with or endorse products.
- Sport offers extensive advertising, **merchandising** or sponsorship opportunities.
- Winning is important, as it creates a link with success.
- Sport is media-friendly/entertaining.

> **Merchandising:** the practice in which the brand or image from one product is used to sell another (e.g. professional sports performers/teams promote various products, including mobile phones, betting companies etc.).

> **Revision activity**
>
> Using a practical example (e.g. association football), draw a spider diagram to summarise the characteristics of sport that make it appealing commercially.

Now test yourself

TESTED

4 Identify the characteristics of commercial sport.

Answer online

The **commercialisation** of sport has grown alongside the use of sport as part of the entertainment industry. Sports have become increasingly aware of their ability to make money from TV via the sale of rights to the highest bidder (e.g. Premier League football to Sky/BT Sport), as well as using this exposure to generate high levels of extra income from business and commerce. Televised sport offers companies an investment opportunity via **sponsorship**, whereby a company puts money into a sport in order to better itself financially. This happens through:

- increased sales and promotion of a product
- increased brand awareness
- improved company image linked to the healthy image of sport
- opportunities to entertain clients via corporate hospitality
- decreasing the amount of tax a company pays, as sponsorship is tax deductible.

The potential positive and negative effects of sponsorship and commercial deals for elite sports performers and the sports they participate in are outlined in the table below.

> **Commercialisation:** the treating of sport as a commodity, involving the buying and selling of assets, with the market as the driving force behind sport.
>
> **Sponsorship:** provision of money and/or support for a commercial return.

Positive effects	Negative effects
Increased wages, prize money and extrinsic rewards	Increased pressure to win and a win-at-all-costs attitude to maintain high-level prize money, extrinsic rewards, wages, sponsorship deals etc.
Increased availability of professional contracts where performers are able to devote themselves full time to sport, training harder and longer to improve performance	An increase in deviant behaviour due to increased pressure to win (e.g. performing when injured or over-training, taking illegal drugs, off-field drinking and gambling)
Performers increasingly in the public eye and increasingly well known, so they need to maintain discipline and behave appropriately to protect a positive image (e.g. on-field via fair play and sportsmanship; off-field via community and charitable work)	Performers treated as commodities, bought and sold for economic reasons; sponsors become too demanding (e.g. via the requirement for performers to make personal appearances at sponsorship events when they should be training)
Increased funding to pay for access to high-quality training support and specialist equipment etc.	Inequality of funding means performers in 'minority sports' (e.g. badminton and table tennis) miss out on funding and full-time professional opportunities

Discuss the impact of sponsorship deals on the behaviour of elite sport performers.

Impact of increased media coverage and commercialisation of elite sport for coaches and managers

Increased media coverage and the associated commercialisation of sport not only influence performers, but they can also positively and negatively impact on the coaches and managers who are in charge.

In terms of the positive effects, coaches and managers gain a much higher profile as a result of high levels of media coverage, which increases public awareness of their role. Such coverage has also led to increased salaries being on offer, particularly in high-profile sports such as football. The increased funding received from sponsors and the sale of media rights, which is then invested into the sport, positively impacts coaches and managers because they are then able to invest some of this money into improving their playing squads, as well as support systems (e.g. training grounds and medical provision). Media coverage of sport also enables coaches to analyse their opponents more, as well as learn from other high-level coaches.

On the negative side, coaches and managers are under intense pressure to be successful and win matches. There is a high level of public expectation to produce positive results and, if not, managers can expect to lose their jobs relatively quickly. When the pressure is on, the expectation to deal with the media (which is often part of media deals such as that between the Premier League and Sky Sports) and answer their questions can be particularly difficult for managers. Inequalities of sponsorship and funding mean that coaches and managers in lower level clubs and minority sports find it harder to attract the best, high-level performers to their clubs/sports, which means they are financially disadvantaged in relation to their higher profile colleagues.

Impact of increased media coverage and commercialisation of elite sport for officials

Increased media coverage and the commercialisation of sport have also impacted in both positive and negative ways on the referees and officials who take charge of sporting contests.

The potential positives for officials include:
- increased profile of officials, which increases public awareness of their important role in ensuring fairness in sport
- an increase in salary and the possibility of full-time job opportunities as part of an elite group of match officials (e.g. in Premier League football)
- increased funding to invest in support systems and training to improve standards of officiating; increased ability to learn from other officials
- increased funding to invest in technology to aid officials in their decision making.

On the other hand, there are also a number of possible negative outcomes of increased media coverage and commercialisation of sport on officials, such as:

- increased pressure on officials to get decisions right (e.g. when TV channels including BT Sport have an ex-professional referee such as Howard Webb giving instant reviews of key decisions via TV replays)
- increased expectation to respond to media enquiries and give interviews explaining their decisions
- risk of possible demotion or loss of job if a 'faulty decision' is highlighted in the media
- technology to aid officials in their decision making not always being available at lower levels of a sport
- officials becoming too dependent on media technology when it is made available to them.

> **Exam tip**
>
> The negative impact of increased media coverage and commercialisation of sport for the official can be remembered via 'OFICAL':
>
> **O** = **O**ver-use/over-dependency on technology
>
> **F** = **F**aulty decisions are highlighted
>
> **I** = **I**ncreased pressure to deal with media queries
>
> **CA** = **C**onstant **A**nalysis of decisions made
>
> **L** = **L**ack of availability of technology at lower levels of a sport

Impact of increased media coverage and commercialisation of elite sport for spectators

REVISED

There are a number of positive effects of media coverage and commercialisation of sport for the sporting experience of spectators, such as:

- increased performance standards; players of a higher standard providing a high level of excitement and entertainment
- improved quality of facilities; larger, higher quality stadia resulting from increased investment
- improved viewing experience via innovations such as changes in ball colour, creation of team merchandise to create team loyalty via the purchase and subsequent wearing of a team's kit
- increased access to watch sport; more opportunities to watch events 'live' as more competitions, events and matches are taking place
- development of more variations of a sport format, which provide alternative viewing experiences
- more funding available to provide entertainment (e.g. cheerleaders/pop stars) at sports events
- rule changes introduced which provide extra interest and extra excitement for the spectator (e.g. Twenty20 cricket)
- increased funding for improved technology at a ground (e.g. video screens) and at home (e.g. interactive technology, HD coverage of sport and referee links)
- increased excitement in the audience while awaiting the decisions of off-field officials (e.g. Hawk-Eye in tennis)
- increased awareness of and knowledge of sport; creation of role models for fans to idolise
- increased elimination of negative aspects of sport (e.g. hooliganism/player violence).

There are a number of negative effects of media coverage and commercialisation of sport for the sporting experience of spectators, such as:

- increased costs to watch sport (e.g. on pay-per-view satellite channels)
- loss of the traditional nature of the sport (e.g. via the wearing of coloured clothing in cricket)
- increased number of breaks in play to accommodate adverts and decisions of officials
- fewer tickets available for the fans; more allocated to sponsors and corporate hospitality
- changes in kick-off times to maximise viewing figures (i.e. scheduled at prime time), which is not always in the best interests of the long-distance travelling fan who wishes to watch an event live
- minority sports likely to receive less coverage; major sports likely to dominate the TV schedules and become 'over-exposed'
- links to team or player merchandise sometimes viewed negatively due to their high cost and regularity of change.

Revision activity

Draw a table identifying the positive and negative effects of increased commercialisation and media coverage on spectators.

Now test yourself

TESTED ☐

6 Explain how the increased level of media coverage of sport and sporting events has positively affected spectators.

Answer online

Exam practice

1 Which of the following statements is a disadvantage of increased media coverage to an official? [1]
   (a) Increased availability of technology to aid decision making
   (b) Increased profile and full-time job opportunities
   (c) Increased pressure to get decisions right
   (d) Increased salaries for those at elite level
2 Discuss the impact of the 'golden triangle' on elite sport. [8]
3 Define the term 'sponsorship' and identify how companies benefit from their involvement in sport. [4]
4 Discuss whether an elite performer should consider the nature of a sponsor before accepting a sponsorship deal. [8]
5 Evaluate the impact of the media and commercialisation of sport on spectators. [8]

Answers and quick quizzes online

ONLINE ☐

Summary

You should now be able to:
- discuss the positive and negative impact of the media, commercialisation and sponsorship on the performer, coach, official, spectator and sport.

7.8 Role of technology in physical activity and sport

Understanding of technology for sports analytics

High-quality **research** is vital to understanding all aspects of sport, exercise and health. When undertaking research and collecting information using technology, you must be able to understand some important terms you might come across during your studies, such as **sports analytics**. Look out for other key terms highlighted below.

> **Research:** a systematic process of investigation and study carried out with the aim of advancing knowledge.
>
> **Sports analytics:** studying data from sports performances to try to improve performance.

Define what is meant by sports analytics.

Quantitative and qualitative research

REVISED

Quantitative research is a formal, objective and systematic process used to gather **quantitative data** (i.e. factual information and numerical data). Most fitness tests used to analyse elite performers use quantitative data, for example the VO_2 max test on a treadmill.

Examples of areas where quantitative data could be gathered to try to prove a hypothesis include the following:
- in sport psychology, the potential positive link between motivational self-talk and improvement in self-paced skills, e.g. a golf putt
- in exercise psychology, research of a quantitative nature, e.g. on a numerical scale, to compare the relative effect of different environments on exercisers' moods: cycle trails in wooded areas vs cycling lanes in urban areas.

Qualitative research is generally focused on words as opposed to numbers. The **qualitative data** collected is subjective, as it looks at feelings, opinions and emotions, for example a group of coaches expressing an opinion when judging a gymnast performing a competitive routine.

Qualitative data is used to try to gain a better understanding of a participant's experiences.

> **Quantitative data:** data that can be written down or measured precisely and numerically.
>
> **Qualitative data:** data that are descriptive and look at the way people think or feel.
>
> **Objective data:** fact-based information which is measurable and usable (e.g. the level achieved on the multi-stage fitness test which links to a VO_2 max score).
>
> **Subjective data:** information based on personal opinion, which is less measurable and often less usable.

Objective and subjective data

REVISED

Objective data is information based on facts. It is measurable and observable and therefore highly suitable and meaningful for decision making when feeding back to sports performers, for example in a performance analysis of a swimmer at the English Institute of Sport (EIS).

Subjective data is information based on personal opinions, assumptions, interpretations, emotions and beliefs. With an emphasis on personal opinions, it is seen as less suitable and meaningful when feeding back to performers, for example a parent talking to their child at half-time during a football match, giving them their opinion on their performance in the first half.

Validity and reliability

REVISED

Data collection when using technology should be both valid and reliable.

Validity refers to the degree to which the data collected actually measure what they claim to measure. To assess the validity of data collection, an important question to ask is: do the data collected measure exactly what they set out to do?

Reliability is when the data collected are consistent, and similar results are achieved when the data collection process is repeated at a later date:

- In quantitative research, reliability can be one researcher conducting the same test (e.g. skinfold measurements) on the same individual on a number of occasions and getting the same or very similar results. Alternatively, it can be different researchers conducting the same test on the same individual and getting the same or very similar results.
- In qualitative research, reliability relates to the same researcher placing results into the same categories on different occasions, or different researchers placing results into the same or similar categories.

Reliability can be affected by errors occurring when researchers do not know how to use equipment correctly, for example in the use of skinfold calipers when assessing body composition. Accuracy can also be affected by poorly maintained equipment, for example weighing devices giving initial incorrect readings which affect calculations such as body mass index (BMI).

The validity of data is requisite for data reliability. If data are not valid, then reliability is questionable. In other words, if data collected are not valid, there is little or no point in discussing reliability because data validity is required before reliability can be considered in any reasonable way.

> **Validity:** an indication of whether the data collected actually measure what they claim to measure.
>
> **Reliability:** refers to the degree to which data collection is consistent and stable over time.

Video and analysis programs

REVISED

Coaches and athletes are using video, DVD or digital technology as a medium more and more to analyse individual technique as well as team performances. At an individual level, video analysis can also be used to analyse gait and biomechanical aspects of performance. Any information gained is also potentially helpful in rehabilitation from injury.

Video motion analysis usually involves a high-speed camera and a computer with software, allowing frame-by-frame playback of the footage on video.

The process of motion analysis has developed into two distinct sport science disciplines:

- Notational match analysis is used to record aspects of individual/team performance. It takes place through the study of movement patterns, strategy and tactics in a variety of different sports. It is used by coaches and sport scientists to gather objective data on the performance of athletes.
- Biomechanics is used to analyse the sporting impact of body movements. It involves quantitative-based study and analysis of sports activities. It is sometimes called kinematics – the study of the motion of bodies with respect to time, displacement, velocity and speed of movement.

> **Video motion analysis:** a technique used to get information about moving objects from video.

The two disciplines use similar methods to collect data and both rely on IT for data analysis. However, the main thing they have in common is the use of measured observation (i.e. quantitative analysis) during or after an event to quantify performance in an accurate, reliable and valid way.

Identify the potential problems a sports coach might have if they choose not to use video analysis programs, but rely instead on their own observation and analysis skills.

Performance analysis (PA) is now acknowledged as an important aid to performance enhancement at all levels, and failure to use it might result in poor immediate decisions being made (e.g. in competition), as well as, in the longer term, in relation to an athlete's training programme.

There are a variety of PA techniques used by coaches and sport scientists to provide them with task, performance and physiological data. Within a training environment, immediate visual feedback software is useful to provide images pre- and post-feedback for the athlete and coach to compare.

In a competitive environment, the coach and performer might look at the statistics of their opponent(s) before discussing the data, alongside any other past experiences against such opposition, to come up with a game-plan to win. In this case, they would look to use particular strategies and tactics to outwit their opponents.

Testing and recording equipment – the metabolic cart for indirect calorimetry

A **metabolic cart** is an electronic medical tool used to measure the body's metabolism through the amount of heat produced when the body is at rest. The metabolic cart uses a process called **calorimetry** to get this measurement. The result can help tell medics more about a person's overall health condition. The various parts of the device, which include a computer system, monitor and breathing tubes, are typically mounted together on a mobile push-cart, hence the name, so that it can easily be moved from one room to another.

Indirect calorimetry is a technique where the headgear from the cart is attached to a subject while they breathe for a specific amount of time. The subject's inspired and expired gas flows, volumes and concentrations of oxygen (O_2) and carbon dioxide (CO_2) are all continually measured. These measurements are then translated into a heat equivalent. It is a non-invasive technique and is regarded as being relatively accurate.

Define the terms 'metabolic cart' and 'indirect calorimetry'.

The two figures (concentrations of O_2 and CO_2) will provide the result for the metabolic cart, which is generally measured as **resting energy**

Performance analysis (PA): the provision of objective feedback to performers trying to effect a positive change in performance. Feedback can be gained on a variety of performance indicators, including the number of passes made, distance run in km, number of shots attempted etc.).

Metabolic cart: a device which works by attaching headgear to a subject while they breathe a specific amount of oxygen over a period of time.

Calorimetry: the measurement of the heat and energy eliminated or stored in any system.

Indirect calorimetry: the measurement of the heat and energy generated in an oxidation reaction (i.e a reaction where oxygen is gained).

Resting energy expenditure (REE): the amount of energy, usually expressed in kcal, required for a 24-hour period by the body during rest.

expenditure (REE). The REE for a patient can vary quite a bit according to a range of conditions. Between individuals, the REE changes with regard to a person's overall weight or height-to-weight ratio. Therefore, due to average differences in size, REE is lower in women when compared to men. Age and gender can also influence the result of this test. In addition, the chemistry of the body in response to various drugs will change the outcome. Smoking and drugs such as amphetamines can both increase someone's REE.

Now test yourself

TESTED ☐

4 Identify different reasons for individual variations in someone's resting energy expenditure (REE) over a period of time.

Answer online

Indirect calorimetry and use of a metabolic cart can therefore help individuals to:

- determine their energy requirements and response to nutrition over time
- calculate energy expenditure, which allows the determination of nutritional requirements/calorific needs
- be classified (or potentially classified) as obese
- calculate their REE, which helps medics determine the amount of food and nutrition needed.

Possible difficulties or sources of error affecting validity and reliability using indirect calorimetry via a metabolic cart include:

- inaccuracies from air leaks
- inaccuracies from measurement or recording errors
- difficulty in using it on children
- overfeeding or underfeeding, based on results received
- single snapshots being worse than average results/studies over a longer period of time
- the fact that the process actually measures consumption, not needs.

Exam tip

Possible sources of error when using a metabolic cart can be remembered via 'LOSE':

L = **L**eakage of air

O = **O**verfeeding or underfeeding may occur post-results

S = **S**ingle snapshots are not as good as average results over longer time periods

E = **E**rrors in taking measurements may occur

GPS and motion-tracking software and hardware

REVISED ☐

GPS software tracking systems are very useful when helping coaches to monitor players during matches, as well as in training. Such systems give coaches a vast amount of information immediately, at the touch of a button on a computer. They track the speed, distance and direction of the individuals concerned.

GPS (global positioning system): a space-based navigation system that provides location and time information.

GPS can also provide data which help improve performance via monitoring success rates in technical performance. In high-contact sports (rugby, for example), it can measure the impact in 'G' forces. It can also help coaches to make objective decisions about possible replacements/substitutions. This can decrease the risk of injury, as GPS can help gauge a performer's fatigue level. If a performer is recovering from injury, GPS can be used to manage workload during their rehabilitation.

In football, GPS tracking of players allows the measurement and monitoring of players' speed and distance performed during a game or a training session. Some GPS trackers can also be used to measure a player's heart rate, pace, recovery time and the amount of dynamic acceleration.

A number of reasons can therefore be given for using GPS technology for player performance tracking, such as:
- It makes better use of training time, to ensure training meets game demands.
- It improves the tactical analysis undertaken at a club.
- It helps a coach compare player performance and potentially pick the best player for the team based on GPS data.
- It helps to get injured players through rehabilitation at a faster rate.

> Describe the different ways in which GPS data can help to improve player performance.

Monitoring data integrity

REVISED

The overall intent of **data integrity** is to ensure data are entered into a system and recorded exactly as intended; when information is retrieved later, it should be the same as when it was originally recorded.

Data integrity can be compromised in a number of ways through:
- human error when data are entered
- errors occurring when data are transmitted from one computer to another
- software bugs or viruses
- **hardware** malfunctions such as disk crashes.

Ways to minimise threats to data integrity include:
- regularly backing up data
- controlling access to data and protecting against malicious intent via security mechanisms
- designing interfaces which prevent the input of invalid data
- taking care when entering data
- using error detection and correction software when transmitting data
- not leaving a computer unattended for unauthorised individuals to access.

> Identify ways in which data integrity can be maintained.

Software: computer software is any set of machine-readable instructions which direct a computer's processor to perform specific operations.

'G' forces: forces acting on the body as a result of acceleration or gravity (e.g. the G-load/force of an American football 'hit' on an opponent).

Data integrity: maintaining and ensuring the accuracy and consistency of stored data over its lifetime.

Hardware: computer hardware is the physical components of computers.

Functions of sports analytics

The answer to the question '*Why* sports analytics?' is fairly obvious: the effective use of sports analytics can help an individual and/or team increase their chances of success and win more frequently and more consistently. The focus should therefore be more about *how* sports analytics can be used to gather new, meaningful statistical information on player performance and/or game details. It is then important to consider how this information can be synthesised and summarised into key points to help improve the efficiency and effectiveness of performance for those involved in sport or physical activity.

Monitoring fitness for performance

Analysing data and assessing fitness levels is common in high-level sport and is becoming more common in lower levels of performance. One function of sports analytics is to gain information to help in monitoring fitness for performance, whether for individual recreational purposes (e.g. monitoring heart rate or amount of calories being burned when training for a marathon) or for elite-sport purposes (e.g. elite marathon runners monitoring key aspects of performance such as distance covered in training, pace of running, sleep statistics, calorie input and output, as well as heart-rate monitoring before, during and after exercise). There are a number of **smart wearable fitness and sports devices** available to aid such performers in their quest to improve performance based on the key information they provide.

> **Smart wearable fitness and sports devices:** devices worn or attached to a performer's body to provide instant feedback on aspects of performance such as distance covered or heart rate (e.g. Adidas MiCoach).

Skill and technique development

Sports analytics can be a highly valuable tool in aiding the skill and technique development of elite performers. An analytics program called Dartfish is one example of how technology can be used to capture, create, analyse and share video content on sports performance. The Dartfish software combines technical, tactical and statistical information to help improve skills and techniques on the spot or identify areas for improvement in future training sessions. It is particularly useful in sports and activities where visual feedback is beneficial for the performer and coach.

Injury prevention

Vibration technology can be used for various purposes, including exercise recovery, injury prevention and rehabilitation. Application of **vibration therapy** can be both direct (i.e. applied to the affected area) and indirect (transferred to the whole body or body part affected).

Advocates of vibration therapy claim there are a number of possible health benefits which can be gained from both whole body and localised vibration therapy, such as:
- improving bone density
- increasing muscle mass/power
- improving circulation
- reducing joint pain
- reducing back pain
- alleviating stress
- boosting metabolism
- an overall reduction in pain/delayed onset of muscle soreness (DOMS)
- maintenance of cartilage integrity where weight-bearing activities are difficult to undertake.

> **Vibration therapy:** can be applied directly to an affected area of the body or indirectly to either the whole body or just the body part affected. It is also known as 'whole body vibration' (WBV). An example is the use of vibration plates to induce exercise effects in the body.

> **Revision activity**
>
> Draw a spider diagram identifying a range of health benefits of using vibration therapy.

All of these benefits help to prevent future injuries.

Identify the possible benefits to health of using vibration therapy.

Electrostimulation can help to prevent injuries by:

- strengthening and toning the muscles (e.g. it can strengthen the muscle groups of the legs to give stability and help prevent injury or recurring injuries to the knees and ankles)
- helping to prevent losses in fitness levels via application to specific muscle groups, which maintains muscle tone during periods of inactivity
- assisting in rehabilitation through the gradual strengthening of injured or weakened muscles via small incremental increases in workload on the muscles (i.e. by inducing stronger muscular contractions)
- helping to get rid of lactic acid after a training session or competition, as well as decreasing muscle tension and potential injury by providing a relaxing effect to muscles.

> **Electrostimulation:** the production of muscle contraction using electrical impulses.

Explain the role of electrostimulation in injury prevention.

Game analysis

Analytics can be used in lots of different sports, e.g. in team games such as netball and basketball, to gather quantitative data, including player performance metrics which measure the amount of court covered during matches by individual players. Elite-level sports have embraced the role of technology and sports analytics in providing them with valuable information on player performance, on the pitch or court. Use has increasingly been made of video and data, captured and displayed on iPads, which is then used to give real-time analysis and feedback to coaches during games. This ultimately aims to give them an edge over the opposition.

On the field or court during games of football and netball, for example, sports analytics can also be used to measure individual performance, which can help improve player performance and fitness after they have finished. Use of small GPS receivers can measure aspects such as distance covered in games, as well as top speeds and/or acceleration speeds achieved by individual performers during matches. The information received from games can help coaches and physiotherapists fine-tune training programmes and optimise rest and recovery times.

The data gained via sports analytics can also assist coaches when looking at tactics, formations and substitutions during games. Access to precise data allows coaches to compare an individual player's performance to their 'normal play', as well as to match team tactics to the squad available to them. It is important to appreciate that as the technology available for game analysis develops further, there is more of a need to be selective and choose the most relevant information to capture. Quality of information is more important than quantity of information.

Talent ID/scouting

Sports analytics can be used to provide qualitative data on individual performers in a range of different sports, for example through written scouting reports commenting on opposition players and/or feedback from players being watched with a view to recruiting them onto a Talent ID programme.

Technology can be used in 'pathway analytics', as a method of systematically profiling and benchmarking the effectiveness of performance pathways across Olympic and Paralympic sports. Talent ID programmes have developed over the years, linking to the specific technical, physiological and psychological requirements of different sports. For example, Tall and Talented requires technically gifted sports performers to be above a certain height for sports such as basketball and rowing. The data on potential recruits needs to be systematically gathered and analysed so it can be used as effectively as possible in identifying the best, most talented athletes who are the 'most likely' to succeed at elite level.

Development of equipment and facilities in physical activity and sport

Assistive and adaptive equipment for elderly and disabled people

In the twenty-first century, mobility limitations resulting from age or disability no longer need to constitute a barrier to participation in sport and physical activity.

The design of assistive or adaptive technology in sport is on the increase. New devices are being created to help elderly and disabled sports enthusiasts to participate at recreational level, and highly advanced equipment is being created for elite Paralympians. In athletics, adaptive equipment such as specially designed wheelchairs are used on the track and, in the field, throwing frames have been designed for use in the shot put and discus.

Assistive devices can therefore enable training and exercise, as well as providing the opportunity for participation in sport. Wheelchairs are an important assistive technology in sport and can be individually designed and adapted to meet the specific requirements of different sports. Sports such as tennis and basketball require lightweight frames to enable fast-paced movements, sharp turns and lots of agility. Contact sports such as rugby require chairs with strong reinforced frames and impact/foot protection.

Prosthetic devices have been developed to meet a number of athletic purposes. For example, prosthetic leg devices (e.g. Springlite) have been designed to assist athletes in running via improved gait efficiency. Prosthetic legs have also been designed for use in cycle racing. The introduction of new materials for prosthetic devices, such as carbon flex-fibre, and new developments in wheelchair technology are positively impacting performance in many sports.

> **Revision activity**
>
> Choose three sports and identify how equipment has been adapted to enable elderly and/or disabled athletes to participate in them.

Technology and facility development – the Olympic legacy

Places People Play is an initiative delivered by Sport England in partnership with the British Olympic Association. It aims to deliver on the Olympic and Paralympic legacy promise to increase sports participation by providing sports facilities for the local community to access and use.

Iconic Facilities is part of this initiative, designed to transform the places people use to play sport in towns, cities and villages across the country. It directs funds into a small number of 'best practice' strategic facility projects designed to increase mass participation in sport across England. Best practice is based on high-quality design and long-term sustainability of a facility which delivers multi-sport provision, with a focus on sporting activities that have high participant numbers.

There have been a number of technological developments in surfaces suitable for such multi-sport provision, with **3G surfaces** increasingly being used. The sand and rubber infill in 3G surfaces gives them playing characteristics similar to those of natural grass. They allow high levels of use in a wide variety of sports and are ideal for sports such as hockey, football and rugby. The benefits of 3G surfaces include the fact that they can be played on more frequently and for longer than natural grass. Synthetic grass also gives consistent conditions, unlike natural grass which can become very worn and unpredictable.

> **3G surface:** third-generation artificial synthetic grass covering for pitches etc.

While there a number of benefits to artificial surfaces being used in sport, one of the main problems in sports like football is that some do not reflect the true bounce of grass. In addition, they have been criticised for being too rigid, leading to joint or ligament injuries. The more recent 3G/4G surfaces have gone some way to rectifying such problems. Even fully competitive games of rugby are now being played on an artificial surface – Rugby Super League team Widnes Vikings has re-embraced artificial turf at its home stadium in Hallam, as has Saracens Rugby Union at Allianz Park.

Discuss the benefits to sport of technological developments in artificial surfaces.

Advances in technology have also led to the development of multi-use games areas (MUGAs). A specific surface for each sport would be ideal, but this is often too expensive and impractical in terms of space for many local authorities, schools and sports clubs. MUGAs made of artificial grass are often the best solution to providing multi-sport opportunities, and increasing participation in sport and physical activity helps the Places People Play initiative deliver on its promise.

The impact of technology on sport, the performer, the coach and the audience

REVISED

Sport

Technology can have a positive impact on sport by helping to increase participation and make it more inclusive. The development of adaptive equipment such as carbon-fibre prosthetic blades and lightweight wheelchairs described above has certainly increased access to sport for people with disabilities. Technology can also benefit a sport by improving the quality of surfaces it is played on, as well as providing meaningful data via GPS systems, which can help in the short- and long-term development of players.

There are also possible negative implications of using technology for sport, including the following:

- Pure data can be misleading at times, for example if a performer has not covered many metres in a game but the tactics and game context are such that it does not require them to do so.
- It can be expensive, so inequalities might exist in terms of access to the latest technology available in a sport, for example only the wealthiest countries and teams are able to succeed. Some might argue that the high costs of technological advances in sport might be invested better in participation initiatives as opposed to a few elite performers.
- It can lead to 'paralysis by analysis'. Players and coaches might become too reliant on data to inform their decision making and unable to react creatively and instantly to on-field problems or issues as they occur.
- It can have a placebo effect. Are athletes simply gaining increased confidence by using equipment, even though it may have limited scientific proof to support it? Is technology acting as a sporting placebo, increasing a player's confidence?

Performer

There are a number of potential benefits of technology for sports performers, which include:

- improved clothing/footwear which can lead to improved performance, for example bodysuits used by athletes have helped sprinters increase their speed (their use in swimming was a little more controversial as they led to some dramatic performance improvements, with several world records being broken in a short space of time following their introduction)
- improved sports equipment which can aid skill/technique development, for example modern-day footballs have been designed to allow more swing and curve, and technological developments in golf have allowed manufacturers to build lighter clubs to increase swing speeds and enable golfers to hit golf balls a lot further and with more control; clubs can now be personalised and designed to meet the individual needs of a golfer, and aerodynamics has improved through driver head designs decreasing wind resistance and increasing club head speed
- improved protective equipment, for example cricket helmets to withstand increasingly fast-paced deliveries
- improved recovery from training (e.g. via **compression clothing**); technology can be used to simulate/counter extreme climatic conditions
- improved recovery from injury and better rehabilitation (e.g. oxygen tents)
- detailed scientific analysis of performance via GPS data to provide meaningful technical and physiological feedback to performers and coaches
- increased knowledge of diet and sports supplements (e.g. carbo-loading; sports energy drinks)
- advances in drug-testing technology to keep up with performers taking illegal performance-enhancing substances
- improved sleep enabling appropriate rest and recovery from training or competition (sleep is important for physiological recovery as well as an individual's reaction time); players at some professional clubs (e.g. in football) who are poor sleepers are given wristbands (e.g. the Fatigue Science Readiband), which use movement sensors to assess sleep quality.

> **Exam tip**
>
> When discussing the impact of technology on sport, you need to clearly identify and talk about both positive and negative effects.

> **Compression clothing:** items such as elasticated leggings, socks or shirts worn to promote recovery by improving circulation. They can decrease the pain suffered from muscle soreness/stiffness and decrease the time for muscle repair.

There are a number of potential negative effects of technology for the sports performer, including the following:

- It can lead to injury or over-aggression, for example from bladed boots or due to the use of protective equipment which makes some performers feel invincible or less inhibited.
- It can lead to cheating, as drugs are taken by athletes who believe they will get away with it, for example taking effective masking agents or a newly developed performance-enhancing substance for which there is no test.
- It can be expensive and unaffordable for some, which leads to potential inequalities and unfair advantages if the technology is not available to all.
- The availability of technological advances aiding performance might be dependent on an individual or team sponsor, which might positively or negatively impact the chances of success. The use of modern technologies in sport may mean that competition at the very highest level is only affordable to the leading top athletes due to the high costs of specialised sports equipment.

Identify the potential negative effects of technology for performers.

Revision activity

Make a list of the positive and negative effects of technology in relation to the sports performer.

The coach

As discussed above, the impact of sports analytics and technology on sports performers can be highly informative as they aid in the detailed analysis of performance for coaches. Video analysis of matches enables an assessment of player performance tactically, technically and physiologically. For example, an in-depth technical analysis can be instantly gained through such programs as Dartfish and Prozone. The detailed information gained can help a coach develop more focused training programmes designed to improve on any weaknesses identified. Whilst technology has its positives, it can prove a hindrance if there is an over-emphasis on performance analysis data. Use of computers is also a possible negative as they are open to potential hacking which might lead to information on weak links in a team being passed on and exploited by the opposition.

Audience/spectator

Statistical enthusiasts can visit many websites to find out various pieces of information on their favourite teams and players. The data collected in different ways can be organised to make it more easily understandable and digestible to fans and spectators, who can gain improved knowledge about the physical, technical and tactical aspects of performance in a sport.

Advances in technology have certainly impacted in positive ways on the audience. Officials are now 'mic'd-up' (e.g. in rugby) so the audience can hear what is being said on the field of play. This increases involvement and excitement in the audience and enhances the viewing experience. Increased interest and excitement also occur as a result of technology being employed to aid officials in their decision making (e.g. Hawk-Eye).

Other advantages for an audience from the increasing use of technology to aid officials in their decision making include the following:

- It ensures the right decisions are reached, with less frustration at incorrect decisions.

- It helps officials communicate with one another and the players, which the audience can sometimes hear (e.g. in rugby matches).
- More accurate timing and distances achieved are quickly communicated to the audience (e.g. via big screens in the stadium).
- There is increased excitement in the audience as they await decisions (e.g. Hawk-Eye at the Wimbledon Tennis Championships).

However, there are also some disadvantages of officiating technology as far as the audience is concerned:

- There may be a loss of respect in the crowd for the official as the 'final decision maker'.
- Costs limit the use of technology at events, which can give an inconsistent experience to spectators, as well as performers.
- Breaks in play can be disruptive for spectators if decisions take too long or there is an over-reliance on technology which leads the official to over-use it. For example, in the opening 2015 World Cup fixture when England played Fiji, the referee Jaco Peyper was criticised for his over-reliance on the television match official (TMO), which seriously slowed down the action and negatively impacted on the viewing experience.

Exam practice

1 Which of the following is a negative aspect of technology when used to aid officials in their decision making? [1]
  (a) Increased performer confidence in the correct decisions being made
  (b) Increased disruption to a sporting event as a result of lots of referee referrals
  (c) Increased excitement in the crowd as decisions are awaited on the big screen
  (d) Increased accuracy of timings or measurements taken
2 Identify two types of adaptive equipment used in athletics. [2]
3 State the disadvantages to the sporting event of the increased use of technology to help officials in their decision making. [3]
4 Technological products are becoming an increasingly important part of modern-day twenty-first century sport. Outline the advantages for performance in sport of using such technology. [4]
5 How have sports spectators benefited from advances in technology? [3]
6 Fitness apps, which are usually based on smartphone technology, are viewed as one way of increasing participation in sport/physical activity. Discuss the use of fitness apps as a way of increasing participation in sport/physical activity. [4]
7 Discuss the impact of modern technology on participation in sport/physical activity. [6]
8 The use of TMOs in sport has been positive for spectators. Discuss. [6]

Answers and quick quizzes online

ONLINE

Summary

You should now be able to:

- explain, using practical examples in sport and physical activity, how technology such as video and analysis programs, a metabolic cart, GPS and motion-tracking software can be used to help collect quantitative and qualitative data to inform and improve performance
- explain how such data can be collected to ensure objectivity, validity, reliability and integrity
- explain the functions of sports analytics/value of analysing data to improve fitness and skill/technique, prevent injury, analyse games and identify talent

- explain the impact of facility/equipment development on participation and performance (e.g. the importance of adaptive or assistive technology in enabling increased access to sport by disabled and elderly people; advances in artificial multi-use surfaces which have improved access to sport as a positive legacy of London 2012)
- discuss the positive and negative effects of technology in sport linked to sports, performers, coaches and the audience.